DISCARDED

Management Education and Humanities

This book is dedicated to the memory of Claudio Ciborra, who, alas, could not stay with us until it was finished.

Management Education and Humanities

Edited by

Pasquale Gagliardi

Barbara Czarniawska

In association with Fondazione Giorgio Cini

Edward Elgar
Cheltenham, UK • Northampton, MA, USA

Published by
Edward Elgar Publishing Limited
Glensanda House
Montpellier Parade
Cheltenham
Glos GL50 1UA
UK

Edward Elgar Publishing, Inc.
136 West Street
Suite 202
Northampton
Massachusetts 01060
USA

A catalogue record for this book
is available from the British Library

Library of Congress Cataloguing in Publication Data

Management education and humanities / edited by Pasquale Gagliardi, Barbara Czarniawska.
   p. cm.
   Selection of papers presented at a conference held in Venice on Sept. 10–12, 2003.
   "In association with Fondazione Giorgio Cini."
   Includes bibliographical references.
   1. Management–Study and teaching–Congresses. 2. Business education–Congresses. 3. Executives–Training of–Study and teaching–Congresses. 4. Management–Social aspects–Congresses. 5. Management–Moral and ethical aspects–Congresses. 6. Education, Humanistic–Congresses. I. Gagliardi, Pasquale, 1936–   II. Czarniawska, Barbara. III. Fondazione "Giorgio Cini."

HD30.4.M3493 2006
650.071′1–dc22   2005052709

ISBN-13: 978 1 84542 475 6 (cased)
ISBN-10: 1 84542 475 1 (cased)

Printed and bound in Great Britain by MPG Books Ltd, Bodmin, Cornwall

Contents

Contributors

Helene Ahl holds a PhD degree from Jönköping International Business School in Sweden, an ME degree from Lund University and an MBA from the Anderson Graduate School of Management at UCLA. She is a Research Fellow at the National Centre for Lifelong Learning (www.encell.se) at the School of Education and Communication at Jönköping University. Her research focuses on learning, from individual, organizational and institutional perspectives. At present she is engaged in a discourse analysis of the concept 'lifelong learning', and her latest publication was a critical literature review of the motivation concept. She has also published within feminist theory and entrepreneurship. Her book *The Scientific Reproduction of Gender Inequality* received an award at the Critical Management Studies division of the Academy of Management in 2003.

Daniel Arenas is Assistant Professor of the Department of Social Sciences at ESADE Business School. He holds an PhD and an MA from the Committee on Social Thought at the University of Chicago, a degree in Philosophy from the University of Barcelona and a diploma from the Program of Executive Development at ESADE. He teaches courses on sociology and business ethics, and also coordinates the Program 'Vicens Vives – Leadership and Civic Commitment' and the humanities courses for undergraduates at ESADE. He has done research in the area of business ethics and corporate social responsibility as well as in aesthetics and political theory. Among the most recent publications are: (with Josep M. Lozano and Alfons Sauquet) 'Educational Programs in CSR' in José Allouche (ed.), *EFMD-Book on Corporate Social Responsibility*, Palgrave McMillan (forthcoming Spring 2005); (with Josep M. Lozano and Conxita Folguer) 'Setting the Context: The Role of Information Technology in an Business Ethics Course Based on Face-to-Face Dialogue', *Journal of Business Ethics* 48, 99–111 (2003), and 'Per què ens importa l'art? El trencaclosques de l'estètica i els valors', *IDEES Revista de temes contemporanis*, 2004, 21, 34–45.

Barbara Czarniawska holds a Swedish Research Council/Malmsten Foundation Chair in Management Studies at Gothenburg Research Institute, School of Economics and Commercial Law, Göteborg University, Sweden. Her research takes a constructionist perspective on organizing, most recently in the field of big city management and finance. She applies narratology to organization studies. Her recent English books are *A Tale of Three Cities* (Oxford University Press, 2002), and *Narratives in Social Science Research* (Sage, 2004). Czarniawska is a member of the Swedish Royal Academy of Sciences, the Swedish Royal Engineering Academy, and the Royal Society of Art and Sciences in Gothenburg. She received the Wihuri International Prize 'in recognition of creative work that has specially furthered and developed the cultural and economic progress of mankind' in 2003.

Niels Dechow is a Lecturer in Management Studies (Accounting) at the Saïd Business School – University of Oxford. Before joining Saïd, he worked in the Danish consulting industry for Deloitte Consulting and KPMG Consulting and later in the United States as Assistant Professor of Accounting at Case Western Reserve University. His current research is based on empirical studies focusing on the implementation and coordination of new management control technologies, concepts and procedures; the (lack of) interaction of consultants and practitioners in transforming management projects into practice; and associated with this, the role of the business school in shaping modern notions of 'good management'.

Pasquale Gagliardi is Professor of Sociology of Organization at the Catholic University of Milan, and Managing Director of ISTUD – Istituto Studi Direzionali. Before launching his academic career, he worked as a consultant with many large Italian corporations. During the 1980s he contributed to the foundation and development in Europe of SCOS, the Standing Conference on Organizational Symbolism. His present research focuses on the relationship between culture, aesthetic knowledge and organizational order. He has widely published books and articles on these topics in Italian and English. Among his publications: *Le imprese come culture* (Isedi, 1986); *Symbols and Artifacts: Views of the Corporate Landscape* (de Gruyter, 1990); *Studies of Organizations in the European Tradition* (Jai Press, 1995), co-edited with Sam Bacharach and Bryan Mundell; *Narratives We Organize By* (Benjamins, 2003), co-edited with Barbara Czarniawska. Professor Gagliardi is at present Secretary General of the Giorgio Cini Foundation in Venice. He also serves on the Editorial Boards of *Organization Studies* and *Organization*.

Silvia Gherardi is Professor of Sociology of Work and Organization at the University of Trento, Italy, where she is responsible for the Research Unit on Cognition, Organizational Learning and Aesthetics (RUCOLA). Her research activities focus on workplace learning and knowing. Her theorethical background is in qualitative sociology, organizational symbolism, and feminist studies. Her most recent book *The Texture of Organizational Knowledge* (Blackwell, 2006) is devoted to the theme of the circulation of knowledge.

John Hendry is a Fellow of Girton College, University of Cambridge, and Professor of Management at the University of Reading. He holds degrees in mathematics (from Cambridge) and history (from London) and has written extensively on intellectual history as well as on business and management. Having worked in both the public and the private sectors, he joined the faculty of the London Business School in 1984, and has since held positions at Cranfield School of Management, Birkbeck College and the University of Cambridge's Judge Institute of Management, where he was director of the MBA Course from 1990–1998. His current research is on the CEO's job in large listed companies and his most recent book is *Between Ethics and Enterprise: Business and Management in a Bimoral Society* (Oxford University Press, 2004).

Daniel Hjorth is Associate Professor of Management and Entrepreneurship at Växjö and Malmö Universities and senior researcher at ESBRI in Stockholm. His previously published works include *Rewriting Entrepreneurship – for a new perspective on organisational creativity; New Movements in Entrepreneurship; Narrative and Discursive Approaches in Entrepreneurship;* and *Entrepreneurship as Social Change*, the latter three being part of a mini-series of four books for which Hjorth has written and worked as editor (together with Chris Steyaert). Hjorth's publications in journals (such as *Journal of Management Inquiry, Journal of Management Education*, or *Human Relations*) display an attempt to make literary studies affect our understanding of creative organizational life.

Anthony G. Hopwood is the Peter Moores Dean of the Saïd Business School, the American Standard Companies Professor of Operations Management, and Student of Christ Church at the University of Oxford. Educated at the London School of Economics and the University of Chicago, prior to moving to Oxford in 1995 Professor Hopwood had held professorships at the London Business School and the London School of Economics. He was also the President of the European Institute for Advanced Studies in Management, Brussels from 1995 to 2003. A prolific author, Professor Hopwood is also Editor-in-Chief of the major international research journal, *Accounting, Organizations and Society*. He has served as a consultant to commercial, governmental and international organizations. Professor Hopwood holds honorary doctorates from universities in Denmark, Finland, Italy, Sweden and the United Kingdom.

Keith Hoskin is Professor of Strategy and Accounting at Warwick Business School. He was initially trained in the humanities in Europe, studying ancient Greek and Latin, and medieval and modern Greek, as an undergraduate. He then went a more social science route as a graduate student in the USA, taking an MSc in Educational Psychology. In his PhD thesis he split the difference by undertaking a historical–theoretical study of rhetoric as educational practice in ancient Greece and Rome. In his subsequent research career he has drawn on both humanities and social science traditions, in particular studying how past educational practices are sedimented in our present ways of learning, acting and thinking. He is currently using this syncretist approach to attempt to understand the nature of, and interplay between, past and present structures, processes and contents in the fields of education, accounting and management. Where possible he looks to use this approach to identify dysfunctional outcomes and suggest less dysfunctional alternatives: as here.

Karin Knorr Cetina is Professor of Sociology at the University of Constance (DE), Visiting Professor at the University of Chicago, and a member of the Institute for World-Society Studies, University of Bielefeld, Germany. In addition to her three degrees, she has received several honors, including Vienna University's Fellowship for the Gifted, and she was a Ford Foundation Post-Doctoral Fellow, a member of the Institute for Advanced Study, Princeton, President of the International Society for Social Studies of Science, and she is a future member of the Center for Advanced Study in the Behavioral Sciences in Palo Alto, CA. She has published numerous papers and books, including *Epistemic Cultures: How the Sciences Make Knowledge* (Harvard University Press, 1999), which received the Ludwik Fleck Prize of the Society for Social Studies of Science and the Robert K. Merton Prize of the American Sociological Association.

Carl Rhodes is Associate Professor of Organization Studies at the School of Management, University of Technology, Sydney. He is author of *Writing Organization* (Benjamins, 2001), co-author of *Reconstructing the Lifelong Learner* (Routledge, 2003) and co-editor of *Research and Knowledge at Work* (Routledge, 2000). His current research focuses on identity at work, the ethics of managing, and organizations in popular culture.

Michel Serres was born in 1930 in Agen, France. In 1949, he went to naval college and subsequently, in 1952, to the Ecole Normale Supérieure (rue d'Ulm). In 1955, he obtained an agrégation in philosophy, and from 1956 to 1958 he served on a variety of ships as a marine officer for the French national maritime service. His vocation of voyaging is therefore of more than academic import. In 1968, Serres gained a doctorate for a thesis on Leibniz's philosophy. During the 1960s he taught with Michel Foucault at the Universities of Clermont-Ferrand and Vincennes and was later appointed to a chair in the history of science at the Sorbonne, where he still teaches. Serres has also been a full professor at Stanford University since 1984, and he was elected to the French Academy in 1990. Through his explorations of the parallel developments of scientific, philosophical, and literary trends, Michel Serres has built a reputation as one of modern France's most gifted and original thinkers.

Ken Starkey is Professor of Management at Nottingham University Business School. His research interests include: strategy and learning, the theory and practice of strategy and organization, organization development, and management education. He is author of 10 books, including *How Organisations Learn* (International Thomson Press, 2004 – with Sue Tempest and Alan McKinlay), and of about 60 articles in journals such as *Sociology, Strategic Management Journal, Academy of Management Review, Journal of Management Studies, Human Relations, Organization Studies* and *Organization Science*. He is former Chair of the British Academy of Management Research Committee and author of a number of reports on the future of management research and management education. He is currently Principal Investigator on an Economic and Social Research Council project 'The Dynamics of Knowledge Production in the Business School'.

Chris Steyaert is Professor of Organizational Psychology at the University of St Gallen. After receiving his doctoral dissertation in Psychology from the Katholieke Universiteit Leuven (Belgium), he was connected to the Institute of Organization and Industrial Sociology, Copenhagen Business School, Denmark and to the Entrepreneurship and Small Business Research Institute (ESBRI), Stockholm, Sweden. He has published in international journals and books in the area of entrepreneurship and organizational innovation. His research themes include organizing creativity, diversity management and difference, language and translation, forms of performing/writing research and the politics of entrepreneurship and human organizing.

Sue Tempest is Senior Lecturer of Strategic Management at Nottingham University Business School. Her research interests include organizational learning, social capital and new forms of organization, management education and the impact of demographic ageing on strategic management. She has published in journals such as *Organization Studies, Organization Science, Human Relations*, and *Journal of Management Studies*.

Lars Vissing initially served in the MFA in Copenhagen and in Danish embassies in Lisbon (1976–79) and Rome (1984–88). Multilateral assignments includes the CSCE (1973–74) in Geneva, and later (1982–83) the GATT, now WTO, also in Geneva. Before taking on the OCSE Chairmanship as Ambassador and Head of the Danish Delegation to the OCSE in Vienna (1996–2001), in 1997, he served five years (1991–96) as DCM and Minister to Bonn. In 2001 he was appointed Ambassador of Denmark to Moscow, and is also accredited to Belarus and the five Central Asian States. Beyond contributions to different reviews on Political Science and History he has published elements of his research on the Italian Renaissance (*Machiavel et la Politique de l'Apparence*, PUF, 1986). Lars Vissing studied in Paris, Copenhagen and Rome. He holds a Doctor's degree (dr. Phil.) from the University of Copenhagen (1984).

Foreword

On 10 September 2003, a group of scholars and interested practitioners gathered in Venice for a three-day conference aimed at debating the role of humanities in the formation of the managerial profession. This conference was promoted and hosted by the Fondazione Giorgio Cini and took place on the Island of San Giorgio Maggiore. The conference was organized in cooperation with ISTUD – Istituto Studi Direzionali, Milan, and the Saïd Business School, University of Oxford. This book has originated from a selection of papers presented at this conference. These papers have been put together and in many cases developed or transformed following the requests of the two editors, who attempted to map a vast and not necessarily homogeneous territory, on which the array of expressed opinions could be situated.

Introductions

1. A role for humanities in the formation of managers

Pasquale Gagliardi

'I felt responsible for the beauty of the world'
Marguerite Yourcenar, *Hadrian's Memoirs*

The community of scholars and experts on management is by now of vast proportions, and its expansion testifies to the widespread and growing interest of developed and developing countries in the creation and diffusion of expert knowledge on management and organizations. It is not surprising that this interest should be so lively and far-reaching, given that management – in all its varieties, functional and sectoral – is among the most widespread professions of our time. But this community is also so large because it comprises a series of sub-communities that can be arranged along a continuum: with interest in theory at one extreme, and interest and involvement in the practice of management at the other.

Broadly speaking, we may say that the members of this vast community gravitate around three main nuclei of interest: management research, management design, and management education. The first nucleus comprises more academically oriented scholars interested in studying management and organizations as social and cultural phenomena; the second, scholars more interested in 'management theory' viewed as normative science (how organizations should be designed and managed); and the third, those more specifically concerned to translate the expert knowledge about management – produced by management researchers and management designers – into management 'practice', through training or consultancy. In this last group, those who study and those who are studied overlap, in that the sub-community extends its off-shoots into companies, where it includes internal consultants, specialists, and even line managers interested in rationalizing their work. These sub-communities often act as separate worlds, each with its own journals, its own 'sessions' (even at single-theme conferences), its own paradigms, and its own reference values (Barley et al., 1988). Academically oriented scholars are often reluctant to concern themselves with the problems and requirements of practitioners, and see problem-solving research

3

as fieldwork of a strategic and restricted sort (Schein, 1987; Gagliardi, 1991). On the other hand, the frequent conceptual weakness of practitioner-oriented discourse – due to excessive haste in translating new ideas into simple causal models – fuels suspicion of other groups, a reciprocal tendency to differentiate and distinguish, and scant interest in communicating. This gives rise to a vicious circle in which everyone loses something: the academics lose the opportunities and creative stimuli that could be derived from more immediate exposure to the reality of management; the practitioners miss chances to access richer and more sophisticated models for the interpretation of organizational reality.

From this point of view, a comparison between management research and management design is illuminating. For a number of years, academic research on management and organizations has been aware that organizational order never arises solely out of a preordained rational project, because organizations are the living product of processes where historical and political, instrumental and expressive, material and symbolic aspects are inextricably interwoven. Processes are then more relevant than structures, and design could be more appropriately seen as a social process and as a dialogic exploration during which differing views of the world, cognitive maps, strategies and interests are set against each other and mediated. Nevertheless, still the most widespread conception in the literature and practice of organizational design is that what has to be designed is a structure, and the structure to be designed is mainly viewed as a system of tasks and roles which can be formally communicated and consciously learnt. These social patterns mediated by mental experiences are still viewed as the main – if not the only – factors working for regularity and persistence in time, and the interplay between physical, symbolic and social structures is largely neglected. What is particularly surprising, in my opinion, is the distance that separates the two extremes of the continuum: management research on the one hand, and management education (and management practice) on the other.

In Europe, the academic study of organizations and management was initially, and for a long time thereafter, indebted to North America for its ideas, epistemologies and models (Djelic, 2001; Shenhav, 1999). This dependence has diminished with time, however. For years, European management research has been in great ferment, gradually acquiring a set of distinctive features with respect to the tradition and models still dominant in the United States (Bacharach et al., 1995). In my view, the three most striking of these features are the following:

1.   There seems to be a widespread and specific tendency to contextualize the phenomena studied: attention has shifted from the organization as

a circumscribed phenomenon analysed mainly in terms of its internal dynamics to the relations between organizational forms and management models – and their socio-institutional context, with its diverse political, cultural, economic and technological aspects.

2. Organizational analysis has grown more 'cultural', open to the most diverse theoretical and methodological approaches, interested just as much in the local and in 'understanding' as in the explanation of the translocal, in the best Weberian tradition. It has become attuned to general trends in contemporary thought, and attentive to ongoing debate on the crisis of science and the nature of knowledge. The values underpinning these inclinations are tolerance, an openness to discussion, and appreciation of cultural diversities and specificities.

3. Above all, analysis of management and organizing has fruitfully sought inspiration in disciplines other than those from which it has traditionally drawn its analytical categories, namely economics, psychology and sociology. The most promising new insights seem to derive from other social sciences like anthropology and cultural studies, but also from disciplines to which the division of intellectual labor has assigned the great heritage of humanistic culture: philosophy, history, literary criticism, linguistics, the study of art and of aesthetic experience.

Only very little of this richness and vitality has been transferred to management education, to management consulting and, as a consequence, to everyday management practice. In the sphere of practice, besides the hasty and often uncritical embracing of managerial fads which the management market ceaselessly produces and consumes, the basic conception of the manager's role and of how it is learnt continues to be the conception adopted and disseminated fifty years ago by the first European business schools and consultancy companies that imported it from North America. This conception portrays managerial competence as the possession of a self-referential set of methods which enable managers to cope rationally with problems that – even if strategic and far-reaching – are and remain practical problems. Such problems have to do with resources and goals, means and ends, and are therefore to a large extent 'technically' governable. This conception – which separates the sphere of politics, of values and emotions, from the sphere of administration, of facts and efficiency – has probably come to predominate because it serves to qualify management as a scientific phenomenon. By virtue of this conception, also education into 'institutional leadership'[1] – which prompted Richard Normann (1976) to liken a manager to a 'statesman' – risks being converted into a set of prescriptions. The majority of management education courses deal with the emotions as part of projects to optimize interpersonal relations. Ethics (in business) is one subject like any other, not a dimension which traverses every managerial function and activity. This construction ignores the fact that each manager, when making any decision, consciously or unconsciously assesses the alternatives available not only on the instrumental level, but also on the more general one of their lawfulness and desirability, and that no choice is morally neutral.

The socialization into the management profession emphasizes the narrowly rational and instrumentalist dimensions, at the expense of moral and aesthetic ones. Yet no profession deserves its name if technical codes are not flanked by ethical and aesthetic ones, with general validity for the professional community, independently of the contexts within which its practitioners work. The profession of manager is then in danger of remaining only 'half a profession', and we should not be surprised that companies often appear to be 'moral mazes' – as shown by Robert Jackall (1989) in his book, which mercilessly explores the world of corporate managers. At the same time, the most widespread practices of management education seemingly postulate that expert knowledge on management can be translated into prescriptions readily transferable to managers. But in this case, too, the simplifications adopted in practice ignore the more problematizing views propounded by academic research (Czarniawska, 2003), which has for a long time distinguished between espoused theories and theories-in-use, emphasized the mysteriousness of the ways in which theories are translated into action, and demonstrated that theories really empowering for action often have inspiring rather than prescribing qualities. What is most surprising is that this 'half professional' – rationalist, calculating, able to combine means and ends in the service of any cause – is increasingly often also proposed as a model for non-profit organizations, whether public or private, where it is evidently more difficult to artificially separate the sphere of ideals, values and collective interests from the technical-administrative sphere of operations.

One therefore discerns a widening gap between the richness and developments of European management research, on the one hand, and the substantial inertia of the conceptions that generally underlie socialization to the profession of management, on the other. This gap concerns both the conception of management imparted by socialization processes and the theories of learning that these processes implicitly adopt.

Conceiving a company solely as an economy, and not as a community as well, is to forget that formal organizations – to which modern society assigns the task of transferring values and collective expectations into collective action – increasingly characterize the social landscape, replacing or contaminating communitarian forms of aggregation, and that today the majority of people spend most of their waking lives in organizations. Conceiving management education solely as training in the management of an economy is to ignore the enormous power of managers in determining the individual and social quality of life in the community – small or large – entrusted to them, in making their organizations pleasant or oppressive places in which to work, in fostering possible human happiness or at least reducing avoidable human suffering.

Leaders can actually perform a crucial role in determining the character of the organization. Organizations, even more than professions, are the most immediate objects of identification for individuals, and the identity of the organization for which one works may be of crucial importance in the overall construction of personal and social identity, determining the esteem in which individuals hold themselves and the prestige that they enjoy in society. And the greater the power that the organization wields over society, the more the choices of the managers who run it influence the lives and destinies not only of its workforce but also of those who live outside it but undergo the effects of these choices as consumers, suppliers, or simply as members of the wider community. It's difficult to imagine that managers can fulfill these responsibilities by using the same cultural baggage that enables them to optimize the use of limited resources in pursuit of specific goals.

It will be objected that these matters are not new, that I am talking about the firm's social responsibilities, an issue long on the agenda, indeed a watchword that has already aroused the interest of the business services industry and already become a commodity, a pre-packaged product with its serving suggestions, to be placed alongside the other ready-made items on the manager's shelf. But I honestly do not believe that what is taught to managers on these matters can really enable them to discharge such a high and serious responsibility.

In *Hadrian's Memoirs*, Marguerite Yourcenar recounts that the great statesman's first thought on being told that he had become emperor was: 'I felt responsible for the beauty of the world'. Exactly: I believe that managers should feel responsible not only for profit and turnover but also for the beauty of that portion of the world which they have the fortune to govern. And I do not think that a manager can be a statesman unless s/he has a profound humanistic culture, a thorough knowledge of history, of philosophy, of art, of the heritage of knowledge and sensibility that humankind has constructed in its history on this continent, and which can be an inexhaustible source of inspiration and creativity. In recent years, ISTUD – an Italian management center specialized in post-experience management education – has organized a series of innovative programs which expose managers of various levels to educational experiences unusual for a business school: purely philosophical speculations, aesthetic experiences, lessons in history. What has struck both trainees and trainers is the extraordinary potential of analogic exploration, critical reflection and creative re-invention that these experiences offer in defining and addressing every-day management problems usually coped with by resorting to stereotyped routines. A humanistic culture will not provide administrators with pre-scriptions or information that can be used immediately to solve specific problems, analytical or relational; nor will it enable them to take technically satisfactory decisions. But perhaps it will help them to evaluate events and persons with greater humility, to view phenomena from a broader perspec-tive, to courageously confront the moral risks and responsibilities involved in doing their job, to rely constantly on a set of values rather than apply algorithms, and to give just as much importance to passion as to reason, to wisdom as to competence.

These expectations towards managers might seem irremediably idealistic, and the confidence placed in the inspiring qualities of humanities could be groundless. However, at least some of the authors who contributed to this volume seem to share both of them. Moreover, without optimism nobody would venture on such a demanding task as trying to reconstruct from scratch the whole system of management education.

NOTE

1. According to Selznick (1957, p. 28), the institutional leader is 'primarily an expert in the promotion and protection of values'. Thompson (1967, p. 11), drawing on Parsons (1960), distinguishes three levels of organizational responsibility and administration: technical, managerial, institutional. The institutional level has to cope with 'a wider social system which is the source of the "meaning", legitimation, or higher-level support which makes the implementation of the organization's goals possible'.

REFERENCES

Bacharach, Samuel B., Pasquale Gagliardi and Bryan Mundell (eds) (1995), *Studies of Organizations in the European Tradition*, Greenwich, CT: JAI Press.
Barley, Stephen R., Gordon W. Meyer and Debra C. Gash (1988), 'Cultures of culture: academics, practitioners and the pragmatics of normative control', *Administrative Science Quarterly*, **33**, 24–60.
Czarniawska, Barbara (2003), 'Forbidden knowledge. Organization theory in times of transition', *Management Learning*, **34** (3), 353–65.
Djelic, Marie-Laure (2001), *Exporting the American Model: The Postwar Trans-formation of European Business*, New York: Oxford University Press.
Gagliardi, Pasquale (1991), 'Organizational anthropology, organization theory, and management practice', *Hallinnon Tutkimus (Finnish Administrative Studies)*, **10** (3).
Jackall, Robert (1989), *Moral Mazes. The World of Corporate Managers*, New York: Oxford University Press.

Normann, Richard (1976), *Management and Statesmanship*, SIAR.

Parsons, Talcott (1960), *Structure and Process in Modern Societies*, New York: The Free Press of Glencoe.

Schein, Edgar H. (1987), *The Clinical Perspective in Fieldwork*, Beverly Hills, CA: Sage.

Selznick, Philip (1957), *Leadership in Administration*, New York: Harper & Row.

Shenhav, Yehouda (1999), *Manufacturing Rationality: The Engineering Foundations of the Managerial Revolution*, New York: Oxford University Press.

Thompson, James D. (1967), *Organizations in Action*, New York: McGraw-Hill.

2. Forming managers? A counterpoint

Barbara Czarniawska

'Who defines beauty?'
Anonymous, written on a plastic cup acquired at the
50th International Art Exhibition, Venice, 2003

Sweden, the country where I live, is experiencing a serious re-make of its social and political structure. The welfare state has remade itself into a market-oriented, liberal social democracy and is beckoning its citizens to follow and remake themselves into 'folk capitalists'. Individualism, free choice and pensions invested in stocks has replaced solidarity, common deliberation and folk savings (see Ohlsson, 2003, for the description of the domestication of financial products in Sweden). As the stock market went down, however, the alliance between these newly acquired identities revealed its precarious character. Luckily, it turned out that social democratic liberals and folk capitalists had a common enemy: CEOs and presidents of large corporations. Right after Enron, a series of scandals shook the trust of the Swedish people in the industry captains. Huge bonuses in face of losses, ridiculous pension funds and 'parachute salaries' that made failure more profitable than success became everyday news.

Neither the establishment of management as a new professional group nor the domination of pension funds on the capital market are new phenomena: the former has a history of at least a century (Chandler, 1977), the other of two decades, at least in the USA (O'Barr et al., 1992). But none of them before came so close, and with such a threatening significance, to the Swedish saver and future pension holder.

In such a societal climate, the idea that management might constitute future elites has a hollow resonance. Educating managers, on the other hand, seems to be of utmost importance, while at the same time the issue of the relation to the past education attempts remains unresolved. Did they fail because the education had failed, or did they fail because they did not partake in it? Are universities compromised or, on the contrary, needed more than ever? After all, there is a widely held opinion in many Western countries that competition from other knowledge-producers is forcing the universities towards a shift from state-financed monopolies to self-financed participants in knowledge-production markets (Czarniawska and Genell, 2002). Each bigger corporation boasts its own 'university'. The questions multiply: by whom, where and how has the present managerial cadre been educated? By whom, where and how ought the future managers to be educated, or who might claim to be able to do so?

My co-editor ascribes to me a cynical view of the world. This honor is too big for my shoulders; much as I admire the Cynics, I am far from being able to follow their harsh principles. To begin with, they did not write (due to which it is easy to hang dogs on their philosophy nowadays); I do, some say too much. To continue, they preached austerity; I have no achievements in this field. The most important tenet of their philosophy was, however, that one ought to look reality in the face and avoid illusions. This is harsh indeed: who can live without illusions? But, says Nussbaum (1997), the Cynics left open 'the invitation to become, to a certain extent, philosophical exiles from our own ways of life, seeing them from the vantage point of an outsider and asking the questions an outsider is likely to ask about their meaning and function' (p. 58).

This idea of an imposed estrangement was taken up by Stoics, anthropologists and ethnomethodologists, to name only a few schools of thought that attempted to throw light on what is taken for granted. I would suggest, therefore, in a more pragmatic vein, that we look at what is taken for granted in management and management education.

To begin with, who do we educate at universities, at schools of business and/or management? Consultants rather than managers, claim some. Why? Because it is easier, because consulting is closer to teaching than management is. (The old joke about looking for the lost keys under a lamppost comes to mind.) What do we teach them? The contents of the US text books, say several authors in this volume. Why, many of us ask, don't we teach them the contents of our research, which is not uninteresting at all? I have given quite a lot of thought to the matter, and came upon several answers (Czarniawska, 2003). As usual, when in doubt, it is good to look for an analogy in history. We seem to be living in a time of transition. What has been said of other transition times? This is what Hanna Pitkin had to say about the times of Machiavelli:

> in times, when there is a great disparity between the inherited ideals and standards, on the one hand, and people's actual activities, needs, and feelings, on the other (. . .) traditional forms and ceremonies are experienced as empty, and they no longer sanctify. Traditional rules virtually guarantee failure, for there is 'such a difference between how men live and how they ought to live that he who abandons what is done for what ought to be done learns his destruction rather than his preservation.' Inherited theories no longer make sense of the world, and actual practice remains chaotic, inconsistent, untheorized. It may be

time for new theory, for the (re)creation of value and meaning. (. . .) But how does one teach in such times of dislocation in judgment and action? (Pitkin, 1984, pp. 307–8).

It is not by chance that, instead of finding an answer, I find but another question. If, like Michel Serres suggests, it is time for a new humanism or, like Karin Knorr Cetina suggests, it is time to start constructing a post-humanism, it is obvious that old answers will not do. It is equally obvious that nobody can provide complete answers on the spot, either. This collection can therefore be seen as posing more questions than answers, and groping for half-answers in the dark. Turning from natural sciences to humanities in this search does not have to be an ideological choice. Social sciences, to which economics and management belong, have learned a lot from natural sciences in the last century or so. Turning in the other direction might be as rewarding, although for different reasons and with different results.

What is there to be found in the humanities that has not been provided by the classics? To begin with, the classics can always be re-read with a fresh eye, as several essays in this book demonstrate. Personally, I have another gain in sight. If, like everybody says, management is an art, is it not obvious that an art needs its art critics? I am not alluding here to our colleagues in critical management studies, whose work I otherwise admire. The difference between their criticism and art criticism is that they assume an ideologically negative starting point in their view of management. Art critics are deeply dedicated to the art they criticize, and they are prone to admiration as much as to a shattering critique. Not always loved by the artists, they are considered indispensable. Sycophants rarely make careers in art criticism. This is, in my eyes, at least one field where management research and education has a lot to learn from humanities.

REFERENCES

Chandler, Alfred D. (1977), *The Visible Hand*, Cambridge, MA: Harvard University Press.
Czarniawska, Barbara (2003), 'Forbidden knowledge: Organization theory in times of transition', *Management Learning*, **34** (3), 353–65.
Czarniawska, Barbara and Kristina Genell (2002), 'Gone shopping? Universities on their way to the market', *Scandinavian Journal of Management Studies*, **18**, 455–74.
Nussbaum, Martha C. (1997), *Cultivating Humanity: A Classical Defense of Reform in Liberal Education*, Cambridge, MA: Harvard University Press.
O'Barr, William, John M. Conley and Carolin Kay Brancato (1992), *Fortune and Folly: The Wealth and Power of Institutional Investing*, New York: Irwin.

Ohlsson, Claes (2003), 'Keep your stocks with your socks: The language practice in domestication of financial products in Sweden', paper presented at APROS, Oaxaca, Mexico, 7–10 December.
Pitkin, Hanna (1984), *Fortune Is a Woman. Gender and Politics in the Thought of Niccolò Machiavelli*, Berkeley, CA: University of California Press.

3. A guide for readers

Pasquale Gagliardi and Barbara Czarniawska

This volume examines three themes that have emerged as central to the contemporary debate on management education: the profession of management; humanism as a philosophy and worldview; and the humanities as an academic field which, as many have suggested, could provide fresh inspiration for management schools' curricula. All three themes are scrutinized in a frame of reference extended between the two points of view presented above: the traditional view, with its tendency to idealize (and even sometimes romanticize) humanism, the humanities and management as a social function; and the past-modern view – as Karin Knorr Cetina calls it – less prone to take these values for granted, inclined to skepticism and to the deconstruction of social and cultural phenomena. While some approaches opt for one of the two extremes, many are situated between the two.

The first part of the book focuses on the state of the management profession at the beginning of the new century. John Hendry begins the discussion, sketching the historical development from bureaucracy to post-bureaucracy. Many things happened on the way, and many factors – among them, technology – contributed to this transformation. But, in his opinion, when things go wrong they go wrong because 'those in leadership positions renege on their moral duties'. Technology takes care of technical problems; management in post-bureaucracy must focus on morality, and so must management education. This kind of education, aimed at developing the capacity of moral judgment but also at construction of a new managerial identity, and developing managers as persons, needs to be grounded in the humanities.

Helene Ahl is not convinced. Hendry ends his chapter with a fictitious example of a woman student, but Ahl doubts whether a female student would receive much help from the humanities. She agrees with Hendry that the identity of an entrepreneur, recently presented as an alternative to the bureaucratic manager, does not solve problems evident in post-bureaucracies. She rests her argument on a short history of the notions of entrepreneurship and entrepreneurs, and discusses the reasons for their present notoriety. At least one aspect of these notions makes them hardly applicable to present conditions: they seem to exclude women by design. Behind the identity of an entrepreneur, as behind the identity of the traditional manager, lie deeply rooted gender stereotypes. In the past the humanities actually contributed to the viability and perseverance of such stereotypes. But, says Ahl, there is hope: the humanities are transforming themselves: from Plato and Aristotle to Foucault and Derrida, and this transformation can give impetus to the construction of new identities of managers and entrepreneurs alike.

This transformation is fully exploited in the chapter by Daniel Hjorth and Chris Steyaert. They attempt to create a *symptomatology* of management, bringing previously unperceived notions into language with the help of images. In this way, they are able to deconstruct the received notion of the managerial profession as a contemporary elite. But are symptomatologists wanted in business schools? Yes, 'to be able to point out a possible life presently missing', the very possibility of new identities that Hendry and Ahl found missing. This chapter, placed as it is in Part 1 to set the (provocative) tone, could as well be in Part 3, as it beautifully illustrates – or rather performs – the role the new humanities can play (and play with) in management education. Before we reach this point, however, a closer look at current management education practice is in order (Part 2).

Ken Starkey and Sue Tempest set the issue of management education in a broader debate on the future of the university. Their provocative thesis runs as follows: universities survive partly because of the financial support given to them by business schools. Consequently, universities will be able to compete for a new role in contemporary society – that of knowledge broker. Business schools will be in the fore of this new role, if they ground it in the unique features of the university as an institution. In such a case, they will have the opportunity to spread and preserve traditional university values – the very values that, according to some critics, the emergence of business schools has threatened. The allegiance to the university in general and to the humanities in particular might prove to be a unique trump card for the European business schools.

Daniel Arenas expresses great sympathy for the humanities, but also formulates a warning against 'rushing enthusiastically to raise a toast to the humanities as if they were able to offer new solutions to organizational problems'. First of all, he says, we need to scrutinize the meaning of the term: does it suggest a concern for humankind (*humanitas*), in which case it includes natural sciences (a point which will be forcefully made by Michel Serres later on), or does it refer to a species in an ivory tower? Instead of deciding either way, management should explore and exploit the very tension between the two meanings. While such an endeavor might have been easier earlier (Arenas quotes historical examples), the present predicament – of the humanities and management education – offers new challenges but also new opportunities. These new opportunities do not mean indulging in nostalgia for the good old days, or attempting to produce a new fixed body of common knowledge, but in cultivating 'a set of attitudes, predispositions and capacities' borrowed from the humanities.

How typical of the modern sciences, natural sciences and the humanities to propose ever new ways of cultivating the subject! Niels Dechow espouses the Eliasian contrast between cultivation (expressed in achievements) and civilization (expressed by adaptation to society) to offer an explanation of the success of management consulting at the expense of management research in the field of management education. As Elias pointed out, the process of civilization continues throughout modernity. Managers want to know how to behave properly when managing, and the consultants can offer them advice on just that. Does it mean that there is no role left for management research in management education? No: Dechow, too, sees the researchers in the role of brokers (or moderators), but in a different game. Instead of peddling cultivation, the researchers should reflect on and interpret the growing variety of attempts to civilize.

Not everybody would agree to surrender the cultivation endeavors in the face of the all-pervading wave of civilization. Let us bring the humanities into the heart of management, proposes Keith Hoskin, whose chapter begins Part 3 of the book, by going back to the classics. Like Arenas, he evokes the ancient notion of *paideia* meant as 'true education; it is what makes people fully human', in the sense of an all-round education in contrast to education fragmented by disciplinary divisions. Hoskin claims that management needs to adopt the way of thinking promoted in the humanities, because the humanities are the custodians of the synthesizing approach of the old *paideia*. In his opinion, both management practitioners and management researchers will benefit from this.

Silvia Gherardi believes that managers might be offered an excursion into the classics for a different reason – to re-create the desire for knowledge for its own sake. The classics, and their consequent elaborations (Gherardi uses the example of Dante's version of the Odyssey), perpetuate and preserve mythical thinking, which 'connects us to the humanity of the past and the future, thereby situating practical knowledge within the stock of knowledge that is our collective heritage.' In this case, the excursion into the world of Ulysses reframes knowledge management into management knowing – a passionate activity.

Czarniawska and Rhodes also go back to the classics, but with a different result: revealing the classics as the sources of 'strong plots', which survive not because they express human nature, but because they are repeated and thus perpetuated by the central past-modern presence: popular culture. Popular culture does not only propagate old plots, however; it also ridicules or subverts them. Consequently, management researchers must compete not only with consultants, as Dechow pointed out, but also with popular culture. Is there any task left for them? Czarniawska and Rhodes agree with Hjorth and Steyaert that management researchers can play a role similar to avant-garde art, experimenting with new forms and transgressing old ones. Their way of bringing the humanities into the heart of management is by using the instruments of literary criticism to understand the practice of management.

The last part of the book, 'Rethinking humanism', attempts to advance beyond the main focus into the future, and beyond management education. The three contributions contained in this part are somewhat unusual for a book on management. The author of the first, Lars Vissing, is a philosopher turned ambassador. From the vantage point of his unique experience, Vissing believes that the medieval division between Church and Empire, between spiritual and temporal powers, remains a positive achievement. He looks therefore with suspicion at the possible new association of management with the humanities, as this move could lead to 're-exporting religion, though in a new version, back to secular affairs'. Vissing agrees that a more balanced approach to management is probably needed, and even that it could come from the humanities, 'but not necessarily and not everywhere'. His unique vantage point adds a new aspect to the skepticism expressed in several contributions to this volume.

Michel Serres claims that the inherited notion of humanism, present in Western culture during the last half millennium, needs to be replaced. The only common language that humankind ever possessed was, and is, that of natural sciences. It is time to begin a new humanist era, not by reverting to the classics, but by putting our hearts into the language of science: 'establishing a common stock of knowledge will gradually unite all people . . . and will eventually encourage spreading of peace in the world.'

Karin Knorr Cetina agrees that the old humanism has ended. Not, however, because it has been in need of new definition, but because its subject has vanished. We live in a post-humanist era, in which post-moral persons act together with non-human objects in post-social environments. The challenge is to make human sciences (including management and all social sciences) talk to and with non-human sciences.

At the end of the journey, and looking back at the various stages, we realize that the map we had when we set out ought now to be redrawn. The question marks, the gray areas and unexplored territories are more numerous than we had imagined. We have learned many things, however, which have whetted our curiosity and fuelled our desire to continue exploring. We hope that this feeling and this sense of purpose will be shared by our readers at the end of their voyage.

PART 1

Managerial profession at the start of the new century

4. Management education and the humanities: The challenge of post-bureaucracy

John Hendry

In this chapter I wish to argue and defend two main theses. The first is that under the twin tyrannies of economic thinking and technique our views of both management and education have become severely distorted. As a result, management education as currently practised, with its emphasis on techniques of economic efficiency, has little or no relevance to the real problems and challenges of management. These, I shall argue, are and always have been the problems and challenges of any socially-located human activity: problems of judgement, of persuasion and of leadership, of personal development and of political action; the classic subject matters of the humanities.

My second thesis is that the recent shift in organizational forms from traditional bureaucracy toward what is sometimes called post-bureaucracy has severely exacerbated this problem, heightening the disparity between management needs and management education and increasing the need for the humanities in the latter. Traditional business bureaucracies were the product of much the same world view as has dominated management education. Because they had to survive in the real world they never took to the extreme version of it. The commitment to technique, in particular, was always balanced by a more pragmatic commitment to getting the job done. But they did tend to mechanize management and to limit the scope for individual human judgement and action. The education provided in our business schools may not have met their real needs, but there was at least an element of consistency. Post-bureaucratic organizations, in contrast, rely heavily on the human qualities of their managers: on qualities of trust and moral awareness, learning and entrepreneurship, judgement and direction. Whereas bureaucracies needed leadership only at the top and only in emergencies, in times of radical change, post-bureaucracies need it every day and at every level, simply to hold together. In educating managers to meet this need, we simply cannot afford to neglect the rich resources of the humanities.

The structure of the chapter is as follows. I shall begin by explaining what I mean by the tyrannies of economic thinking and technique. In the next section I shall look at the evolution of management. More specifically, I shall look at the characteristics of business organizations and how they have been shaped by these cultural forces; I shall examine the shift from bureaucracy to post-bureaucracy; and I shall explore how this has impacted on the role of the manager and the challenges of management. In the following section I shall look at management education in the same cultural light, exploring how and why it has got stuck with an outdated (and never accurate) notion of management, addressing the need for substantial reform if it is to address the challenges of post-bureaucracy, and identifying the humanities as the most obvious resource for such a reform. I shall finish the chapter by addressing some of the practical impediments to a humanities-based management education.

THE TWIN TYRANNIES: ECONOMIC THINKING AND TECHNIQUE

Economic thinking frames the world in terms of financially measurable costs and benefits, and in terms of property rights and agency relationships. It privileges private property over the common good, and arm's-length market over face-to-face interpersonal relationships. It prioritizes short-term over long-term interests, and treats money as the measure of all good. For sociologist Ralph Fevre (2000), this economic thinking is just one manifestation of an increasingly prevalent 'common sense' mode of thinking that takes its ground in opinion polls, the media and other outwardly 'sensed' sources of 'common' knowledge and rejects or ignores both the moral world of the emotions and the critical world of reason. An alternative view, drawing on cultural theory (Douglas, 1996), sees it as rooted in the ideology of market culture, with its characteristic ethic of economic self-interest (Hendry, 2004a). According to this view economic thinking has always had a place in civilized societies, which have always needed to trade in order to grow and prosper (Landes, 1999). But it has until relatively recently been confined to carefully delineated market subcultures within predominantly hierarchical cultures characterized by non-economic values and the ethic of obligation. Ever since the Enlightenment of the eighteenth century the influence of the economic mindset has been growing, but only towards the last quarter of the twentieth century, as traditional moral authorities collapsed, cultural barriers were eroded, and business and finance became the dominant institutions of society, did it seriously challenge hierarchical modes of thought.

But challenge them it did. Over the last thirty years the economic mindset has come to dominate not only our thinking about business and public administration, but also political thinking in general. Assumptions that were first introduced by economists to artificially simplify the analysis of purely economic phenomena (the assumptions, for example, of *homo economicus*, of the financial measurability of utility, of efficient markets, and of equilibrium conditions) are now taken for granted and employed willy-nilly across the realm of social life. Artificial measures of economic value have become ends in themselves, driving out less measurable but more meaningful goals of personal and social development and well-being. Economy has replaced humanity as the core value of political discourse. Human rights, though much trumpeted, serve merely as economic costs did in the past, to set a practical limit on the extent to which the ideal (the economic ideal, now) can be realized (Hendry, 2004a).

Zygmunt Bauman (1989) and Richard Stivers (1994) draw attention to another feature of contemporary culture. For Stivers, the key feature of contemporary society is not so much the rise of economic or 'common sense' thinking as the growing domination and worship of another product of the Enlightenment age, technology. Technology, broadly understood to include everything from machines to psychotherapy, has become the solution to all our problems, promising us success, survival, happiness and health. But like common sense thinking, its triumph has been at the expense of both critical reasoning and individual moral engagement.

The two main expressions of technology identified by Stivers are bureaucracy, or organizational technique, and psychological technique. Bureaucracy replaces context-dependent moral norms and critical decision making with general and abstract rules, to be followed without question. Judgement is subjugated to technique; ends are eclipsed by means. The classic example is the Holocaust, as analysed by Bauman (1989): an evil that was made possible only by thousands of ordinary people dutifully following the bureaucratic rules, asking no questions, just trusting the system and doing what they were told. For Bauman as for Stivers, 'bureaucracy's double feat is the moralization of technology, coupled with the denial of the moral significance of non-technical issues.' (p. 160).

Psychological techniques, manifest everywhere from advertising and PR to therapy and self-help, are equally powerful. Again judgement gives way to the application of technique, critical reason is overridden and what were traditionally the core problems of moral practice – how should I live my life, how should I respond to the needs of others – are replaced by the purely technical problems of therapeutic technique and image manipulation.

Although they share similar historical roots, the ideologies of economic thinking and technique are not always in tune with each other. Indeed the bureaucratic organization is in many respects the product of a hierarchical, not a market culture. Its structure is modelled on that of the hierarchical society and its characteristic morality is also that of the hierarchy: to be good in this context is to act in the interests of the community as a whole, which means in practice to act in accordance with traditional moral values and norms (Rohr, 1988; Hendry, 1999; Grey and Garsten, 2001). But that doesn't normally mean acting on one's conscience. By and large it means acting on the direction of recognized moral authorities. When things go wrong it is not merely because the technology disables moral thinking, though it can certainly do this, but also because those in leadership positions renege on their own moral duties, and exploit the social structure for their own private ends.

The tension between economic thinking and bureaucratic technique is also very visible in the contemporary rhetoric of enterprise culture, which has taken bureaucracy as one of its main targets (du Gay, 1996; 2000). It is striking, though, that recent attempts at deregulation and the dismantling of public sector bureaucracies seem to have led to more bureaucratic technique rather than less, and in particular to a veritable explosion in the bureaucratic techniques of audit and accountability. I have suggested elsewhere that one way of understanding this is in terms of the cultural confusion of our 'bimoral' society, in which obligation and self-interest, market and hierarchy, vie for predominance (Hendry, 2004a; b). The notions of economic thinking and 'enterprise' that dominate contemporary society are not those of a pure market culture, in which entrepreneurs are self-oriented and unaccountable, but of a market culture corrupted by bureaucratic technique. And the notions of technique that equally dominate are not those of a pure hierarchical culture, in which the moral ideal is of mutual obligation and service to the community, but those of a hierarchical culture corrupted by economic self-interest. In these corrupted forms economic thinking and technique sit comfortably together.

THE EVOLUTION OF BUSINESS AND MANAGEMENT: FROM BUREAUCRACY TO POST-BUREAUCRACY

The institution in which economic thinking and technique most naturally came together, historically, was the business organization, and especially the large business organization, which through most of the twentieth century was typically bureaucratic in structure. Businesses are by nature economically oriented, and even though economic thinking has never been as dominant, or at least as apparent, in industrial corporations, which operate at the heart of society, as in the culturally more peripheral arenas of international trade and finance, it has always had a place in the corporate world view. From the early twentieth century onwards the scale, geographic spread and manufacturing focus of the large corporations also pushed them relentlessly towards technique, in the form of the mechanization and rationalization of both production and administrative functions (Chandler, 1962).

The model of business management that emerged from this process is a very familiar one. As Alasdair MacIntyre observed twenty years ago,

> Managers themselves and most writers about management conceive of themselves as morally neutral characters whose skills enable them to devise the most efficient means of achieving whatever end is proposed. Whether a given manager is effective or not is on the dominant view a quite different question from that of the morality of the ends which his effectiveness serves or fails to serve. (MacIntyre, 1985, p. 74.)

At the core of the model is a conception of the business enterprise as a mechanism for coordinating economic inputs and activities and of the manager as a morally neutral technician engaged in a world of purely rational problem solving in the pursuit of efficiency.

From MacIntyre's own perspective, the 'dominant view' described above is misleading in one respect. Managers are not really, in his view, the innocent, morally neutral technicians they claim to be but manipulative political actors: they are in effect the villains of the piece. Approaching things from a rather different perspective, and with a rather greater knowledge of what managers actually do, however, Stanley Deetz (1992) sees MacIntyre's 'dominant view' as essentially accurate. Business bureaucracies, he suggests, are cultures within which managers are held responsible only for the means by which corporate goals are achieved and not for the goals themselves. Like it or not, he argues, bureaucratic managers are effectively locked into a kind of purely instrumental means-oriented reasoning, from which all questions of values, whether the values of the corporation, of the manager or of the community, are rigorously excluded. The central job of a manager is to mediate between conflicting interests, choosing between options, selecting and rejecting staff, allocating resources between competing projects, and resolving differences of judgement or opinion. But even though many of these conflicts arose from differences of values, the definition of the managerial role is defined so as to give no place to such values, or to the emotions that go with them. The interests of the manager thus lie in the process of mediation rather than in its specific outcomes, and in particular in processes that can be seen as 'objective' or value-neutral. They are led, consequently, to mechanize as far as possible their decision processes, and to translate conflicts into the value-neutral form of cost–benefit analysis and economic pricing decisions, the techniques of economic efficiency.

Both Deetz and MacIntyre were writing as theoreticians, and the reality of bureaucratic management was never quite as starkly economic-technical as they portrayed it. Melville Dalton's (1959) mid-century empirical study of bureaucratic business management showed managers responding to the limitations of bureaucratic technique by subverting or working round the bureaucracy and exercising judgement, breaking the rules and explicitly addressing the moral consequences of that. Other classic studies, such as those of Mintzberg (1973) and Kanter (1977), also show managers in mixed modes, subject to the demands of economic thinking and technique, certainly, but also making judgements, providing leadership, teaching, learning and managing people.

Bureaucracies are designed to suppress individuality: it's the office that counts, and in a smoothly functioning bureaucracy who holds that office should be secondary. They are also designed to capture and codify knowledge, so that as far as possible people can apply a well-developed rule or technique without having to work things out from scratch. They are intentionally both morally and creatively disabling, because as in the army (an archetypal form of bureaucracy) unpredictable idiosyncratic decisions can put everybody's welfare at risk. So the greater part of bureaucratic management is about technique, and in a business context that technique naturally draws on the foundations of economic thinking. But limiting the scope for personal discretion is not the same as eliminating it, and bureaucracies still have to be managed and led. The techniques can only do what they were designed for, and when things go wrong, or when circumstances change, judgement and leadership are still required.

This became apparent when, in the late 1970s and 1980s, things did change, and increasingly powerful information and communications technologies allied to the freeing of global markets quickly destroyed the carefully accumulated competitive advantage of many bureaucratic corporations. Under these pressures, established techniques ceased to be effective and the community of interests that held the corporations together morally began to break down. Companies continued to demand loyalty from their employees, but they could no longer afford to give it in return. Employees continued to profess loyalty and commitment, but with their security shattered they were increasingly forced to look after their own interests in a competitive struggle for survival. Robert Jackall's (1988) empirical study of moral attitudes in two very traditional bureaucratic business organizations, *Moral Mazes*, illustrates this well. From his introductory account Jackall seems to have thought he was portraying the morally disabling effects of bureaucracy in general, but both companies were evidently in sharp decline, collapsing under the pressure of competitive forces to which their leaders, and their systems, had no response. In these circumstances neither economic thinking nor technique were much in evidence: the guiding logic was that of personal survival.

In the twenty years since Jackall's study, the organization and management of business have evolved significantly. The initial response to the failure of bureaucracy was very much in line with the political and public sector rhetoric of enterprise. Bureaucracy was vilified and, led by Peters and Waterman (1982) 'in search of excellence', consultants and their clients set out in search of an organizational mechanism for delivering accountable (and so controllable) enterprise (Hendry and Hope, 1994). Unlike politicians and public sector organizations, however, businesses must perform in order to survive, and when this approach failed they soon tried other ways of combining hierarchies with markets, organization with enterprise. They ended up by discovering that much of what was previously done (or supposedly done) by managers could now be done through internal markets and information systems, and that much of what was done (or not done) by the bureaucratic structure would have to be done by managers.

Contemporary business organizations take a wide range of forms, from the highly rigid and bureaucratic to the highly flexible and, to use Henry Mintzberg's evocative term, adhocratic. In cultural and moral terms, however, most are hybrid forms. On one hand, most business organizations today retain significant elements of bureaucracy, in particular a strong vertical dimension. Apart from the CEO, every manager has a boss; and every manager is a boss. The ensuing vertical relationships are marked, as they always have been, by significant power differentials. And because they are relationships between people, living in a society that recognizes and values the principles of traditional morality, these power differentials carry perceived moral obligations. Most managers still feel some moral duty to serve their employers and support their bosses, by working hard and to the best of their ability. They also feel some moral responsibility towards the employees who report to them.

On the other hand, these same business organizations are also structured according to the rules of the market. Self-interest is expected and even encouraged. In particular, managers are expected to look after their own careers, and many are employed on contracts that offer little or no security. The dominant ideology presented by the corporation is that of the free market, with employees treated as free agents, and on this view of things the power differentials carry no moral obligations. Employees are free to change their jobs, and employers are free to change their staff: it all comes down to supply and demand.

Linking these two cultural elements are organizational devices that fit properly into neither: teams and networks. Many contemporary businesses still look from the outside rather like traditional bureaucracies. But for the most part they are no longer structured round the rigid reporting lines and tightly defined 'offices', each responsible for a specific task, of classical bureaucracy. Job definitions are now much broader and more flexible, channels of communication take the form of extended networks, and the core operating structure is the team. For teams to work effectively, they need high levels of freedom, autonomy, and flexibility, all of which are anathema to traditional bureaucracy. They also need to operate as traditional moral communities with high levels of mutual trust, loyalty and commitment, all of which is anathema to market culture. In the right cultural context they can be extraordinarily effective, and it is no accident that they have flourished in a society torn between the ideals of market and hierarchy, but they are also inherently vulnerable to the tensions of that society.

What is the role of management in such organizations? Research in this area is still in its infancy, but one thing we can be sure of is that today's managers are not morally neutral problem solvers. Indeed being a manager, in contemporary organizations, is beset by moral tensions. In bureaucratic organizations, most of a manager's responsibilities could be subsumed under a responsibility to their immediate superiors. But in post-bureaucracy these responsibilities are quite separate, and pull in different directions. Contemporary managers are responsible directly for the company's performance, of which they are made constantly aware, and on the basis of which they are often paid. They are responsible to the team members with whom they work, who rely on their contributions and high level of commitment; and to the employees who report to them and rely on their support. Without the paternalistic care that was offered by the old bureaucratic corporations, they have heightened responsibilities to their families and to others who rely on their friendship or support, and heightened responsibilities to themselves – for developing their careers, for building and sustaining their incomes, and for generally looking after their own interests.

Some of these tensions affect all employees, and are simply more pressing in the case of managers, whose hours are not limited and whose jobs are never finished. Most obvious here are the tensions between work and home, between the needs of the family and the demands of the job, and the tensions in teams whose members are both colleagues (for the project in hand) and competitors (for a place on the next project team) (Watson and Harris, 1997; Sennett, 1998). But managers are not merely employees and team colleagues; they are also bosses. They have to manage teams and they have, crucially, to hire, promote and fire, or 'release' employees. In theory this should be easier in a market culture, where there is no explicit commitment beyond the terms of a contract, but the theory does not take account of the power differentials and the reality of human relationships. Managers have to ask their reports for loyalty and commitment, even though they cannot offer it in return. They can give friendship and support, and create a trusting relationship. Indeed, if they are to get the most out of their employees, they must do this: it is what management is all about. But they must do it knowing that they may have to take hard, market-based decisions and to renege on the implicit moral contract, and that they may not be able to give help and support if and when it is really needed.

At the top of the organization, these tensions are compounded by others, as senior managers have to take responsibility for other stakeholders as well as for shareholder performance, and to live out the curious and contradictory role of the contemporary chief executive or CEO. They must act as their predecessors acted, as stewards of the corporation, but in doing so their judgement is constrained. The market culture, which gives priority to shareholder returns, requires them to take very hard decisions, many of which go against traditional moral principles. Their pay is structured so that these decisions are handsomely rewarded, but in a way that just heightens the tension. If a CEO makes a thousand people redundant, enhances performance and gets paid a million pounds extra for that performance, he (or very exceptionally she) is castigated by the popular press as self-interested and, in traditional terms, immoral. If he looks after the firm's employees and the communities that depend on them, he is also castigated, this time by the financial institutions, as self-interested, and as failing in his traditionally moral commitment to shareholders. In a pure market culture, of course, self-interest is moral, not immoral, so the latter criticism is inherently unfair; but in today's society it is what you get. Like football managers, CEOs also get the sack when performance falters, whether or not they are at fault.

Managing all these tensions presents numerous challenges, not all of which are yet well understood. There is now widespread recognition of the need for the development of entrepreneurial and career self-management skills alongside the traditional functional and technical skills of management. But important as these are, they are not at the core of the new management challenge. The core of that challenge is to combine enterprise with humanity, to channel and direct the entrepreneurial energies that are now being released so as to serve both the needs of the company – which is a challenge in itself – and, beyond that, the needs of society at large.

Part of this is a challenge of leadership. The demands of business leadership have not changed. Leaders still need, in John Kotter's (1990) classic formulation, to provide direction, including a vision for the company and a strategy for achieving it; to communicate that direction and align people behind it; and to motivate and inspire people to keep moving in that direction, despite all the barriers and distractions that get in their way. Whereas in the past leadership was needed only for change, however, it is now needed for stability as well. Provided that it was going in the right direction an old-fashioned bureaucracy needed little leadership; it was change that was the problem. In more flexible organizations, where entrepreneurial self-interest pushes people in their own directions and where moral tensions pull them in multiple directions, just holding the organization together is a leadership challenge.

The nature of the organization also impacts on the kinds of leadership that can be effective. Both bureaucratic and market cultures tend to favour strong individual leadership and those who reach the top of contemporary business tend to be highly competitive individuals. Once at the top they are held personally to account in a way that isolates them further from their colleagues, and pushes them towards autocratic styles of leadership. The effectiveness of flexible organizations, however, depends critically on the freedom and autonomy that they give their employees, and attempts at autocratic leadership are almost invariably counter-productive. At the other end of the leadership spectrum, empowering styles of leadership can be tremendously effective for small organizations and for the leadership of communities where the interests of those being empowered are of paramount importance. But a business is not just a community. It has specific objectives to meet, and these objectives will not always correspond to the interests of its employees. Moreover, achieving consensus by mutual adjustment is too slow a mechanism to respond effectively to rapidly changing competitive environments in large, complex companies.

Contemporary business leaders have to find ways of combining genuine autonomy with control, and empowerment with clear direction. In practice, this means following the dictates of empowering or servant leadership, listening to people, understanding them and building on their own individual aims and objectives; treating them openly to build up trust and trustworthiness. But it does not mean following their wishes. Business leaders have in the end to call the shots, and to take responsibility for their calls.

Another part of the contemporary management challenge is explicitly moral, in the traditional sense. Bureaucracies may have disabled people's moral faculties, but contemporary business organizations simply crowd them out. In amongst all their other responsibilities, managers are now held explicitly responsible for upholding traditional moral standards in the business, for what is usually called 'business ethics'. But the disciplinary forces identified by critical sociologists of management and bureaucracy are still present and in a society in which moral engagement is getting progressively more difficult, in a business culture in which self-interest is ardently promoted, and in jobs in which the immediate, instrumental demands are manifold and all absorbing, finding space for the traditionally moral can be incredibly difficult. Many of the recent scandals of business ethics could surely have been averted if some of those in the management ranks had simply *noticed* what was going on at board level. But they were all far too busy, far too preoccupied with more immediate concerns, to give such moral issues brain-space.

Moral management, then, is no easier in post-bureaucracy than it was in bureaucracy, but in a central and critically important sense, morality is now what management is all about. In contemporary organizations, the technical problem solving and pursuit of efficiency that dominate existing conceptions of managerial work can be carried out primarily through IT-based market mechanisms. To be effective these mechanisms need the support of skilled technicians, and they also need to be regulated, but the discretionary skills of technical managerial problem solving are fast becoming redundant. And with the technical side taken care of, the task of the manager becomes precisely that which was previously forbidden: the political and moral task of determining purposes and priorities, reconciling divergent interests, and nurturing interpersonal relationships. The economic advantages of flexible organizations come from giving people the freedom to act as entrepreneurial agents, but these advantages can only be realized and sustained if they are set in the context of a traditionally moral community based on mutual trust and respect, active moral awareness and concern, the recognition of diverse needs and interests, and the fair treatment of those needs and interests. In old-fashioned bureaucracies, traditional moral duties and obligations were built into the rulebook, but contemporary management is all about breaking the rules, and finding new ways of doing things. The moral dimension has to be managed directly, by managers, through the medium of personal relationships.

At the heart of this new model of management is the building of trust, or more accurately of trustworthiness. Only if people trust each other will they share their knowledge and insights and so learn from each other, allowing the organization to capture the benefits of their individual enterprise. In a knowledge-based economy, the ability to learn is the ultimate source of sustainable competitive advantage and managing learning is the third key component of the contemporary management challenge. In bureaucracies, knowledge was stored in the structure and culture of the organization and passed easily from one generation to another. The problem, when it arose, was unlearning, or shaking off the institutionalized assumptions and routines that had once proved effective but no longer worked in a radically changed environment. In more flexible organizations, knowledge is held by transient individuals and in temporary teams, and learning needs much more active management. Part of this can be done through distributed information systems. Because the knowledge that counts tends to be tacit know-how rather than codified information, however, both learning and unlearning also have to be managed directly, through the management of personal relationships. And the skills required here are much the same as those required to meet the other challenges of leadership and moral management: listening, empathy, personal engagement, open and honest communications, and demonstrable trust and trustworthiness.

THE DEVELOPMENT OF MANAGEMENT EDUCATION

The history of management education differs from that of management in two significant respects. In the first place the business school model of management was always, for quite understandable reasons, much closer to the MacIntyre-Deetz stereotype than was management itself. In the second place, when management changed, management education didn't.

Though many a manager has sheltered behind the conception of management as technique, that conception has always been most strongly advanced by business school academics and by the management consultants they train. There are obvious reasons for this. Analytical techniques are what these people are good at, what they enjoy doing, what they value, and what they can teach and sell. On one hand the conception of management as technique enhances the perceived expertize and reputations of business school teachers. As long as management is all about technique, they are the experts. If it were about something else – leadership, for example, or moral judgement – they would be at best commentators or critics. Moreover, since analytical techniques are eminently examinable, the conception also affords them easy control over their potentially troublesome students. On the other hand, the conception gives the students, as consumers, a clearly identifiable product that allows them to claim professional expertize, and in due course to charge for it.

It is no surprise, then, that management education reflects both the instrumental rationality of bureaucracy and the disciplinary controls associated with this. Consistent with the conception of the manager as a morally neutral technician, management education imparts a series of instrumental techniques, by means of which the 'manager' can rationally analyse and so, by implication, control the social world in which she operates. Whether on the ubiquitous MBA, in undergraduate or executive education, the curriculum is dominated by the rationalizing techniques associated with the principal business functions of finance, accounting, marketing, operations and so on. Even topics such as organizational behaviour, business ethics or change management, which seem at first to promise some escape from technical specialization, are framed in terms of technologies of control.

This orientation can be traced back to the very beginning of business school education a century or so ago. Drawing on the Prussian Cameralist tradition of education for the civil service (Small, 1909), both of the pioneer American business schools, Wharton and Harvard, emphasized the application of scientific method and the reduction of management to science and technique (Spender, 1997). At first this approach, led by academics and designed to advance the students' general knowledge of the scientific principles of business conduct, was complemented by courses led by business practitioners, which were intended to convey specialized knowledge of particular industries, but they appear to have been quickly squeezed out. For the first half of the twentieth century management education can be characterized as the communication of a blend of accounting and production techniques, economics, law and statistics, together with elementary organizing principles or rules of thumb. Later in the century, under the influence of the Graduate School of Industrial Administration at Carnegie, it focused more on the communication of social science research, and on training in the techniques associated with that research (Gordon and Howell, 1959; Mintzberg, 2004).

The exception to this rule was Harvard, where the use of practical examples became institutionalized with the development of the case study method, which was first used in the inaugural 'business policy' course of 1912 and subsequently extended to other areas of the curriculum. Harvard students studied, and to some extent still study, cases rather than theories or techniques, and this approach was accompanied by a rhetorical emphasis on craft learning. Every industry, every firm, every situation was different, it was argued, and would-be managers should prepare for this by analysing as many 'real' situations as possible (Andrews, 1987). The original aim of case teaching, however, apart from keeping an early generation of students, who could not see the relevance of the social science core, was to provide examples in which scientifically-based learning could be applied. Moreover the emphasis was always on carefully pre-selected 'objective' features of the case study rather than on the messy, subjective reality with which real managers have to deal (McNair and Hersum, 1954; Mintzberg, 2004).

Eventually, even the Harvard business policy tradition succumbed to the tyranny of technique, as 'business policy' was replaced by that idealization of technical-rational analysis and control, 'competitive strategy', in which naïve economic rationalizations are proffered as a basis for the direction and management of large complex organizations and for global industry domination. In Harvard at least, the course in competitive strategy, which was first run by Michael Porter in the 1980s and finally usurped business policy completely in 2000, was still case-based; but it had little to do with management. It was, quite explicitly, a course in economic thinking and technique, and the cases were designed and used to illustrate and apply that technique.

While the emphasis of management education was in some ways an accurate reflection of the largely bureaucratic world of business in the mid-twentieth century, it was never an appropriate response even to that world. Even in strictly bureaucratic settings, managers routinely faced problems that were inherently messy, that did not fall into functional categories, and that could not be solved simply by the application of analytical techniques. Indeed, as Dalton (1959) pointed out almost fifty years ago, in a business setting bureaucracy itself creates such problems. As the rigidities of the bureaucratic structure fail to cope with the rapidly changing needs of customers, the unreliability of machines and the inability of real humans to fit the demands of theoretically defined 'offices', managing *in* a bureaucracy almost inevitably requires managing *round* a bureaucracy. Even in the strictest bureaucracies to be a 'manager' has always been to carry some autonomy and discretion, and some responsibility (or at least accountability) for others. However circumscribed their options, managers have never been, and could never have been, reduced to machines. They have always been people: socially interdependent and self-conscious agents, whose work has entailed a critical measure of human interaction, and who have brought to that work unique habits of thought, perception and feeling, grounded in unique life histories.

With this human context come values and political interests. As the proponents of Critical Management Studies have pointed out, management has always been politicized (Alvesson and Willmott, 1992; Fournier and Grey, 2000; Parker, 2002). However impartial managers have sought to be, their actions have always been informed by personal and social values and political interests. Impartiality itself has always been a value judgement. So while techniques may have been a necessary part of management education, the notion that they were ever sufficient, like the notion that technical expertize automatically conferred managerial control, was always an illusion, and in the end a self-defeating one. Indeed, by ignoring the social realities of organizational life and reinforcing the structural rigidities and disciplinary tendencies of the bureaucratic form, management education may well have contributed significantly to its demise.

These observations suggest that even before the shift from bureaucracy to post-bureaucracy, management education was in need of reform. Though relatively recent, the call for a 'Critical Management Education' that pays attention to values and context and explicitly acknowledges the politicized nature of management practice (Reynolds, 1997; Dehler, Welsh and Lewis, 2001; Grey, 2004), was as relevant to bureaucratic as it is to post-bureaucratic management. In particular, the urgent need for a reorientation from technique to practice advocated by John Roberts and implemented in the University of Cambridge MBA in the early 1990s, was largely independent of the particular kind of business organization for which managers are being developed (Roberts, 1996). The same is true of the similar reorientation from analysis to management advocated by Henry Mintzberg and colleagues and embodied in the International Masters Programme in Practising Management, run jointly since the mid-1990s from McGill, Lancaster, INSEAD, Bangalore and a consortium of Japanese universities (Mintzberg and Gosling, 2002; Mintzberg, 2004). Though they have yet to be copied on any significant scale, these innovations were long overdue even when they were launched, and they remain as relevant as ever in the present context.

Post-bureaucracy also brings with it, however, some additional and more specific challenges for management education, and in what follows I should like to address these in terms of three particular aspects of the educational task: the development of a knowledge base, the creation of a new managerial identity, and the development of the person.

All education includes the communication of a knowledge base of some kind, and management education is no exception. The knowledge normally propagated in business schools, however, has two particular characteristics. The first is that it masquerades as technique. To take one familiar example, Michael Porter's *5 Force* model of industry competition (Porter, 1980) is founded on a basic knowledge of how markets work and is itself an expression of our knowledge of some of the principal sources of market imperfections, the factors that differentiate the real, complex markets found in most industries from the simple 'perfect' markets of economic theory. This knowledge is surely of relevance to anyone engaged in business: it is a necessary and important part of the curriculum. But it is not presented as knowledge. It is presented as a technique for achieving competitive success, in such a way that the great majority of the millions of students who learn the model remain quite unaware that it has anything to do with market imperfections. It is a bit like teaching surgeons the best way to cut open an organ without teaching them anything about how the organ works or is constructed. In a similar way, knowledge about patterns of consumer behaviour gets hidden behind the techniques of marketing, and knowledge about the relative values of different patterns of financial returns gets hidden behind the techniques of finance. In the de-bureaucratized and de-specialized world of contemporary business, managers need more than ever to know something about how markets work, how consumers behave and how investments create returns. But to the extent that we do have scientific knowledge of these things it is that knowledge they need, not the quack remedies based loosely upon it.

The second characteristic of the knowledge communicated, however distortedly, by business schools is its claim to scientific status. I am not concerned here with issues of epistemology or the social construction of knowledge. I take it for granted that all knowledge is socially constructed but also that for many practical purposes that doesn't matter. Whilst I would argue that managers should be made critically aware of the contingent nature of the knowledge they imbibe, that should not get in the way, in business schools any more than in medical schools, of the transmission of accepted knowledge. Again, I take it for granted that much of what passes for empirically-based knowledge in the social sciences is shot through with hidden, unrealistic assumptions and un-stated conditions, but that does not mean it should not be taught. Moreover, the problems attendant on teaching it seem to be essentially the same in a post-bureaucratic as in a bureaucratic world. What is different, what is changed by the shift to post-bureaucracy, is the relative importance of explicitly non-scientific knowledge, of the knowledge associated with the humanities.

As I have already argued, managers have always had to make judgements. But in a bureaucratic setting, and in a society in which behaviour was governed by the rules of traditional moral authority, the need for such judgements was relatively limited. If the rulebook did not specify a solution, the culture of the organization, or failing that the culture of the society in which it operated, often did. The behaviour of those for whom a manager was responsible could also be relied upon to follow certain rules, as individual personalities were to some extent subsumed under tight social norms and constrained by the well-defined roles they filled. Only for the very few, for those charged with leading a radical change of an organization's culture, for example, was it necessary, or indeed possible, to go beyond the readily available repertoire of paradigmatic judgements and behaviours.

In post-bureaucracy, in contrast, and in a society in which moral norms are contested, that repertoire is no longer available and every manager has to take on to some extent the responsibilities of leadership. Today's managers need not only to know something about how things work in general (the established, scientific bit of management education) and in particular industries or cultures. They also need a knowledge base on which to draw when making judgements about human specifics: about how particular individuals will behave in particular circumstances, about how they will respond to each other's actions or to the words or actions of the manager, about the conditions under which they might be trusting or trusted. Managers need, in other words, some knowledge of human nature in its many and various conditions, and of the diversity of human characters; of human potential and of human foibles. They need to make decisions that cannot be cast as cost–benefit analyses, to reconcile conflicting evidences and take account of diverse and ultimately incommensurable factors. They need to make decisions that are neither right nor wrong in themselves, but that will serve to hold together a particular variety of personal and political interests. And the disciplines that can provide a foundation for these kinds of judgements, both in terms of the knowledge they build and in terms of the methods they employ, are of course the humanities: above all history (especially, perhaps, political and social history) and literature (which can be seen as a kind of exploratory or fictional history), together with those parts of the social sciences that favour rich explorations of the human condition over the development of simple statistical laws: social anthropology, for example, and historical and interpretive sociology.

In the context of what we have been discussing so far it does not matter greatly which of these humanities, or which topics within them, are drawn upon by the management teacher. A number of writers have argued for the use of business and management history to set contemporary management practices and contemporary management ideas in context (for example Anthony, 1986; Clegg and Ross-Smith, 2003). Others have made a strong case for the use of novels in exploring organizational behaviour (for example Czarniawska-Joerges and Guillet de Monthoux, 1994; Willmott and Knights, 1999). But histories, biographies, myths, plays, novels and ethnographies can also all be used to help people explore the human condition, and to help them understand their fellow humans as individual and idiosyncratic characters. Drama and the performing arts can be used to provide workshop situations in which hard knowledge (getting the lines right), humanistic knowledge (developing an interpretation of those lines) and management itself (creating a coherent and energizing performance) are all brought together. What matters is not so much what specific resource is employed, as how it is employed, first by the teacher and subsequently by the manager.

In the post-bureaucratic context, the humanities also have another rather more specific but critically important role to play in management education: as contributing to the development of a new managerial identity.

The established identity of the manager as bureaucratic technician is evidently far too narrowly circumscribed and too socially and morally impoverished to be of use either to contemporary businesses or to contemporary society. Accepting this identity, conferred on them by the business schools, would-be managers effectively disqualify themselves from taking on the managerial responsibilities that are now called for in flexible business organizations. This disqualification leaves a moral and political vacuum at the heart of these organizations, disabling their growth and development and isolating them from the needs of the societies that depend upon them.

There is already one alternative identity available: the identity of the entrepreneur. With the growth of an enterprise culture, this identity has in recent years been thrust not just upon managers but also more generally upon people of all kinds, and in all walks of life (du Gay, 1996). Contemporary business organizations, with their strong market orientations, strongly encourage their employees to take on both the identity and the behaviour pattern of the entrepreneur, and those aspiring to succeed in the world of business, whether through their own ventures or through careers in management, now typically cast themselves as entrepreneurs. Business schools, protecting their own particular interests, still tend to make entrepreneurship itself into a set of techniques, but responding to market demand they too talk the enterprise talk and many students now emerge with a kind of split identity: the manager both as morally neutral technician and as self-interested market entrepreneur.

The entrepreneurial identity serves several functions. Some of the students go on to be real entrepreneurs, but they are often the ones for whom the education provided by the business schools is something of an irrelevance. They go there for the credibility and networking benefits conferred, not to learn. Some others adopt the entrepreneurial identity as a face-saving mask to hide their disappointment at not getting the jobs they had hoped for on graduation. For those who do go into management, and for the business schools themselves, it invests technique with a bit of glamour, a seemingly contemporary edge. Unfortunately, that is about all it does do, because for all the hype, the identity of the entrepreneur is ultimately no better suited to the contemporary responsibilities of management than that of the technician. Of course managers have to be enterprising, just as they have to be technically competent, but the essence of management lies in the governance of enterprise, not in its pursuit. The identity of the entrepreneur is every bit as disabling, in terms of the management needs of our businesses and the needs of the societies in which they operate, as the identity of the technician.

If managers are to fill the roles we need them to, they need a new identity. Specifically, they need an identity that empowers them to manage: to exercise judgement, to reconcile interests, and to build and lead communities of trust. But identities cannot simply be manufactured from thin air. They must be rooted in tradition and illustrated by example. The identity of the manager as technician was deeply rooted in traditions of engineering and public administration (book-keeping and financial allocations) that can be traced back to ancient times. The identity of the manager as entrepreneur draws on equally longstanding traditions of individual enterprise, of trading and financial risk-taking for profit. The role of management in post-bureaucracy also has ample precedents, in traditions of responsible political leadership and governance, of public service and productive wealth creation. But if we are to forge a new identity for managers, management will first have to be reconnected to these traditions.

This reconnection may take many forms, but the underlying task is surely historical. By taking people away from the messy immediacy of the present, history can bring distance and clarity to the nature of the managerial role, and help them to distinguish it from the equally important but quite different roles with which it is generally confused. By drawing attention to the relevant traditions it can also give value to the role, showing why it may be worthy of respect and how, within it, that respect may be earned. Of course, history never gives us answers. Its interpretations and lessons can and must be debated. But it does provide a ground for debate, a ground that is noticeably lacking in existing business school curricula.

A third role for the humanities concerns the development of the person. One of the consequences of the tyranny of economic thinking discussed earlier is that education has come more and more to be seen as primarily concerned with enhancing the economic productivity of those educated. In Britain, for example, the 2003 'white paper' (HMSO, 2003) setting out government policy on higher education took it for granted that the primary if not the sole purpose of a university education was to increase the country's economic productivity and national competitiveness. Moreover, when the minister responsible seemed to suggest that some subjects in the humanities, such as history and classics, might be of 'ornamental' value only, and not therefore appropriate for state funding, academics in these fields quickly mounted an economic defence. In a country with a thriving tourist industry and lots of picturesque medieval castles and churches, it was argued, history is an earner.

Set aside the irrelevance of 'national' competitiveness in a globally integrated society and globally marketed educational sector, such contemporary economic conceptions of the role of education are seriously undermining our society's considerable achievements and need to be very vigorously challenged. University education is, or at least should be, about much more than economic competence. It is also about responsible citizenship and about the personal growth and development of individual human beings, and this applies just as much in a business school as in any other part of the university.

There are two points to be made here. The first is independent of the move to post-bureaucracy. In educating people to be managers we should also be educating them to be responsible members of society, setting an example, helping others, contributing to the social and political processes by which people are elected or otherwise appointed to leadership and governance roles and where appropriate taking on those roles themselves, whether in local charities and sports clubs, in local or national politics, or in national or international civil society organizations. And we should be helping them to grow, to develop, as far as possible, their own life projects. The outcome of these processes, if successful, is not knowledge in the scientific sense but wisdom. And if it's wisdom we are looking for, we are much more likely to find it in the humanities than in the techniques of economic efficiency.

The second point is specific to contemporary organizations. I noted above that while bureaucratic offices tend to subsume personalities under well-defined roles, post-bureaucracy gives free reign to personalities. This does not necessarily mean that those personalities are revealed. As Sennett (1998) has pointed out, flexible organization can all too easily be destructive of true character, forcing people to respond to its multiple and changing demands by constantly reinventing themselves, and losing themselves, in the process, in the parts that they act. What Sennett describes is, however, the pathology of post-bureaucracy, just as what Jackall describes is the pathology of bureaucracy. If post-bureaucracy is to work, it needs managers with character, with moral integrity, and with wisdom. And if managers are to hold on to those qualities in the frenzied setting of the contemporary organization they need to arrive in good shape, developed and strengthened, as people, by the educational process.

CONCLUDING REFLECTIONS

The case for the humanities in management education seems to me to be a powerful one, and one that is made all the more powerful by the shift from bureaucracy to post-bureaucracy. But the difficulties of implementing a humanities-based education should not be underestimated, and I shall conclude by addressing some of these.

One major difficulty arises from the fact that most management students nowadays start out with an extraordinarily limited prior grounding in the humanities. High school provides snippets of history and literature, but often no more than that. So a British MBA student, for example, may have a distant memory of some aspects of early modern British history, and of the origins of World War II. But she is very unlikely to have enough history to contextualize any text that might be adopted, or for that matter to contextualize contemporary world events. Similarly she may have read a few poems, and a few novels, and seen a few films and plays. But she is again very unlikely to have read enough to 'read' a piece of literature on any but the most surface levels. Now it could be said that a similar situation pertains in the established business school curriculum. It is a common observation that a master's level course in management is made up of high school level modules. But there is a difference. Understanding through the humanities is a cumulative process of reference, cross-reference and reflection in which each new reading is lit by earlier ones and in turn sheds new light upon them. If Europeans who have been well educated in the humanities (what used to be called 'educated people') engage on an analysis of human nature and human relationships they will take 'as read' a whole corpus of literature, including for example the Greek dramatists and philosophers, the Latin poets and essayists, the Bible and much of Shakespeare and the major poets, playwrights and novelists of their own particular culture. A historian or novelist also relies, to a greater or lesser extent, on her readers being able to pick up such references. But most MBA students simply do not have them. There is no common vocabulary of reference on which to draw, and not even the Iliad or Oedipus, Hamlet or Faust can be taken as read. Everything has to be built from scratch. Within the time constraints of an MBA course, say, this imposes tremendous constraints.

A second difficulty concerns the resources available within the humanities. Given the limited exposure of students (and quite possibly teachers) to the humanities as a whole, and given the need to win students over by quickly demonstrating relevance, one might naturally look for writings that engage directly with business and management. But these are very rare indeed. Business may have neglected the humanities but the humanities have also neglected business. Very few fictional writers have explicitly treated business and management subjects, and when they have they have almost always been both uninformed and unsympathetic (see for example Pollard, 2000). There is a literature of business history, but with a very few exceptions this is largely devoid of human content.

A third obvious difficulty concerns the faculty. If business schools are to deliver humanities-based education they need teachers who are themselves 'educated', in the old sense, at home in and ideally engaged, as practitioners or critics, in the humanities, not just social scientists who happen to have a liking for novels or films. But the primary criterion for appointment to any faculty position is research, and the management academy barely recognizes research in the humanities. So there is a serious problem of academic legitimacy.

Finally, if business schools are to develop the person, and not just provide her with a convenient mask, they need faculty members who can engage as people, and provide role models from which aspiring managers can learn. If management is to move beyond technique, and indeed beyond enterprise, this is perhaps the greatest challenge of all for management teachers. As the philosopher and theologian Martin Buber, himself a great teacher, used to observe, it is not so much what a teacher (or, in our terms, a manager) says that matters, but how she acts, and especially how she interacts with her students (Buber, 1975; and see also Hodes, 1975, p. 135 ff).

As long as management was conceived as a technical activity, business schools could rely on their own technical strengths. Once it becomes reconceived in terms of leadership, governance and inter-personal relationships, business schools will find that they need also to deliver on these dimensions. This doesn't mean that every member of the business school faculty should be a good manager. It does mean, though, that business schools will need to be sensitively managed and that they will need on their faculties people who can act as management exemplars, people who do not simply hide behind their technical expertize but who engage morally with and demonstrate personal commitment to their students and colleagues, listening to their needs and concerns, reconciling conflicting demands, and actively leading a class or group to maximize its learning potential. They will need to start taking education seriously.

REFERENCES

Alvesson, Mats and Hugh Willmott (eds) (1992), *Critical Management Studies*, London: Sage.

Andrews, Kenneth R. (1987), *The Concept of Corporate Strategy*, 3rd edition, Homewood, Ill: Irwin.

Anthony, Peter (1986), *The Foundation of Management*, London: Tavistock.

Bauman, Zygmunt (1989), *Modernity and the Holocaust*, Cambridge: Polity.

Buber, Martin (1975), 'Education' and 'The education of character', in *Between Man and Man*, London: Fontana.

Chandler, Alfred D. (1962), *Strategy and Structure*, Cambridge, MA: MIT Press.

Clegg, Stewart R. and Anne Ross-Smith (2003), 'Revising the boundaries: management education and learning in a postpositivist world', *Academy of Management Learning & Education*, **2**, 85–99.

Czarniawska-Joerges, Barbara and Pierre Guillet de Monthoux (eds) (1994), *Good Novels, Better Management: Reading Organizational Realities in Fiction*, Chur: Harwood Academic.

Dalton, Melville (1959), *Men who Manage: Fusions of Feeling and Theory in Administration*, New York: Wiley.

Deetz, Stanley (1992), *Democracy in an Age of Corporate Colonization*, Albany, NY: SUNY Press.

Dehler, Gordon, Anne Welsh and Marianne Lewis (2001), 'Critical pedagogy in the new paradigm', *Management Learning*, **32**, 493–511.

Douglas, Mary (1996), *Natural Symbols: Explorations in Cosmology*, London: Routledge.

du Gay, Paul (1996), *Consumption and Identity at Work*, London: Sage.

du Gay, Paul (2000), *In Praise of Bureaucracy*, London: Sage.

Fevre, Ralph W. (2000), *The Demoralization of Western Culture: Social Theory and the Dilemmas of Modern Living*, London: Continuum.

Fournier, Valerie and Christopher Grey (2000), 'At the critical moment: conditions and prospects for critical management studies', *Human Relations*, **53**, 7–32.

Gordon, Robert A. and James E. Howell (1959), *Higher Education for Business*, New York: Columbia University Press.

Grey, Christopher (2004), 'Reinventing business schools: the contribution of critical management education', *Academy of Management Learning & Education*, **3**, 178–86.

Grey, Christopher and Christina Garsten (2001), 'Trust, control and post-bureaucracy', *Organization Studies*, **22**, 229–50.

Hendry, John (1999), 'Cultural theory and contemporary management organization', *Human Relations*, **52**, 557–77.

Hendry, John (2004a), *Between Enterprise and Ethics: Business and Management in a Bimoral Society*, Oxford: Oxford University Press.

Hendry, John (2004b), 'The cultural confusions of enterprise and the myth of the bureaucratised entrepreneur', *International Journal of Entrepreneurship and Innovation*, **5**, 53–8.

Hendry, John and Veronica Hope (1994), 'Cultural change and competitive performance', *European Management Journal*, **12**, 401–6.

HMSO (2003), 'The future of higher education', Cmnd 5735.

Hodes, Aubrey (1975), *An Encounter with Martin Buber*, London: Penguin.

Jackall, Robert (1988), *Moral Mazes: The World of Corporate Managers*, New York: Oxford University Press.

Kanter, Rosabeth Moss (1977), *Men and Women of the Corporation*, New York: Basic Books.

Kotter, John D. (1990), *A Force for Change: How Leadership Differs from Management*, New York: Free Press.

Landes, David (1999), *The Wealth and Poverty of Nations*, London: Abacus.

Learned, Edmund P., Roland C. Christensen, Kenneth R. Andrews and William D. Guth (1965), *Business Policy: Text and Cases*, Homewood, Ill: Irwin.

MacIntyre, Alastair (1985), *After Virtue: A Study in Moral Theory*, 2nd edition, London: Duckworth.

McNair, Malcolm P. and Anita C. Hersum (eds) (1954), *The Case Method at the Harvard Business School*, New York: McGraw Hill.

Mintzberg, Henry (1973), *The Nature of Managerial Work*, New York: Harper & Row.

Mintzberg, Henry (2004), *Managers, Not MBAs*, London: Financial Times Prentice Hall.

Mintzberg, Henry and Jonathan Gosling (2002), 'Educating managers beyond borders', *Academy of Management Learning & Education*, **1**, 64–76.

Parker, Martin (2002), *Against Management*, Cambridge: Polity.

Peters, Tom and Robert Waterman (1982), *In Search of Excellence*, New York: Harper & Row.

Pollard, Arthur (ed.) (2000), *The Representation of Business in English Literature*, London: Institute of Economic Affairs.

Porter, Michael E. (1980), *Competitive Strategy*, New York: Free Press.

Reynolds, Michael (1997), 'Towards a critical management pedagogy', in John Burgoyne and Michael Reynolds (eds), *Management Learning: Integrating Perspectives in Theory and Practice*, London: Sage, pp. 312–28.

Roberts, John D. (1996), 'Management education and the limits of technical rationality: the conditions and consequences of management practice', in Robert

French and Christopher Grey, *Re-Thinking Management Education*, London: Sage.

Rohr, John (1988), 'Bureaucratic morality in the United States', *International Political Science Review*, **9** (3), 167–78.

Sennett, Richard (1998), *The Corrosion of Character*, New York: Norton.

Small, Albion W. (1909), *The Cameralists*, Chicago: University of Chicago Press.

Spender, John Christopher (1997), 'Underlying antinomies and perpetuated problems: an historical view of the challenges confronting business scholars today', working paper available at home.earthlink.net/~jcspender.

Stivers, Richard (1994), *The Culture of Cynicism. American Morality in Decline*, Oxford: Blackwell.

Watson, Tony and Pauline Harris (1997), *The Emergent Manager*, London: Sage.

Willmott, Hugh and David Knights (1999), *Management Lives: Power and Identity in Work Organizations*, London: Sage.

5. Women and humanities: Allies or enemies?

Helene Ahl

Whether those who govern work organizations are labeled leaders, managers or entrepreneurs, is contingent upon the fashion of today, write Czarniawska-Joerges and Wolff (1991). They suggest that these three roles serve three different symbolic purposes: the leader acts as a symbol embodying people's hope of control over destiny, the manager introduces order into a chaotic word, and the entrepreneur creates entire new worlds.

What they actually do cannot be neatly separated. Leaders do not really lead all by themselves, and heroic deeds are more often the result of collective action than one person's sole efforts. Managers are not impersonal and neutral order-creating machines, and management techniques include both leadership and power over people. Entrepreneurs need both followers and some degree of order to create new worlds. Practitioners thus play all three roles, but in daily discourse they are seen as separate, since they serve different symbolic purposes. Czarniawska-Joerges and Wolff (1991) suggest those central roles in the organization are seen as enactment of archetypes, in the sense of Krefting and Frost (1986, p. 164): 'universal, idealized, larger-than-life symbols that contain the essence of human experience and that help individuals develop an emotionally satisfying picture of the world'. The leader is thus an archetype symbolizing the personal causation of social events, the manager answers to the need of order, and the entrepreneur makes dreams come true and embodies people's hope for a better life.

If the central person in the organization, whether labeled a leader, a manager or an entrepreneur, answers people's needs as expressed in archetypes and fills certain symbolic purposes, what about a woman filling such a role? I will discuss this issue by looking closer at research on the entrepreneur, which, after almost a century in the backwaters, is the most fashionable role currently.

The entrepreneur was the central figure in the epoch of the early capitalism, but was replaced by the leader towards the middle of the last century. The leader was replaced by the manager in the 1970s. At that time, the entrepreneur was more likely to be seen as a marginal figure, a person of low moral status, self-interested, egotistical, tempted to cheat on taxes and exploit others. This has now changed dramatically. Today, the entrepreneur is center stage, promising revitalization of industry, alleviation of unemployment, and economic growth and prosperity. With the welfare state in decline, governments all over Western Europe, and especially the European Union put great hopes in entrepreneurship. Accordingly, they institute programs fostering entrepreneurship, and they supply start-up assistance, entrepreneurship training and seed financing. The universities are catching up as well. Entrepreneurship is now a rapidly growing academic field, and private as well as public funding for entrepreneurship research is increasingly available (Cooper et al., 2000).

CLASSICAL AND CONTEMPORARY TEXTS ON ENTREPRENEURSHIP

How is the entrepreneur constructed in research? The classical texts on entrepreneurship are mostly concerned with delineating the *function* of entrepreneurship. Hébert and Link (1988) explain how economists have envisioned it, beginning with Cantillon who in the early 1700s defined the entrepreneur as someone who engages in exchanges for profit and exercises business judgment in the face of uncertainty. Such people could be producers, merchants, arbitrageurs or even robbers. Cantillon's followers added the role of innovator. The role of the capitalist was seen by some as a separate function, but for others, such as Adam Smith, it was equated with entrepreneurship. Saint-Simon saw the entrepreneur as the astute business leader who piloted society into the era of industrialism. The entrepreneur was both a skilled manager and a visionary.

Walras, a French economist (1834–1910), developed the theory of general static equilibrium. He did not see the entrepreneur either as the capitalist, or as the firm manager, but as an intermediary between production and consumption, drawn to situations of disequilibrium where opportunities for profits reside. An economy in a state of equilibrium would, however, make him [sic] superfluous.

The classical texts also debated the role of risk. US economist Knight (1885–1972) differentiated between insurable risk, of which probabilities could be calculated, and uninsurable uncertainty, the most important of which was future demand. The entrepreneur was defined as taking the latter kind of risk. The reward for this kind of risk was conceptualized as 'entrepreneurial gain', which is profit minus interest on invested capital, insurance against business losses, and the wages of management (Hébert and Link, 1988).

The most influential definition on entrepreneurship is attributed to Schumpeter (1883–1950). His main contribution to economics was the theory of 'economic development', which is different from general equilibrium theory. Economic development comes from within the capitalist system, and it comes in bursts rather than gradually. It is accompanied by economic growth, but in addition, it brings qualitative changes or 'revolutions', which radically transform old equilibriums. 'Add successively as many mail coaches as you please, you will never get a railroad thereby', said Schumpeter (1934/1983, p. 64). Adding a railroad, however, would displace other means of traffic, which made him label this process 'creative destruction'.

Schumpeter suggested that innovation and economic development can be achieved in five different ways: (1) the introduction of new goods, (2) the introduction of new methods of production, (3) the opening up of a new market, (4) the conquest of a new source of supply of raw materials or half-manufactured goods, or (5) the carrying out of a new organization of any industry, such as the creation of a monopoly or the breaking up of one.

Even if the economists aimed at theorizing entrepreneurship as a function in the economy (as 'the market', or 'interest rates'), none of the above writers resisted the temptation to characterize the entrepreneur. Schumpeter devotes a whole chapter to a description of such a person, who belongs to a special, unusual type. Many men can sing, he says, but the Carusos are rare. Firstly, his intuition and daring makes an entrepreneur make the right decision even though he does not have complete information. Secondly, he has the ability to go beyond fixed habits of thinking. 'This mental freedom presupposes a great surplus force over the everyday demand and is something peculiar and rare in nature', writes Schumpeter (1934/1983, p. 86). Thirdly, he is able to withstand the opposition coming from the social environment against one who wishes to do something new.

What motivates this unusual figure? Schumpeter sees three motives. The first is, 'the dream and the will to found a private kingdom, usually, but not necessarily, also a dynasty' (p. 93). He says that this is closest to a medieval lordship possible to modern man, in that it offers a sense of power and independence. The second motive is the will to conquer: 'the impulse to fight, to prove oneself superior to others, to succeed for the sake, not of the fruits of success, but of success itself. From this aspect, economic action becomes akin to sport – there are financial races, or rather boxing-matches' (p. 93). 'Finally', writes Schumpeter, 'there is the joy of creating, of getting things done, or simply of exercising one's energy and ingenuity. This is akin to a ubiquitous motive, but nowhere else does it stand out as an independent factor of behavior with anything like the clearness with which it obtrudes itself in our case. Our type seeks out difficulties, changes in order to change, delights in ventures.' (pp. 93–4).

This fascination with the person carries through to contemporary entrepreneurship research, which inherited the definitions of entrepreneurship from economics, with Schumpeter as the most important source of inspiration. With an understanding of entrepreneurship as 'creative destruction' (Schumpeter, 1934/1983); 'pure alertness to as yet unexploited – because unnoticed – opportunities' (Kirzner, 1983); or 'the pursuit of opportunity without regard to resources currently controlled' (Stevenson, 1984), many envisioned entrepreneurship as an act of creativity, innovation and ingenuity. Entrepreneurs were seen as risk takers and sometimes as daredevils. Earning a good personal profit is implicit, as is the contribution to economic growth in society. The definitions clearly center on process: 'creative destruction, pursuit of opportunities, alertness to opportunities, breaking equilibrium'. The person who accomplishes this is seen as unique and important for society.

Consequently, most of the early research on entrepreneurs focused on who this person was, rather than on what this person did. The idea was that by identifying such a person it would be possible to select would-be entrepreneurs and thus stimulate entrepreneurship for the benefit of the economy. This is commonly referred to as the trait approach, and it dominated entrepreneurship research for several decades. It has been very productive in outlining the characteristics of entrepreneurs, but disappointingly unproductive in finding out how they differ from others, wrote Gartner (1988, p. 22), who, reviewing the psychological research, found out that 'when certain psychological traits are carefully evaluated, it is not possible to differentiate entrepreneurs from managers or from the general population based on the entrepreneur's supposed possession of such traits.

Attempts were then made to shift the focus solely to the function and away from the person (Gartner, 1988; Low and MacMillan, 1988), but the person kept coming back again and again. It was argued that businesses are not started by themselves. The entrepreneur is and must be an indispensable ingredient in a theory of entrepreneurship (Carland et al., 1988; Shane and Venkataraman, 2000). Consequently, even contemporary research is very much preoccupied with the characteristics of the entrepreneur.

Also, the texts that focus on the function of entrepreneurship have not been able to differentiate entrepreneurship from leadership or management. The empirical psychological research on real life entrepreneurs failed to distinguish entrepreneurs from leaders and managers. In real life persons, the roles are intertwined, but the archetypes and the symbolic purposes they serve are different. This may provide a reason for why researchers continue looking for the entrepreneur.

A FEMINIST DECONSTRUCTION OF ENTREPRENEURSHIP

In the discussions about the entrepreneurs, they were described in words that lead the thought to a man, not to a woman. It is not only the frequent use of the male pronoun (this was standard in science until the 1980s), but also the way he is described. I am not the first to point out that entrepreneurship is a male gendered concept. It might be argued that this is because entrepreneurs have traditionally been men. Several authors hold, however, that this is not the case, but that women entrepreneurs were made invisible (Sundin, 1988; Sundin and Holmquist, 1989; Javefors-Grauers, 1999; Stider, 1999). Other authors discuss male gendered measuring instruments (Moore, 1990; Stevenson, 1990), gendered attitudes to entrepreneurs (Nilsson, 1997), or male gendered theory (Reed, 1996; Mirchandani, 1999). In any case, one needs only to read through the definitions of entrepreneurship to see that it is a male gendered concept. I made a compilation of all the words used to describe the entrepreneur in the texts reviewed above, and compared them to Sandra Bem's (1981) research. Bem developed a sex-role inventory, widely used in American psychological research, and also quoted in the entrepreneurship research reviewed by me. The inventory captures what Americans generally considered typical masculine and feminine traits. It was validated for use in Sweden by Persson (1999). The words marked with an asterisk in Tables 5.1 and 5.2 were found not to distinguish between masculinity and femininity in Sweden – but the others did. Table 5.1 below compares the masculinity-words with the words describing the entrepreneur.

As Table 5.1 demonstrates, the masculinity words correspond very well to the entrepreneur words. There is a match for every word except athletic. For the femininity words there is no such fit. In fact, several of the femininity words do instead correspond to *opposites* of the words describing the entrepreneur. Table 5.2 shows the result of such a match. It turned out that the two femininity words most associated with the non-entrepreneur words were 'yielding' and 'gullible'. Both words reinforce how language positions women as 'less' than men and as subordinated men. Most of the positive words associated with womanhood in Bem's list – affectionate, sympathetic, understanding, compassionate, warm, tender, and so on – are not present in the discussion about entrepreneurship. These were neither among the list of words describing the entrepreneur, nor among the list of opposite words. I think it is quite safe to conclude that entrepreneurship is a male gendered construct; it is not neutral. This does not mean that entrepreneurs (or men) are as described above. It is a particular, culturally constituted, and time and space bound version of masculinity[1]

Table 5.1 Masculinity words compared to entrepreneur words

Bem's masculinity scale	Entrepreneur
Self-reliant	Self-centered, Internal locus of control, Self-efficacious, Mentally free, Able
Defends own beliefs	Strong willed
Assertive	Able to withstand opposition
Strong personality	Resolute, Firm in temper
Forceful	Unusually energetic, Capacity for sustained effort, Active
Has leadership abilities	Skilled at organizing, Visionary
Willing to take risks	Seeks difficulty, Optimistic, Daring, Courageous
Makes decisions easily	Decisive in spite of uncertainty
Self-sufficient	Independent, Detached
Dominant , Aggressive*	Influential, Seeks power, Wants a private kingdom and a dynasty
Willing to take a stand	Stick to a course
Act as a leader	Leading economic and moral progress, Pilot of industrialism, Manager
Individualistic*	Detached
Competitive*	Wants to fight and conquer, Wants to prove superiority
Ambitious*	Achievement oriented
Independent*	Independent, Mentally free
Analytical*	Exercising sound judgment, Superior business talent, Foresighted, Astute, Perceptive, Intelligent
Athletic*	

that is communicated and reproduced through the theorization of the entrepreneur.

Not only is the construct male gendered, it also implies a gendered division of labor. Being an entrepreneur – strong-willed, determined, persistent, resolute, detached and self-centered – requires some time, effort and devotion to a task (energetic was also on the list), leaving little time for the caring of small children, cooking, cleaning and all the other chores necessary to survive. Performing entrepreneurship in the sense described above requires a particular gendered division of labor where it is assumed that

Table 5.2   Femininity words compared to opposites of entrepreneur words

Bem's femininity scale	Opposites of entrepreneur words
Affectionate	
Loyal	Follower, Dependent
Sympathetic	
Sensitive to the needs of others	Selfless, Connected
Understanding	
Compassionate	
Eager to soothe hurt feelings	
Soft spoken	
Warm	
Tender	
Gentle	Cautious
Loves children*	
Does not use harsh language*	
Flatterable*	
Shy*	Cowardly
Yielding*	Yielding, No need to put a mark on the world, Subordinate, Passenger, Irresolute, Following, Weak, Wavering, External locus of control, Fatalist, Wishy-washy, Uncommitted, Avoids power, Avoids struggle and competition, Self-doubting, No need to prove oneself
Cheerful*	
Gullible*	Gullible, Blind, Shortsighted, Impressionable, Makes bad judgments, Unable, Mentally constrained, Stupid, Disorganized, Chaotic, Lack of business talent, Moody
Childlike*	

a wife (or some woman anyway) does the unpaid, reproductive work associated with the private sphere (Collinson, 1992; Mulholland, 1996). Perhaps not all of Schumpeter's entrepreneurs had a family, but founding a dynasty certainly required one.

There exists a certain discourse on entrepreneurship, which is similar to the discourse on masculinity. There is also a discourse on womanhood, which is in conflict with the discourse on entrepreneurship. Most of the words used above to describe a woman associate with a different archetype, namely the mother. These two discourses are likely to have some bearing on studies of women's entrepreneurship, to which I will now turn.

THE ENTREPRENEUR IN RESEARCH ON WOMEN'S ENTREPRENEURSHIP

Looking for the construction of the female entrepreneur, I analyzed 81 research articles on women's entrepreneurship published between 1982 and 2000 (Ahl, 2004). I included all articles on the topic in the four international entrepreneurship research journals identified as leading by the entrepreneurship research community (Ratnatunga and Romano, 1997). These were *Journal of Business Venturing, Entrepreneurship Theory and Practice, Journal of Small Business Management* and *Entrepreneurship and Regional Development*. Because of frequent citations in these, an additional 13 articles from other journals were included. The articles are mainly from the USA (64 per cent) or from the Anglo-Saxon sphere (83 per cent). They are divided about equally between descriptive and explanatory studies. Cross-sectional survey studies comparing men and women through statistical analysis dominate. Half of the studies make no attempt at connecting to established theories. The remainders are based in psychology, sociology and/or management theory/economics. References to feminist theory are absent from the majority of the papers and only four papers have an explicit feminist point of departure.

A number of unstated assumptions seem to underpin research on entrepreneurship. The first, and almost universal assumption, is that entrepreneurship is a good thing, leading as it does to economic growth and full employment (Birch, 1979). The rationale for studying women entrepreneurs in the reviewed articles is largely (in 88 per cent of the reviewed articles) the same – how can they contribute to employment and economic growth? Since equality arguments were largely absent, I concluded that these were either not interesting, or not legitimate as reasons for studying women's entrepreneurship.

If the rationale behind entrepreneurship research is a search for contributions to economic growth, and the topic is women's entrepreneurship, then women's contributions must of course be compared to something. They are compared to men. It turns out that women's businesses are concentrated in the retail and services sectors (rather than manufacturing) and they are on average a little smaller, grow a little slower and are somewhat less profitable than men's businesses. However, when controlling for sector and size of business, men and women actually have similarly growing companies and their growth ambitions (or lack thereof) are alike (Davidsson, 1989). Nevertheless, the reviewed texts portray it as a female problem. Somehow men get to be free riders on their few growth-oriented fellow businessmen, while the women are marked out as the non-growers.

Women's smaller average contributions are then constructed as a problem and as a further reason for investigation. What can be done to make them perform better? A logical next step would be to look for the reasons for their lesser performance. Those who look for structural reasons, for example discrimination by money lenders, obtain mixed results. Women seem to be discriminated against by banks in several studies, but the explanations appear to be structural again: they own the types of businesses that banks associate with higher risks.

If structural barriers do not offer an explanation, maybe there is something about women that does? Indeed, a majority of the studies look for differences between men and women entrepreneurs. Obviously, characteristics held to be necessary for successful entrepreneurship would be the first thing to study.

This is where the archetypal entrepreneur enters the picture. The words used to describe the entrepreneur – bold, rational, calculative, firm, strong willed, achievement oriented, detached, and so on – are reflected in the measuring scales and the hypotheses of the reviewed research. He is accompanied by the archetypal mother. Studies trying to figure out the personality of female entrepreneurs typically envision two possible versions. They call one of them masculine and the other feminine, or one entrepreneurial and the other feminine, and then administer various tests to see how men and women entrepreneurs score.

One example of this is a study which modeled two possible ways of management. One model assumed that men and women managed in an identical way; it was called 'the successful entrepreneur'. The other model assumed that 'women behave differently as entrepreneurs and managers' (Chaganti, 1986, p. 19), and it was labeled 'the feminine entrepreneur'. Already the labeling indicates that a feminine model is an exception, of lesser value, and that the other one serves as a norm. The model tells the story of the successful entrepreneur (who is not feminine), who is detached, rational, calculative, bold, decisive, aggressive and result-oriented. The feminine model is the opposite of that: modest in goals, weak in expertise, irrational (does not use experts or hire trained personnel), unassertive, and emotional.

In fact, my analysis of the research problems and hypotheses showed that well beyond half of the articles focused explicitly on some sort of problem or shortcomings associated with women. Women are discussed as having a psychological make-up that is less entrepreneurial, or at least different from a man's. They are thought of as having less motivation for entrepreneurship or for growth of their businesses. They are hypothesized as having insuffi-cient education or experience, being risk-averse, having unique start-up difficulties or training needs or not networking optimally. They are thought to use less than optimal, or perhaps 'feminine' management practices or strategies, to behave irrationally by turning to unqualified family members for help, and to attribute loan denials to gender bias instead of flaws in the business plan (Ahl, 2004).

The conception of women as being *less* than something is thus prevalent in this research. Less than what? For the most part, 'less than a man' is explicitly stated but sometimes authors write 'less than entrepreneurs in general'. Knowledge of the latter is largely derived from research on males (Stevenson, 1986) so for practical purposes the propositions are the same.

However, the research results tell a different story. Across a long range of psychological, attitudinal and other background factors, there were many more similarities between male and female entrepreneurs than there were differences. Characteristics held to be typical for entrepreneurs such as need for achievement, risk-taking propensity, independence and inner locus of control were similar for men and women, and so were management practices, networking patterns and information needs. The start-up process was also very similar for men and women. Differences were found within groups of female entrepreneurs, between different occupational groups and between entrepreneurs in different countries.

This does not, however, lead some authors to depart from the idea that men and women are different. I found three ways of trying to save the idea of the existence of gender differences, in spite of scant such results. The first, which I label *making a mountain out of a mole-hill* entails overempha-sizing the few differences that are actually found and ignoring the similar-ities and the overlaps between the sexes. The second strategy is to explain the lack of differences by stressing that women entrepreneurs are different from ordinary women, even if the authors have no research results on 'ordinary women'. I call it *the self-selected woman* strategy. The idea is that women entrepreneurs who have made it in a harsh environment are likely to be tougher than ordinary women. Another version of the self-selected woman strategy is to distinguish between 'normal' women entrepreneurs, and those who display a pattern more associated with success, such as running a large business or one in manufacturing. The underlying idea in these studies is to see if there are differences between the woman entrepre-neur who behaves like a regular woman entrepreneur, and the one who is more successful, that is, not like a regular woman.

The third strategy, which I call *the good mother* strategy, is to cherish the small differences found and from these, combined with general know-ledge on women and women's life situations, mold an alternative, female entrepreneur model which is characterized by being relational, ethical and caring. She is said to be well equipped for today's business life which is characterized by the need for networking, the need for ethical considerations and the need to compete for skilled personnel. The good mother strategy turns women's proposed differential disadvantages into advantages, but it does not challenge the man/woman dichotomy and the gendered understanding of entrepreneurship. The 'feminine' column is still different, but not necessarily 'in lack'; rather, it is complementary. The 'male way' is still a norm, albeit not as positive as in earlier versions.

These three strategies serve the purpose of maintaining the idea of the existence of essential gender differences even though the research results indicate the contrary. It is as if the assumption of essential gender differences, or as if the ideas of the archetypal entrepreneur and the archetypal mother have more power over the mind than result figures in tables measuring personality.

The assumption that men and women are different goes hand in hand with the assumption that essential, inner, stable characteristics that affect behavior do indeed exist. This assumption is highly questionable as shown not only by feminist scholars, but also by psychologists. Attitudes, defined as 'predispositions to behave in a characteristic manner with respect to specified social objects or classes of such objects' (King and McGuinnies, 1972, p. 8) have been shown to be neither stable, nor related to behavior (Wicker, 1969; Abelson, 1972). They are constructed, not merely revealed, in the generation of a response to a judgment or a choice task (Payne et al., 1992). Such a position, however, would render much entrepreneurship research invalid, since attitudes (in this case presumably varying with gender) are one of the most popular research areas. Essentialist assumptions go hand in hand with an objectivist epistemology. Questioning one means questioning the other, and it also means questioning the methods used. If stable inner characteristics do not exist, or at least do not affect behavior, there is not much sense in measuring such things on Likert scale surveys.

There are other assumptions working in the same direction. One is the assumed division of a public and a private sphere of life, where women are assumed to take responsibility for the latter, making it an obstacle for their entrepreneurship, while men seem to go untouched by such matters. Research on entrepreneurship without a gender focus hardly mentions family. When research focuses on women entrepreneurs, however, it becomes apparent that life consists not only of work, but also of home, family and children. Women entrepreneurs are asked how they balance work and family. Giving the woman the responsibility for the private sphere means that she must work double shifts and it means that she cannot compete with male competitors in the same business on equal terms. She is given a secondary, complementary role in business while men's responsibility for children is rendered invisible.

Another assumption is the individualist take on entrepreneurship, positioning legal structure, family policy, social and cultural norms, and so on as irrelevant. This blocks collective solutions to problems perceived as private. It also severely restricts the study of entrepreneurship. The other side of the coin of the archetypal entrepreneur as the lone hero, is that individuals are to be blamed by society at large or, even worse, to blame themselves for all the problems in the world, while institutional arrangements remain largely unquestioned. The neglect of social aspects also means that the power perspective is lost. Issues of women's subordination to men are seldom touched upon and there is no talk of collective action to change gender inequalities.

WHY DOES RESEARCH CONSERVE THE CURRENT SOCIAL ORDER?

The archetypical entrepreneur seems to be alive and well in the reviewed research. He is in fact so strong that he causes serious researchers to defend him in spite of scant evidence of his actual existence. The archetypal mother stands beside him in the minds of the researchers, and the result is that women's entrepreneurship is positioned as something less, as an alternative or a complement or, at best, as some unused resource. Instead of giving women entrepreneurs a place in the limelight, this research reinforces women's subordination to men. I have no reason to believe that this was the intention of the authors. Then why did it turn out this way? The way to give women a voice in a field where they are marginalized is to speak *through* the normal discourse – which oppresses women. The unstated assumptions discussed above are the most important underpinnings of such discursive practices, and the foremost of these are the archetypal male gendered entrepreneur and the assumption of essential gender differences. Yet other discursive practices play a role as well.

The disciplinary regulations, to use Foucault's (1972) terminology, favor theories that concentrate on the individual and/or the individual firm. They include certain methodological preferences, namely surveys and statistical analyses that favor analyses of differences. They also include an objectivist epistemology which, combined with the search for essential gender differences and the male norm, renders women secondary. The training and socialization of researchers may reinforce the disciplinary regulations, and so does institutional support in terms of research funding and research centers. Funding is increasingly available for entrepreneurship research, but the interest is either in growth (government funding) or business performance (private funding). None of these focus on gender relations or power issues. Women become only a variable in the growth equation where they are rendered inadequate. The writing and publishing practices further support this. Researchers' careers depend on getting published in mainstream journals. If these encourage discursive practices as outlined above, the articles submitted will conform. I analyzed the composition of the editorial boards in my four main journals and found that they were comprised mostly of US scholars, many of them served on more than one board, and most of them went to the same entrepreneurship research conferences. They form a discourse community which is likely to attract research that shares its assumptions and reject studies based on different ones.

Now, is this a US 'normal science' problem? After all, there is a great deal of critical and feminist scholarship around, and there are alternative journals. Even within the mainstream journals, there are critical voices. I found a number of European articles and some of them, most notably the British ones, openly questioned the individualist and gendered assumptions and the methods used by their colleagues. They expressed a much larger awareness of issues such as gender/power perspectives, class issues, and institutional matters. These arguments were not taken up by the mainstream writers, however, even if they published in the same journal. It was as if the debate against the instrumental view was a debate only among a small number of European writers.

Is it perhaps a problem which will diminish with time, then, as research gets more sophisticated? There is reason to worry that this will not be the case. Europe is currently importing the 'publish-or-perish' system from the USA, ranking journals and counting researchers' articles published in A-journals. For a scientist it is therefore a good idea to publish in these journals. The review boards will only accept articles that fit their assumptions and that use approved methods, however, and the writer must write accordingly. One might of course, as a European writer, choose to publish somewhere else, but this works against the idea of international research and it could also work against the researchers' career interests. North American mainstream research traditions dominate the field of entrepreneurship research.

Elsewhere I argue for an expansion of this research area to include factors related not only to the individual, but also structural, historical, cultural, legislative and institutional factors (Ahl, 2004). I also argue for more comparative, international work. More importantly, I suggest a shift in epistemological position, from objectivist to constructionist, from gender as something that *is*, to gender as something that is *done*, from gender as something firmly tied to bodies to gendered anything – concepts, jobs, industries, language, disciplines, businesses and so on. Instead of looking at physical men and women and using their sex as an explanatory variable, one can look at how gender is *accomplished* in different contexts. Study objects would be how individual men and women perform gender in daily interaction and/or the gendering of institutional orders and how they are constructed and reconstructed. Business legislation, family policy, support systems for entrepreneurs, cultural norms, how childcare is arranged, gendered divisions of labor, and so on would also be objects for study. Such studies would show how gender/power relations are constructed, which, I believe, is more fruitful than looking within individuals for the reasons for gender imbalances.

DOES IT MATTER WHAT THE RESEARCHERS SAY?

What does this entail for women entrepreneurs? After all, the study related above focused on about a few thousand pages covering women entrepreneurs published in journals that very few, if any, practitioners (and not that many scholars, either) bother to read.

In fact, research results cause serious trouble insofar as they perpetuate the traditional assumptions about women and workplaces. My study concentrated on the archetypal entrepreneur, but it was clear that I could have described the leader or the manager as well – all three functions were included in the description of the entrepreneur, and empirical research could not differentiate between them. The male gendering of the entrepreneur is just as applicable to the manager or to the leader (Calás and Smircich, 1996). The symbolic purposes that the leader or the manager or the entrepreneur fulfils are different from each other, but they are all strongly male gendered. This means that the conclusions of Czarniawska-Joerges and Wolff (1991) might be further specified: the leader is the man who acts as a symbol embodying people's hope of control over destiny. The manager is the man who introduces order in a chaotic world. The entrepreneur is the man who makes dreams come true and embodies people's hope for a better life.

Since 'man' is an integral part of the archetypes, this implies that a woman is not eligible. Of course a woman can be a leader, a manager or an entrepreneur, but in the minds of others, she will not do as the symbolic leader, manager or entrepreneur. And as far as symbols matter, as far as they answer to people's needs for archetypes, there will be great obstacles for real life women leaders. The absence of women at the top in most organizations bears witness to this, as does the way women in top positions are treated and evaluated.

The reproduction of male dominated elites has been explained by the term *homophily*, which means that people prefer to interact with others who are similar on given attributes such as sex, race, education, power and social status (Ibarra, 1992; Lindgren, 1996). This implies that people in top positions tend to reproduce themselves. However, the male gendered archetype is just as important as an explanation. Because of its persistence, the choice of a man for a leadership position is perceived as 'natural' and usually goes unquestioned. Arguments are always needed in order to select a woman – be they equality arguments, arguments about a particular woman's superiority, or arguments about women as providing something 'different' and complementary to men. The latter argument draws on the archetypal woman/mother that women leaders always have to deal with.

As women, they have difficulties fulfilling the symbolic purpose of the male archetype, but they have equal difficulties escaping the female archetype. As women, they are expected to be all the things in the feminine column in Table 5.2 above. This is usually a drawback, since these things are 'not-entrepreneur'. However, these things are sometimes constructed as an advantage – women leaders are supposed to supply the top layers of management with the ingredients necessary for good leadership that men are not perceived as equally capable of, such as participative management, good personnel relations and ethical judgment. These are all said to be good for business. The arguments are the same as in the 'good mother' strategy used by the reviewed entrepreneurship research. Yet, in the end, this is also a drawback. People usually do not get to the top by being all the things in the feminine column. And once they are there, it is no easy feat to suddenly shift personality. As a result, women leaders are neither perceived as 'real leaders', nor are they perceived as 'real women' but have to endure being labeled derogatory terms, such as bitch, iron lady, or Madam Saddam. The business case for women leaders does not question the male gendering of elite positions; it only supplies a female gendered complement.

Being a woman and a leader at the same time means that one has to position oneself simultaneously with regard to two conflicting discourses, that of a leader and that of a woman. Men do not have this problem. When a woman enters a male dominated area, she is therefore usually forced to (or feels compelled to) affirm her womanhood simultaneously. She is seen, not as a leader, but as a *woman* leader, implying that these are two different things (Höök, 2001). The assumption of essential gender differences has a hard grip on women's choices.

The assumptions discussed here and the discursive practices in which they are embedded are not consciously used by men against women. In fact, women share them, and thereby co-reproduce their subordination. Fagenson and Marcus (1991) found, for example, that women did not perceive other women as being cut for entrepreneurship. Such practices make a powerful impact *because* they are taken for granted (Foucault, 1995). They form what people hold as true and act upon, and therefore they have social effects. The discourse of the archetypal entrepreneur, the archetypal mother, and the assumption of essential gender differences make very effective obstacles for a more equal gender balance in top positions.

Changing the situation would require two things. The first is to make the discursive practices transparent. Something which is not taken for granted can be questioned and then lose some of its grip on people's reality construction. This discussion is already taking place in feminist circles, in gender research and in women's advocacy groups, but this is seldom where decisions on recruitment for leaders are made, so the circles need to be widened. There is also reason to issue a warning: it is quite easy for the issue to be co-opted and changed. Such was the case when The Confederation of Swedish Enterprise took up diversity in business as an issue. They write that 'stimulating diversity in working life is a question of being business minded . . . it contributes to creativity and fresh ideas'.[2] Their arguments for more women are the same. Women are supposed to contribute with something different; otherwise there is no point in having them. The same thing happened when the Swedish government discussed support programs for women entrepreneurs. It was partly justified by their businesses supplying something unique and different. Women were seen as particularly well cut for restructuring the care sector from public to private (Proposition 1993/94:140). So the assumption of gender difference was as intact as ever.

Naturally, what is also required is to abolish these assumptions. It is very easy to make the case that they have no base in research results on how men and women actually are configured (Doyle and Paludi, 1998), but such claims have been made for a long time with no result. The reason why constructions of gender seem resistant to change may be that constructions of femininity and masculinity are such an integral part, if not the most important part, of people's identity construction. Questioning what it is to be a man and a woman means questioning who one is, and that is a very uncomfortable thing to do. Taking things for granted gives a sense of ontological security, writes Giddens (1991). It brackets out threats and anxiety, it maintains social stability and it provides a stable frame of reference for the creation of one's identity. If this frame of reference is changed, one will experience great uncertainty and discomfort.

The research result on entrepreneurial traits discussed earlier, which said that mean differences between men and women are non-existent or very small, does not imply that all men and women are similar. It means that the variation within each sex is much larger than the mean difference between the sexes. It means that there are extremely decisive and result oriented men *and* extremely decisive and result oriented women. It also means that there are wishy-washy go-nowhere men just as there are wishy-washy go-nowhere women. One finds great variety among people, but this variety is not hinged upon gender. Abolishing assumptions about gender differences does not entail the abolishing of variety. In fact, it would probably allow more variety, since it would open up for more than two fixed categories to mold ones identity upon. Legislation, quotas, affirmative action, a progressive family policy and other measures taken to increase women's participation in the elites have only carried us so far. Questioning how one thinks about gender, identity and oneself is therefore a necessary assault on both men's and women's resistance to women's participation in the elites.

WOULD A TURN TO THE HUMANITIES HELP?

This question may be answered with a yes, with a no, or a maybe, all depending on how one interprets the term 'humanities'. The theme of this book is management education and humanities, and the idea is that the humanities in education would help making management better or more beautiful. My first question then is if management and humanities can meaningfully be described as two separate constructs. If the one is going to improve the other, there must first be a division between them. Second, they must be envisioned as entities that can interact somehow. Can this be achieved?

Looking for help in dictionaries and encyclopedias, I find that the most common way of defining humanities is as a collection of subjects. The Oxford paperback thesaurus says that it is (liberal) arts, literature, classics, classical studies, and classical literature. Merriam-Webster's online dictionary defines humanities as, 'the branches of learning (as philosophy, arts, or languages) that investigate human constructs and concerns as opposed to natural processes (as in physics or chemistry) and social relations (as in anthropology or economics)'. Looking further in the Encyclopedia Britannica, I learn that the separation of humanities from social or natural sciences is a 19th century phenomenon. Italian humanists in the 15th century were more concerned with distinguishing between the secular and the divine. *Studia humanitatis* were studies of grammar, rhetoric, poetry, history, moral philosophy and ancient Greek and Latin studies, all of which the humanists thought to be essentially humane and classical studies rather than divine ones. Contemporary divisions concern, however, not only three groups of subject matters, but also the methods of investigation used. Whereas the physical sciences strive for formulating general laws and examine the world and its phenomena objectively, without reference to human meaning and purpose, the humanities do not; they are devoted to the unique value of the particular within its cultural and human contexts, according to the Encyclopedia Britannica (2004).

After reading sociology of science texts, such as Latour and Woolgar (1979), it seems doubtful to me if the separation between human constructs and concerns as opposed to natural processes is at all meaningful. Latour and Woolgar (1979) clearly demonstrate how the formulation of natural science is in every way a human construct. The distinction between human and social sciences seems equally obscure, and for the same reasons. Many camps of the social sciences try to emulate the natural sciences in their search for general laws (management is a good example), but such a search has proven refractory. An understanding of language as constitutive rather than representative (Saussure, 1983) implies that the questions 'asked' to 'social reality' are themselves human constructs and they, as well as the 'answers received' can never be anything else. This means that *all* subjects could be sorted in the category of humanities, which makes the distinction between the three groups pointless. As many texts in this volume demonstrate, the classical texts of management have actually vacillated between a rational, instrumental view, and a more humanistic approach. This oscillation seems furthermore to be connected to the economy. The humanistic paradigm has dominated in times of recession, and a rational, more mechanistic one has dominated in times of economic growth (Dechow and Fogarty, 2003). One cannot meaningfully sort a subject into one group or the other.

But one does not abandon a several thousand-year-old tradition swiftly. The fact that it has survived for so long means that it is an institution to be reckoned with. Setting epistemological and other objections aside and accepting humanities as a group of subjects different from management, the question asked here is if the humanities can assist in creating a room for women in management. If one looks at the classics, the answer is negative. The writings of Plato and Aristotle are full of contempt for women. Hirdman (2001) quotes Plato who asks if there is any known human activity for which men are not better equipped than women. She also quotes Aristotle's *Politics* where he explains that men, by nature, are better fit for decision making than women, just as the old and mature are better fit for managing than the young and immature. The so-called first democracy in Greece was also for free men only; it was not for women and not for slaves. The classic literature is largely by, for and about men. Not until feminist scholars began revising the history of art and literature were female writers and artists included. Still, less than 10 per cent of the 870 writers included in the appendices to Harold Bloom's (1994) much acclaimed *The Western Canon* are women. From the viewpoint of getting more women into management, the classics are not a good source of inspiration. It might inspire a backlash rather than a step forward.

The humanities may be useful in a different way, however. Questioning the construction of management is a first step in changing it, and this may in turn open up for more women. From the viewpoint of deconstructing management as a male gendered profession, the humanities prove to be an excellent source of inspiration. The analysis in this chapter was largely inspired by Michel Foucault and Jacques Derrida. It seems to me that the same sort of analysis could fruitfully be extended to the theme of this volume. Several contributions give an optimistic account of the value of integrating humanities studies to the management school curriculum. The problems to be solved with this move seem dire, indeed. Management is positioned as too technical, one-sidedly rational, coldly calculative, unethical, immoral, brutal and cruel. The signs of this are many. Egotistic and short-sighted managers have devised reward systems for themselves based on cash flow rather than performance, so even mismanagement leads to astronomic rewards. Workers are ruthlessly exploited in the developing countries, and job security is withering away in the developed economies. The environment and our long-term survival are threatened by short-sighted profit interests. There is a loud call for an 'other', to counterbalance all the shortcomings of management. Indeed management has even been called 'half a profession' if not complemented by this other.

But how does this 'other' manifest itself? The terms used by several authors in this volume call for: ethics; values and emotions; morality; people-orientation; integrity; responsiveness; face-to-face relationships; virtue; compassion; empathy; sensibility; more humane attitudes, capacities and predispositions; communal priorities; understanding cultural, symbolic and emotional elements; trust, care and passion. This list is remarkably similar to the list of words in Bem's (1981) femininity index quoted earlier. To be loyal, sympathetic, sensitive to the needs of others, understanding, warm and compassionate are all feminine virtues. It seems to me as if the call in this book is actually not for humanities, but for femininity, but that one is looking in the wrong place. A turn to the humanities does not develop the feminine virtues. Instead of making management better or more beautiful, it is likely to bring about another reproduction of male hegemony in management.

NOTES

1. Connell (1995) discusses the currently dominant version of masculinity as *hegemonic* masculinity. It is defined as 'the configuration of gender practice which embodies the currently accepted answer to the problem of the legitimacy of patriarchy, which guarantees (or is taken to guarantee) the dominant position of men and the subordination of women'. He stresses that few men embody it, sometimes not even members of the ruling classes but perhaps rather movie stars or sports stars, but that many men support it anyway (labeled

complicity) since they gain from it – they 'benefit from the patriarchal dividend, the advantage men in general gain from the overall subordination of women' (Connell, 1995, p. 79). See Hearn (1999), and Nordberg (1999) for a critical discussion of the concept of hegemonic masculinity.
2. Retrieved from www.svensktnaringsliv.se, 13 June 2003.

REFERENCES

Abelson, Robert P. (1972), 'Are attitudes necessary?', in Bert T. King and Elliott McGinnies (eds), *Attitudes, conflict, and social change*, New York and London: Academic Press.
Ahl, Helene (2004), *The scientific reproduction of gender inequality: A discourse analysis of research texts on women's entrepreneurship*, Copenhagen: CBS Press.
Bem, Sandra L. (1981), *Bem Sex-Role Inventory*, Palo Alto, CA: Mind Garden.
Birch, David (1979), *The Job Generation Process*, Cambridge, MA: MIT Press.
Bloom, Harold (1994), *The Western Canon: The Books and School of the Ages*, New York: Harcourt Brace.
Calás, Marta and Linda Smircich (1996), 'From "the woman's" point of view: feminist approaches to organization studies', in Stewart Clegg, Cynthia Hardy and Walter Nord (eds), *Handbook of Organization Studies*, London: Sage, pp. 218–57.
Carland, James W., Frank Hoy and Jo Ann C. Carland (1988), ' "Who is an entrepreneur?" is a question worth asking', *American Journal of Small Business*, Spring, 33–9.
Chaganti, Radha (1986), 'Management in women-owned enterprises', *Journal of Small Business Management*, **24** (4), 19–29.
Collinson, David L. (1992), *Managing the Shopfloor. Subjectivity, Masculinity and Workplace Culture*, Berlin: Walter de Gruyter.
Connell, Robert W. (1995), *Masculinities*, Cambridge: Polity Press.
Cooper, Arnold C., Gideon D. Markman and Gayle Niss (2000), 'The evolution of the field of entrepreneurship', in G. Dale Meyer and Kurt A. Heppard (eds), *Entrepreneurship as Strategy*, London: Sage, pp. 115–33.
Czarniawska-Joerges, Barbara and Rolf Wolff (1991), 'Leaders, managers, entrepreneurs on and off the organizational stage', *Organization Studies*, **12** (4), pp. 529–46.
Davidsson, Per (1989), *Continued Entrepreneurship and Small Firm Growth*, Stockholm: Stockholm School of Economics.
Dechow, Niels and Tim Fogarty (2003), 'The idea of research-based education and the role of the business school in the formation of intellectual elites', paper presented at *The role of humanities in the formation of new European elites*, Cini Foundation, Venice.
Doyle, James A. and Michele A. Paludi (1998), *Sex and Gender: The Human Experience*, (4th edn), San Francisco: McGraw-Hill.
Encyclopedia Britannica (2004), Retrieved December 8, 2004, from *Encyclopædia Britannica Online*, http://search.eb.com/eb/article?tocId=9041479.
Fagenson, Ellen A. and Eric C. Marcus (1991), 'Perceptions of the sex-role stereotypic characteristics of entrepreneurs: women's evaluations', *Entrepreneurship Theory and Practice*, **15** (4), 33–47.
Foucault, Michel (1972), 'The discourse on language' (L'ordre du discourse), in *The Archaeology of Knowledge and The Discourse on Language*, New York: Pantheon Books, pp. 215–37.

Foucault, Michel (1995), *Discipline and Punish*, trans. Alan Sheridan, Second Vintage Books Edition, May 1995 edn, New York: Random House.

Gartner, William (1988), ' "Who is an entrepreneur?" is the wrong question', *American Journal of Small Business*, Spring, pp. 11–32.

Giddens, Anthony (1991), *Modernity and Self-Identity: Self and Society in the Late Modern Age*, Stanford, CA: Stanford University Press.

Haraway, Donna (1991), *Simians, Cyborgs, and Women*, London: Free Association Books.

Hearn, Jeff (1999), 'The hegemony of men: on the construction of counter-hegemony in critical studies on men', in Per Folkesson, Marie Nordberg and Goldina Smirthwaite (eds), *Hegemoni och Mansforskning*, Karlstad: Institutionen för samhällsvetenskap, Karlstads Universitet.

Hébert, Robert F. and Albert N. Link (1988), *The Entrepreneur: Mainstream Views and Radical Critiques*, New York: Praeger Publishers.

Hirdman, Yvonne (2001), *Genus – om det Stabilas Föränderliga Former*, Malmö: Liber.

Holgersson, Charlotte and Pia Höök (1997), 'Chefsrekrytering och ledarutveckling som arenor för konstruktion av ledarskap och kön', in Anita Nyberg and Elisabeth Sundin (eds), *Ledare, Makt och Kön. SOU 1997:135*, Stockholm: Fritzes.

Höök, Pia (2001), *Stridspiloter i Vida Kjolar*, Stockholm: EFI, Handelshögskolan i Stockholm.

Ibarra, Herminia (1992), 'Homophily and differential returns: Sex differences in network structure and access in an advertising firm', *Administrative Science Quarterly*, **37** (3), 422–47.

Javefors-Grauers, Eva (1999), *AB Adam and Eva – en studie av familjeföretag inom ICA, Lic. uppsats*, Linköping: Linköpings universitet.

King, Bert T. and Elliott McGuinnies (1972), 'Overview: social contexts and issues for contemporary attitude change research', in Bert T. King and Elliott McGuinnies (eds), *Attitudes, Conflict, and Social Change*, New York and London: Academic Press.

Kirzner, Israel M. (1983), 'Entrepreneurs and the entrepreneurial function: a commentary', in Joshua Ronen (ed.), *Entrepreneurship*, Lexington MA: Lexington Books, pp. 281–90.

Krefting, Linda and Peter J. Frost (1986), 'Untangling webs, surfing waves and wildcatting', in Peter J. Frost, Larry F. Moore, Meryl R. Louis, Craig C. Lundberg and Joanne Martin (eds), *Organizational Culture*, Beverly Hills: Sage, pp. 155–68.

Latour, Bruno and Steve Woolgar (1979), *Laboratory Life: the Social Construction of Scientific Facts*, Beverly Hills: Sage.

Lindgren, Gerd (1996), 'Broderskapets logik', *Kvinnovetenskaplig Tidskrift*, (1), 4–14.

Low, Murray B. and Ian C. MacMillan (1988), 'Entrepreneurship: Past research and future challenges', *Journal of Management*, **14** (2), 139–61.

McCloskey, Deirdre (1998), *The Rhetoric of Economics* (2nd edn), Madison: The University of Wisconsin Press.

Merriam-Webster's online dictionary (2004), Retrieved December 8, 2004, http://www.m-w.com/dictionary/humanities.

Mirchandani, Kiran (1999), 'Feminist insight on gendered work: new directions in research on women and entrepreneurship', *Gender, Work and Organization*, **6** (4), 224–35.

Moore, Dorothy (1990), 'An examination of present research on the female entrepreneur – suggested research strategies for the 1990's', *Journal of Business Ethics*, **9** (4–5), 275–81.

Mulholland, Kate (1996), 'Entrepreneurialism, masculinities and the self-made man', in David L. Collinson and Jeff Hearn (eds), *Men as Managers, Managers as Men*, London: Sage, pp. 123–49.

Nilsson, Pernilla (1997), 'Business counselling services directed towards female entrepreneurs – some legitimacy dilemmas', *Entrepreneurship and Regional Development*, **9** (3), 239–58.

Nordberg, Marie (1999), 'Hegemonibegreppet och hegemonier inom mansforskningsfältet', in Per Folkesson, Marie Nordberg and Goldina Smirthwaite (eds), *Hegemoni och Mansforskning*, Karlstad: Institutionen för samhällsvetenskap, Karlstads Universitet.

Payne, John W., James R. Bettman and Eric J. Johnson (1992), 'Behavioral decision research: a constructive processing perspective', *Annual Review of Psychology*, **43**, 87–131.

Persson, Roland S. (1999), *Exploring the Meaning of Gender: Evaluating and Revising the Bem Sex-Role Inventory (BSRI) for a Swedish Research Context (BSRI-SE)*, (INSIKT 1999:1), Jönköping: Högskolan för Lärarutbildning och Kommunikation.

Proposition (1993/94: 140), *Bygder och Regioner i Utveckling*, Stockholm: Riksdagstryck.

Ratnatunga, Janek and Claudio Romano (1997), 'A "Citation Classics" analysis of articles in contemporary small enterprise research', *Journal of Business Venturing*, **12**, 197–12.

Reed, Rosslyn (1996), 'Entrepreneurialism and paternalism in Australian management: a gender critique of the "self-made" man', in David L. Collinson and Jeff Hearn (eds), *Men as Managers, Managers as Men*, London: Sage, pp. 99–122.

Saussure, Ferdinand de (1983), *Course in General Linguistics*, London: Duckworth.

Schumpeter, Joseph A. (1934/1983), *The Theory of Economic Development*, (reprint 1971 edn), New Brunswick: Transaction Publishers.

Shane, Scott and Sankaran Venkataraman (2000), 'The promise of entrepreneurship as a field of research', *Academy of Management Review*, **25** (1), 217–26.

Stevenson, Howard (1984), 'A perspective on entrepreneurship', in Howard Stevenson, Michael Roberts and H. Irving Grousbeck (eds), *New Business Venture and the Entrepreneur*, Boston, MA: Harvard Business School, pp. 3–14.

Stevenson, Lois (1986), 'Against all odds: the entrepreneurship of women', *Journal of Small Business Management*, **24** (4), 30–36.

Stevenson, Lois (1990), 'Some methodological problems associated with researching women entrepreneurs', *Journal of Business Ethics*, **9** (4–5), 439–46.

Stider, Annelie Karlsson (1999), 'Hemma hos firmafamiljen', *Kvinnovetenskaplig Tidsskrift*, **20** (1), 21–31.

Sundin, Elisabeth (1988), 'Osynliggörandet av kvinnor - exemplet företagare', *Kvinnovetenskaplig Tidsskrift*, **9** (1), 3–15.

Sundin, Elisabeth and Carin Holmquist (1989), *Kvinnor som Företagare*, Malmö: Liber.

Wahl, Anna (1992), *Kvinnliga Civilekonomers och Civilingenjörers Karriärutveckling*, Dissertation, Stockholm: Stockholm School of Economics.

Wahl, Anna (ed.) (2003), *Mansdominans i Förändring: om Ledningsgrupper och Styrelser*, Stockholm: SOU.

Wicker, Allen W. (1969), 'Attitudes v. actions: the relationship of verbal and overt responses to attitude objects', *Journal of Social Issues*, **25**, 41–78.

6. American psycho/European schizo: Stories of managerial elites in a hundred images

Daniel Hjorth and Chris Steyaert

'Write with slogans', Gilles Deleuze and Félix Guattari
'No learning can avoid the voyage', Michel Serres

This chapter presents a series of images – in the form of pictures, paintings, citations, dialogues and slogans – to question the dominant account on managerial elites increasingly inscribed in the educational programmes of American and European business schools and to imagine other versions of what it means to educate and to form managers. What we want to do with the critical readings of images of management is to create a symptomatology – to bring the previously unperceived into language. We seek not to describe an illness, but to invent a critical diagnosis of health (as Deleuze puts it). We search to portray a tendency towards elitism that will intensify a symptomatology. The use of images in this chapter answers to two tactics of writing which together help us intensify a symptomatology: 1) we use images much like the anecdote is used in new historicism: as a resonant fragment (often picked from marginal, odd work) that reveals something crucial in the larger picture from which it is drawn (Greenblatt, 1997); and 2) they operate like a tactic in Michel de Certeau's sense, that is as a 'transformative "insinuation" of an anomalous supplementary element into a prescribed order' (Ahearne, 1995, p. 163). Our hope is set on those that, like clinicians, can go after these symptoms keeping in focus the critical diagnosis of health we seek to bring about in this chapter.

The chapter unfolds in five parts. In the *first* part, we introduce our symptomatological approach and relate to the symptoms as we can cut them out of the images of two movies and novels, namely 'American Psycho', directed by Mary Harron and based on the book by Brett Easton Ellis (1991). The second movie is then 'Kafka', directed by Steven Soderberg and based on various works of Kafka, 'our European schizo' – struggling with the impossible necessities of language in the context of the hopelessness of infinite hope. With these images, we enter business schools and compare the tools of management with the powers of literature. We ask the question: 'are symptomatologists wanted in business schools?' The *second* part, departing from a painting by George Grosz, an ironic comment on the elitist pillars of society during the interbellum, is a review of images that situates the upcoming of managerial and professional elites in the history of elites – the military, the clergy, the aristocracy, the intellectuals and those that blur elitist classes. In the *third* part, we force a transition, and, confronted with the explosion of current new elites – from the bobos (bourgeois bohemians) to the creative class – we cut open discourses and make them bleed. The *fourth* part presents a series of alternative literary images – people without qualities, harlequins, masked clowns, angels and troubadours as we find them in the writings of Musil, Bakhtin and especially Serres. The *closing* part urges us to engage intensively with elites and to transform education in business schools into education in becoming faceless, education into third-space activities. Education is then thought of as forming a people to come, a virtual collective; open to its process of actualizing, where they are relationally constituted in experiences of everyday practices.

A symptomatology, as described in Deleuze and Guattari (1986; 1987), has to be two-phased: not only critical (tracing the consistency and mode of expression of a text/image) for it threatens to move towards generalization which ends up in judgement, but also clinical in the affirmative and nomadic sense of seeking difference, spaces of non-identity, anomaly. Deleuze searches a different form of criticism – a clinic without psychoanalysis (psychoanalysis which for Deleuze is negative, characterized by reduction) and interpretation, a criticism without linguistics or significance (Deleuze, 1997) and turns to literature, which we think is the chance the humanities offer to transform education in business and professional schools. Why literature? First, 'literature is a passage of life that traverses outside the lived and the liveable' (Deleuze, 1997, p. 1). Second, '[T]o write is not to recount one's memories and travels, one's love and grief, one's dreams and fantasies' (ibid., p. 2); neither do we write with our neuroses, which do not constitute passages of life, but states we fall into when our desire to create, the fabulation or delirium which creates a possibility of life is blocked. 'Literature', Deleuze says, 'appears as an enterprise of health' (ibid., p. 3). Third, health as literature, as writing, consists in fabulation, the function of which Deleuze describes as 'inventing a people who are missing': 'The ultimate aim of literature is to set free, in the delirium, this creation of a health or this invention of a people, that is, a possibility of life. To write for [the benefit of] this people who are missing' (ibid., p. 4). Finally, Deleuze stresses that literature opens up a kind of foreign language within language (Lambert, 2000).

Literature thus appears as an enterprise of health. The poet is a physician, and literature a practice of world health: 'Health as literature, as writing, consists of inventing a people who are missing' (Deleuze, 1997, p. 4). The people who are missing in the worlds of business schools, those for the benefit of whom we should be working in our educational programmes, are those we try to invent in this writing/imaging. We tactically bring forth the symptoms, the resonant anecdotes, so as to be able to point out a possible life presently missing. We seek the minoritarian writing that describes the transformative forces of the inferior, of the non-chosen, of a people characterized only by movement, by being re-composed by the entrance of every new member, a people beyond the possibility of resting on a position defining what they are (as with being majoritarian). Lambert (2000) summarizes Deleuze's view of the writer's work as follows:

> To raise the false to a higher power [which] is to discover the principle of fabulation that governs even truthful representation, to turn this principle into a critical force which addresses the intolerable situation of 'a people who are missing'. Accordingly, literature bears within its fragmented body – scattered, torn to pieces, or 'dispersed on the four winds' – the seeds of a people to come. These seeds are germs of a 'collective assemblage of enunciation', which, Deleuze often declares, are real without necessarily being actual, and ideal without necessarily being abstract'. (Lambert, 2000, p. 162, using Deleuze, 1989a).

Also Vattimo turns to fabulation and suggests that there is no sense in *simply denying* the world a unitary reality, rather, it makes sense to 'recognize that what we call the "reality of the world" is the "context" for the multiplicity of "fablings" – and the task and significance of the human sciences lie precisely in thematizing the world in these terms' (1992, p. 25). We should consider participating in these fabulous worlds. We are interested in the creative possibilities of our images not because they are unique events in human history, but precisely because human creativity is widespread, a democratic, social possession. As such our symptomatology operates not only in two phases – the critical and the clinical as discussed above – but also in two directions: 1) it insinuates that elitism has nothing to do with human creativity, and 2) from this we turn around and say that affecting appointed elites (such as managers) with images of possible lives (of literature) simultaneously has a deconstructive effect on their status as elite(s) and opens up for their creative transformation into a missing people to come: 'If we cannot pretend (any longer?) to unveil the lies of ideologies and strike an ultimate stable foundation, we can still emphasize the plurality of "tales" and put it to use in freeing ourselves from both the inflexibility of monological tales and the dogmatic systems of myth' (Vattimo, 1992, p. 26). With Deleuze, Guattari and Vattimo, we understand the task of the humanities – our task – is to stress life as literature and to participate through performance. This way we intensify the literary and the non-literary as 'each other's thick description' (Greenblatt, 1997, p. 21, gesturing toward Geertz's famous concept). In performing, we bring into life the most suppressed of knowledge: that our research texts as well as the literary texts are things made, shaped by human imagination 'and by the available resources of narration and description' (ibid.) that helped in composing them. When we perform, more obviously than when we write, the aesthetics of knowledge creation is made overt.

Performance is then a form of getting healthier. As 'symptomatology is always an affair of art' (Deleuze, 1989b, p. 10), this text cannot be but a mixture, a performative fabulation where images, music, pauses and voices intermingle. We prefer to see this chapter 'performed', played out not as a form of theatre, but as a faceless expressivity that connects with the light and shadows of a room, the laughter and silence of an audience, whispering and now and then holding its breath. Through performing, the text itself evolves through people experiencing the space it uses, the speeds and slownesses of the speaking. It forms a murmuring of understatements and a shouting of exaggerations, a cutting in with slogans and a zooming out with pauses. From a majoritarian perspective, when 'the audience' consists of management students, the performance represents a becoming-mute and becoming-faceless, answering to the loss of management vocabulary and de-centring of the managerial subject. A preparation for a people to come.

This is to develop a minor literature, foreign in its own language. This language, in our performances, is extracted primarily from management and organization studies. This language is regulated and disciplined by the operations of institutions and cultural (academic) habits; 'majoritarian formation of the "public sphere", which gives enunciation weight and reference' (Lambert, 2000, p. 163). A minor language will then always be like the story of metamorphiosis that pulls Gregor (the character in Kafka's story) into an inevitable becoming, and haunted by its imaginary or fabulous openness/possibility. This is our pedagogical problem: a minor language seems to be going away, vanishing, centrifugally striking, and like the tactician, to be unable to keep/capitalize on her victories but instead always travel, and travel lightly. Why, asks the mainstream management writer and practitioner, why should we bother? We hope we are able to show that in a minor language/literature/life, the virtualities/imaginations/fabulations set us on a path to health/creation. Re-locating us in the intensities of becomings, in the heterogeneity of the public, we become minor, moving on like tacticians, or so we hope.

As we operate with a minoritarian language, ask not what orders or identities this assemblage of images we have set forth to emphasize a point of instability (elitism in management) have. Recasting the issue of ostensive vs.

performative approaches in research, we point out that a minority is not identified by a definition or supreme principle. It is defined by the nature of the grouping, by how it is moving and being moved by the entrance of new members. This minor language in management, the language of art-images, the images we provoke of the aesthetics of knowledge creation, we like to perform as a politics of becoming-minoritarian (a transformation) of management. Such a politics works with performing literature/art or fabulation to increase the possibilities of management, to increase the variation of managerial existence. Such performances need minoritarian art and literature, the stuff of the Humanities that operate in the service of experimentation, and to play it out with the students of business schools. We urge them: imitate not the fixed interpretations and resist coding; follow flows, revolutionary active lines of flight, and lines of absolute decoding. Deleuze (1995, p. 24) explains:

> we're considering a problem to do with the close link between capitalism and psychoanalysis on the one hand, and between revolutionary movements and schizoanalysis on the other. We can talk in terms of capitalist paranoia and revolutionary schizophrenia, because we're not setting out from a psychiatric understanding from these works but rather from their social and political determinations [. . .]. Schizoanalysis has one single aim: to get revolutionary, artistic, and analytic machines working as parts, cogs, of one another.

This is how the K-function (of Kafka's minor literature), the becoming minor, can come into the accredited 'programmes' of standardized business schools. The role of the Humanities is to engage us with literature, language and life, and to experience that language is not there to communicate, represent or to govern, but to disrupt tradition, to produce and to sound what we cannot recognize, that before which our language stutters: a life possible. Literature opens up to sensations and affects, deterritorializing people from order-words and codings, bringing us back to the intensities that form us, 'to the sounds, marks and affects from which meanings emerge' (Colebrook, 2002, p. 116). This is our proposal: more literature and more movies for students. These are our suggestions: let's give an HRM course as a sign pointing at the machine of capitalism with Arthur Miller's 'Death of a Salesman', and make Willy Loman into a conceptual persona. Let's give the ABC of sales and marketing by screening 'Glengarry Glen Ross' (directed by James Foley and based on the play by David Mamet, 1991). Financial management and 'American Psycho', Operations Management and 'Schindler's List' (directed by Steven Spielberg, based on the book by Thomas Keneally, 1993), Entrepreneurship and 'Citizen Kane' (directed by Orson Welles, 1941), Accountancy and 'Kafka' (the Soderbergh movie, 1991). More novels, more movies, more plays. Students should have a choice.

PART ONE: BECOMING SYMPTOMATOLOGISTS

Early morning, Venice, an isola

–   Images can be used in a literary–clinical sense to investigate the current
    context of the formation of managerial elites. By linking the critical
    and the clinical, literature and life, we reach out to a symptomatology
    that is not a diagnostic of a particular way of living but that is an
    assessment of the potentialities in life. Just as doctors and clinicians,

Figure 6.1   Fils de l'Homme (Son of Man), *René Magritte (1964)*
© *Prolitteris, Zurich*

artists and novelists, moviemakers and painters can be clinicians of civilization, they can be so even more radically as art works give them new means.

– The question is: are there any symptomatologists wanted in business schools?

A sunny day in 1987, Wall Street

– *Voici*, today's dominant elite, the managerial elite. The scene, a group of brokers for whom money is never a limit, and, through being exactly the

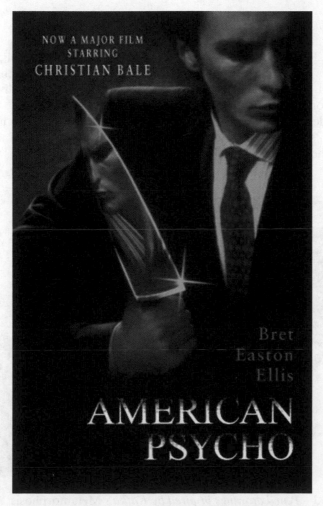

Figure 6.2   American Psycho, *Bret Easton Ellis, Macmillan Ltd*

limit of life allowing an obsession with self-appearance, with finding expression through the labels of their clothes, the style of their signifiers. Money is the language of machismo, giving free access to everything; restaurants, women and murder.

–   Luxury, as intensification with the surface, has to come in place of seeing eyes, tasting mouths.
–   The background dominates, the props, the formats, the restaurant menus, the spreadsheets.
–   The absence of a face.

A night in Prague, dusty corridors

–   The K-function and its razorblade sensation. More novels, movies, plays – let students have a choice. Texts and language that break through the dominant discourse of management and its divisions, a minorization of these major languages.
–   Students becoming artists of their self, allowing their own minorization, sidestepping their grand roles as future managers and managers of the future.

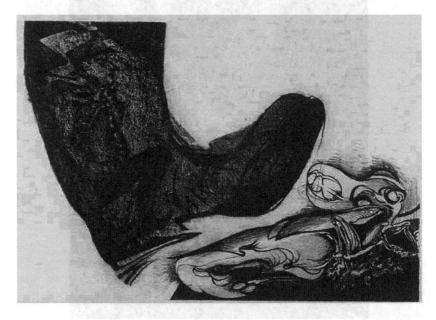

Figure 6.3   Pencil drawings inspired by Kafka's Metamorphosis, *Martin Linnartz (1992)*

–   Great explorers of the possibilities of life, of power of living. Becoming symptomatologist through literature is a matter of health, vitality.

Back in Venice

–   And what about that hat. Really – is it not only in the place of a crown?
–   Of a crown?
–   Yes, is this not a symbol for superiority? Would there still be religious reasons for this cover-up?
–   And one hand is almost completely darkened.
–   The light, the light comes from the other side. But of course, it is a rather grey background. Not threatening but surely dark clouds.
–   And a red tie.
–   He carries the slick grace of the business-card men that sunny day on Wall Street. He is clean, lean, and perhaps prudent. Like a still life.
–   And as a still life, always on the brink of breaking up.
–   I believe he is held back. Maybe by fear, but most likely by duty.
–   Who?
–   L'Homme, 'the man' as Magritte named the painting.
–   He seems capable of action. A man with specific qualities. Well-educated. One who knows something important. Important enough to wear the uniform.

Figure 6.4   Fils de l'Homme, *Magritte (1964)*

– To know is to wear uniform. When knowledge resembles instruments,
  we become uniform. We are armed forces.
– Who's his enemy?

Back on Wall Street

– The business school is where a power of expert knowledge is fused with
  an economism of making everyone accountable. This is where economics and behaviourism cross-fertilize and form such a productive
  power. The professional identity of the manager is so intimately connected to the social role of the one who can enable, the one who can do.

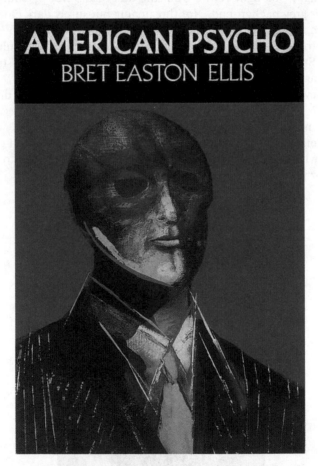

Figure 6.5   American Psycho, *Bret Easton Ellis, Macmillan Ltd (original
               printing)*

– It is merely about picking the right tool at the right moment. Merely doing this, like a pop star grabbing the microphone to say something, is already, has to be, the beginning of another success story.

Prague, early morning

– In the buzzing, swarming and polymorphous bubbling and extravagant creativity of capitalism, system-thinkers find themselves always to be targeting metamorphoses that in effect transform who we are and what

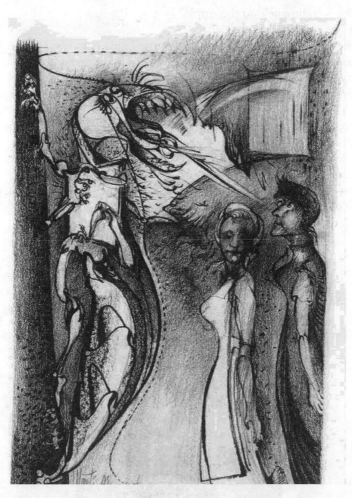

Figure 6.6   Pencil drawings inspired by Kafka's Metamorphosis, *Martin Linnartz (1992)*

we could become all the time. Instead of fighting this productive power, we learn from Kafka that we can affirm the subversive, the transformative, and engage in minorizing processes that put in our hands the power of invention without securing a homeground or appropriating a place.

– We are urged to travel lightly, never keep what we win, and always operate by slogans.

Venice, dark clouds in the background

– Who is hiding behind the Apple? Is it Mr Psycho
– Or Mr. Schizo?
– When Hardt and Negri in Empire, quote *Louis-Ferdinand Céline*, 'there is no escaping American business', we would like to add school; there is no escaping American business schools.
– European business schools currently take up very willingly the dream of a European elite. They apply (finally) to themselves the methods and approaches they have been preaching elsewhere: strategic visions, new cultures, e-learning pedagogies and quality management.
– A fierce competition among each other to rank as high as possible in the top ten ratings.
– No need to point out that the European elite will look very American.
– No chance to escape American business schools indeed.

Figure 6.7   Fils de l'Homme, *Magritte (1964)*

PART TWO: A HISTORY OF MAJORITARIAN ELITES

Venice, a museum

– As the latest elite, managerial and professional elites have joined the societal 'party'. Elites forming the pillars of society, as the German

Figure 6.8 Stützen der Gesellschaft *The Pillars of Society (1926),*
George Grosz © Photo RMN © ADAGP

dadaist and satirist George Grosz painted them in 1926 with a *cutting* realism, a work that nowadays hangs in one of Venice's museums.
–   Painting with slogans.
–   Do we need a history of elites in society to dissect the managerial elites of today?
–   Apparently, according to Grosz, it is the military, the clergy, and the press who provide the seemingly brainless politicians with instructions to govern the chaos of the interbellum. Probably there is no better period than the fin-de-siècle and the interbellum to reflect upon processes of elitarian formation.
–   Grosz would know, as his paintings, together with those from Paul Klee and Max Ernst, were confiscated and shown in the Art Exhibition 'Entartete Kunst', opened by Mr Goebbels personally on 19 July 1937.
–   A generation of avant-garde wiped out: expressionism, impressionism, Dadaism, 'neue Sachlichkeit', surrealism, cubism and fauvism.
–   History on elites was then written as never before.

The elite of the military

–   The first elite, if such a chronological hit parade is needed, is probably the military supporting the emperor and the empire. They go by the name of elite troops or personal guards rather than by the proletarian names of gladiators and soldiers.
–   The ones being paid – 'des sous' – for fighting. So also in the inter-bellum where a military career was among the finest options for the sons of good families.

Figure 6.9   Military

–   Ask Robert Musil, whose first step to open up for a life of writing, was a matter of stepping aside his military education. Stepping aside the *Zeitgeist.*

The elite of the clergy

–   The zero degree of elitarianism could be ascribed to the religious class. Sitting on their thrones as Kings, the popes have joined the elites

Figure 6.10   Study After Velasquez's Portrait of Pope Innocent X, *Francis Bacon (1953), purchased with funds from the Coffin Fine Arts Trust; Nathan Emory Coffin Collection of the Des Moines Art Center, 1980.1.*

instead of the masses. Their screaming open mouths produce an echo of power and property, emprisoned by lines of light.
–   As frightened negative heroes rather than lines of flight in people's lives, they forget the legend of Francis of Assisi. While the church was compromising itself when capitalism was nascent, he was radically stepping aside.
–   Stepping aside into a joyous life instead.

The elite of aristocracy

–   With their crowns, the royals and aristocracy distinguish themselves from the crowds. They don't need arms or religion to establish their impact.

Figure 6.11   Portrait of Louis XIV *(1701), Hyacinthe Rigaud,* © *Photo RMN*

- They embody power with their blue blood.
- Incapable any longer of stepping aside themselves, today, they hang on, with a little help from the paparazzi, to the establishment, exemplary to the Hollywood aristocrats and the media stardom.

The elite of intellectuals

[Here we ask you to imagine an image of Sartre.]
- Substitute blood with brains, and you get intellectual elitarianism.
- Rather than in castles, you find them in cafés.

Elites blurring

- And then there are those that blurr the classification of elitarian classes, carrying a crown of stars.
- Journalist, you said?
- *Sì, ma non solo*: I am prime minister, premier.
- *Ah, interessante! Ma anche capitalista?*
- *Si, no, industriale* – a business man.
- Trying not to see with the eyes squeezed.
- Trying not to speak with the lips pressed together, suppressing a cry or is it a casual joke?
- Trying not to hear, pressing the fingers in the ears.
- Elites without senses.

Figure 6.12   Berlusconi

PART THREE: BREAKING MAJORITARIAN ELITES

Any business school

– And so far our history of the elite, of generals, of popes, of aristocrats, of intellectuals, of those who bet on many horses simultaneously . . .

Figure 6.13   Skrik (The Scream), *Edvard Munch (1893),* © *Munch Museum/Munch-Ellingsen Group, BONO, Oslo, OACS, London 2005*

- You feel excluded by history, by this *beau monde*, by *the crème de la crème*, by the hand-picked?
- Getting a little anxious?
- No problem, any business school can help you in pole position for the high society.
- Are business school students then . . . intellectuals?
- There is a tension we admit, that we can bring back to the end of the 19th century, the time where the *Bildungsbürgertum* (the so-called intellectual bourgeoisie) felt intimidated by the upcoming success of the *Wirtschaftbürgertum* (the so-called business bourgeoisie) and feared a moral crisis provoked by the material orientation of the new industrialists and the massification of society. With the rise of the machine and the masses, they feared, as Oswald Spengler expressed it, an '*Untergang des Abendlandes*' (The Decline of the West), they feared, as Ortega y Gasset expressed it, *La rebellion de las masas* (The Revolt of the Masses).

Back in Venice

- With every new class joining the elite club, its crisis becomes rewritten. The question is always what is it that makes me among the chosen, electus, elite.

Figure 6.14   Fils de l'Homme, *Magritte (1964)*

-   No basis is better than any other: weapons, blood, brains, money, a picture in the papers.
-   Can we not think of a society without the concept of elites?
-   Is there any other way to portray and imagine those that take part in the adventure we call education?
-   The stakes are high.
-   Any possibility altering the revolt of the elites, as Christopher Lasch accuses the professional and managerial elites of betraying contemporary democracy?
-   Let's face that new elite of professionals and managers.
-   You and me!
-   Or should we rather study the apple?

Any TV screen

-   *Les élites nouveaux sont arrivés.*
-   The multiplication of managerial and professional elites.
-   In the media.
-   In IT.
-   In show business.
-   In sports.
-   So many new versions since the Yuppies and the BCBGs, that is the 'Bon Chic Bon Genre'.

Figure 6.15   The Hollywood sign

- The creative class.
- The bourgeois bohemians. The bobos.
- All in the fast lane.
- Part of the jet set. The glitterati.

PART FOUR: MINORIZATION AND IMAGES OF A PEOPLE TO COME

- Let us break into language, give me that knife so I can cut discourses open and make them bleed, make words stutter.
- A Borgesian heterotopia, a collection that doesn't collect: with angels.
- And . . . troubadours.
- And harlequins.
- Masked clowns.
- *Und Frauen ohne Eigenschaften.*

Figure 6.16   Natura Morte Vivante: Still Life Fast Moving © *Salvador Dalí Museum, St. Petersburg, Florida. All rights reserved.*

- Every image is a rhizome that connects the unconnected and the unconnectable, a surrealist tableau that draws upon signs, a clean table-cloth, birds, fruitscales, apples, motifs, knives. Cut! Cut!
- End of the image. Thank you.
- No, not like that, I meant, Carve out! Cut! Cut!
- Cut! Cut! Cut!

Image 1: Mann ohne Eigenschaften

- Woman without face. Effacing the face. No qualities – that is what Musil had been spinning out two thousand pages about.
- Effacing realities, increasing possibilities. Before his death, his work had died already as his books got banned in Germany and Austria in 1938.
- Could we expect this to be a routine decision of the managerial elite at that time in charge?
- Ulrich, a comic anti-hero, was not acceptable in a time that longed for heroes.
- I heard that before Musil invented literature, he invented a chromatometer.
- Then he goes on inventing with precision and soul a new language –

Figure 6.17   Der Mann ohne Eigenschaften *(Book cover), Artist: Mucha, Rewolt Taschenbuch Verlag*

essayistic literature in the hothouse atmosphere of fin-de-siècle Vienna with its amoral *Gefühlskultur*.

– A value vacuum with people weightless.
– Against which Musil – with a Kafka metamorphosis – draws a woman without references, without possessions, without qualities, without gender, without laws and says, letting every bond and bonding go.
– 'I am No One'.
– Teach the soldier so to speak!
– And business students. Business students!

Image 2: harlequins [quotes from Serres, 2000]

– Cut! Cut! Cut!
– 'Even when it is unique, a language remains a mixture, a schizophrenic

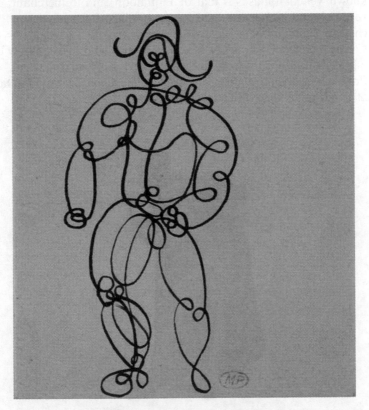

Figure 6.18 Au Lapin Agile (Harlequino) *(1905), Pablo Picasso,* ©
Photo RMN © Sucession Picasso

mélange, a Harlequin costume in which very different functions of language and distinct centres of powers are played out, blurring what can
be said and what can't be said'.
- Harlequin, Speak! Make me speak multiplicity!
- Harlequin, crossbred animal, had to die a thousand deaths to get there,
torn up beneath her derisory dressing . . .
- Politicians, journalists, business people, die a thousand deaths before
you speak, before your lips open.

Image 3: masked clowns

- Ha! This is Pantaloon.
- Indeed. From the *Merchant of Venice*, we know of the central role of
merchants in Venice and it could not be a surprise that one of the best-
known Venetian masks is that of Pantaloon, an old merchant, often
very rich and highly esteemed by the nobility, but sometimes a merchant in ruin.
- Carnival creates a double of life, an inventive comment on how life is
taking its toll. It is a special and specific art of provoking.
- Pro-vocare, when the voice calls forth, when a voice is raised in favour
of a new possibility with a teasing laughter.

Figure 6.19   Pantaloon, trad.

- A carnivalesque provocation opposes the dominant view by installing a second one that upsets, transforms or simply doubles it.
- A carnival, in the middle of life, where one finally can say what one always wanted to say, and where one dares to say so, masked, disguised, being different.
- Stand up, dear aristocrats, and make fun. Make fun of yourself.

Image 4: angels

[Imagine Angels, never fully absent, never fully present, always in the(ir) wings.]

- Cutting language is pruning the wings, so words fly lighter, more elegantly. Put on your wings, like an Icarus, and fly in between. Only in between.
- And write an educational programme in slogans. Start with: we need to . . .
- We need to multiply, embrace the angels, these plural and minorising Hermeses, always busy in the acts of caring, carrying, connecting, bringing messages, talking to us in our sleep.
- We need to listen to the angels to make space for the troubadour of knowledge.

Image 5: troubadours *[quotes from Serres, 2000]*

- 'Pling, pling'.
- Ah, troubadours. For them, cutting in language means make words sing.
- Troubadour comes from the latin *tropare*, which *originally* meant 'composing tropes' or songs. Now it refers to a literary activity that consists of invention, creation, *trouvaille*.
- Troubadours conceive the poet as a 'trouveur' of words, sounds, rhymes, as a kind of craftswoman of artisan word plays and playing with words.
- The troubadour of knowledge is a *conceptual persona* in Serres' philosophy of education and learning. His pedagogy is connective, a mixture, a crossbreeding between arts, sciences and humanities.
- His tone is instructive, 'ready sentences' for teachers to introduce their classes and to give away what students as troubadours do and do not do, what teachers, equally troubadouresque, do and do not do: 'Depart, take the plunge'.
- Taking the plunge implies crossing the middle, sensing the middle, leaving shores and all reference points, settling into its foreign life for good.

Figure 6.20   Troubadours, trad., cut-out

– 'Yes, depart, divide yourself in parts', repeats the teacher.
– It helps to think of the troubadour, to unlearn that the teacher knows and that the student should and could equal that knowledge, to enter into creation yourself: 'the goal of instruction is the end of instruction, that is to say invention'.
– There is no need for schools and pedagogues, only for water and swimmers. The knowledge society is a swim club without membership. We do not belong to schools, paradigms, and give up our positions. We cannot go on excluding people from learning by programming and disciplining them. The *lehrstuhl* is a boat, a non-place, ein *Piratenschiff*. Run your courses as movements.
– Learning by heart is then inventing through love. Teachers and students simply swim along. Our only teachers are those who tell us 'do with me', and are able to emit signs to be developed in heterogeneity rather than propose gestures for us to reproduce.
– Do with us.

PART FIVE: BECOMING LITERARIAN (INSTEAD OF ELITIST)

Faceless face/death mask

- The woman without qualities is an image of the inventive possibilities. She bears no traces of instruction, carries no heritage of disciplinary knowledges, is not weighted down by the duties of her professional identity.
- Like fungus, rhizomatically cooperating with cracks and interstices, we are setting off in all directions, like adventurers without plans.
- We seek possibilities to nurture the birth of that third person in us that makes our attempt to secure a place for what we are impossible.
- We drink from the wells of literature and strive to excel in the fables we tell.

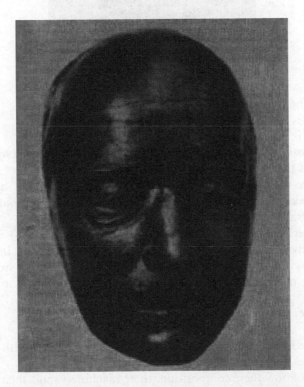

Figure 6.21 The Death Mask of Robert Musil, *www.xs4all.nl/~jikje/ New/pics.html*

Becoming apple

Figure 6.22   Fils de l'Homme, *Magritte (1964)*

- Nothing is hidden behind the apple.
- There is no face.
- There is facelessness.
- The possibilities of a face, of multiple faces, are promised by the location of the apple.
- To face the moment of creation. Life of literature, life of art, crosses the traces of our life revealed and hidden in our face, and makes us into masks, into the faceless.
- Learners, engaged in the formation of future administrative elites, have to cultivate a desire to sneak up on popes and politicians like Francis Bacon's brush: minorising the dominant (majoritarian) story, create masks, make the main story become subverted by its footnotes.

Becoming bird

- We need to intensify our relations with elites, not least, with managerial elites, with the elites of management.
- Get to know their composition, their machinery, and their favourite operations.
- Become a neighbour, a parasite.

Figure 6.23 L'Homme au chapeau melon (Man with bowler hat), *René Magritte (1964) © 2005, Prolitteris, Zurich*

- Practise their favourite principle and make them fly.
- Seek to get into every scene, and pull it towards the ob-scene.
- Become a virus, transform bodies.
- Travel lightly, intensely, imagine all.
- Become a Don Quixote.

'The aim of writing is to carry life to the state of a non-personal power', Gilles Deleuze and Claire Parnet (1987), *Dialogues.*

REFERENCES

Ahearne, Jeremy (1995), *Michel de Certeau: Interpretation and its Other*, London: Polity Press.

Bakhtin, Michail (1968), *Rabelais and his World*, Cambridge, MA: Harvard University Press.

Bakhtin, Michail (1981), *The Dialogic Imagination*, Austin, Texas: University of Texas Press.

Braeckman, Antoon, Raoul Bauer and Jacques De Visscher (2001), *Onbehagen met de Moderniteit. De Revolte van de Intellectuelen 1890–1933*, Kapellen: Uitgeverij Pelckmans.

Brooks, David (2000), *Bobos in Paradise. The New Upper Class and How They Got There*, New York: Simon & Schuster.

Buchanan, Ian and John Marks (eds) (2000), *Deleuze and Literature*, Edinburgh: Edinburgh University Press.

Colebrook, Claire (2002), *Deleuze*, London: Routledge.

Deleuze, Gilles (1989a), *Masochism: An Introduction to Coldness and Cruelty*, trans. Jean McNeil, New York: Zone Books.

Deleuze, Gilles (1989b), *Cinema II: The Time Image*, trans. Hugh Tomlinson and Robert Galeta, Minneapolis: University of Minnesota Press.

Deleuze, Gilles (1995), *Negotiations*, New York: Columbia University Press.

Deleuze, Gilles (1997), *Essays Critical and Clinical*, Minneapolis: University of Minnesota Press.

Deleuze, Gilles and Félix Guattari (1986), *Kafka. Toward a Minor Literature*, Minneapolis: University of Minnesota Press.

Deleuze, Gilles and Félix Guattari (1987), *A Thousand Plateaus. Capitalism and Schizophrenia*, London: Athlone Press.

Deleuze, Gilles and Claire Parnet (1987), *Dialogues*, trans. Hugh Tomlinson and Barbara Habberjam, London: Athlone.

Ellis, Bret Easton (1991) *American Psycho: a Novel*, New York: Vintage Books.

Florida, Richard L. (2002), *The Rise of the Creative Class: and how it's Transforming Work, Leisure, Community and Everyday Life*, New York: Basic Books.

Greenblatt, Stephen (1997), 'The touch of the real', *Representations*, **59**, Summer, 14–29.

Hardt, Michael and Antonio Negri (2000), *Empire*, Cambridge, MA and London: Harvard University Press.

Lambert, Gregg (2000), 'On the uses and abuses of literature for life', in Ian Buchanan and John Marks (eds), *Deleuze and Literature*, Edinburgh: Edinburgh University Press, pp. 135–66.

Lasch, Cristopher (1995), *The Revolt of the Elites and the Betrayal of Democracy*, New York: Norton.

Ortega y Gasset, José (1984), *The Revolt of the Masses*, Notre Dame, IN: University of Notre Dame.

Serres, Michel (2000), *The Troubadour of Knowledge*, Ann Arbor: The University of Michigan Press.

Spengler, Oswald (1998), *Der Untergang des Abendlandes: Urmisse einer Morphologie der Weltgeschichte*, Munich: Beck.

Vattimo, Gianni (1992), *The Transparent Society*, Cambridge: Polity Press.

MOVIES/IMAGES

Movies

'American Psycho' (2000), directed by Mary Harron, written by Bret Easton Ellis (Novel).

'Kafka' (1991), directed by Steven Soderberg, written by Lem Dobbs.

'Glengarry Glen Ross' (1992), directed by James Foley, based on play by David Mamet who also wrote the screenplay for the movie.

'Schindler's List' (1993), directed by Steven Spielberg, based on the book *Schindler's Ark* by Thomas Keneally, screenplay by Steven Zaillian.

'Citizen Kane' (1941), directed by Orson Welles, screenplay by Orson Welles and Herman J. Mankiawicz.

Paintings

René Magritte, *Le Fils de l'Homme / The Son of Man* (1964), oil on canvas, New York, Harry Torczyner Collection.

René Magritte, *L'homme au chapeau melon / Man with bowler hat* (1964), oil on canvas, New York, A. Carter Pottash Collection.

Martin Linnartz (St. Agnesstraat 4, 6241 CB Bunde), Paintings inspired by Kafka's *Metamorphosis* (1992).

George Grosz, *Stützen der Gesellschaft / The Pillars of Society* (1926), oil on canvas, Berlin, Nationalgalerie, Staatliche Museen zu Berlin.

Francis Bacon, *Study After Velazquez's Portrait of Pope Innocent X* (1953), Oil on canvas, Des Moines Art Center, Iowa.

Hyacinthe Rigaud, *Portrait of Louis XIV* (1701), oil on canvas, Paris, Louvre Museum.

Edvard Munch, *Skrik (The Scream)* (1893), tempera on panel, Oslo, Nasjonal-galleriet.

Salvador Dalí, *Natura Morte Vivante / A Lively Still Life* (1956), The Salvador Dalí Museum (Reynolds Morse Collection), St Petersburg, Fl, USA.

Pablo Picasso, *Harlequino*, titled *Au Lapin Agile*, painted in 1905, Metropolitan Museum of Art, New York.

Troubadours: trad., cut-out

Photographs

Berlusconi, Silvio (AP, undated).

Musil, Robert, *Der Mann ohne Eigenschaften I* Book cover, Rowohlt Taschenbuch Verlag, GmbH, Mai 1994 – Taschenbücher – 1040 S.

Pantaloon (traditional image of Venice carnival character). http://www.carnivalofvenice.com/documento.asp?DocID=26

Death mask: The Death Mask of Robert Musil: http://www.xs4all.nl/ ~jikje/New/pics.html

PART 2

Management education: Is a humanist
reframing possible?

7.   The business school in ruins?

Ken Starkey and Sue Tempest

In this chapter we call for a broader debate about the idea and ideal of the business school and its mission, rooted not just in notions of economic rationality but in a more broadly cultural framework. It is our contention, somewhat quixotic perhaps, that it is in the business school that new possibilities lie for re-framing the integration of different forms of knowledge, and for reconciling the tensions between management as science and management as art. We speculate on the constitution of the idea of a manager and of the practice of management grounded in knowledge of social sciences and liberal arts reaching out to the physical sciences (engineering, medicine, pharmaceutical sciences, for example) to capitalize upon new knowledge possibilities. We suggest that, contrary to what its critics claim, it is in the business school that our best hope lies of integrating the two cultures of the sciences and the arts. This aspiration might provide the basis for a uniquely European configuration of the business school idea with important implications for the future formation of European elites.

Our argument is more positive about the potential of business schools than recent formulations. Ironically, as the business school becomes more dominant as a global idea it stands accused of failing to deliver on its promises. In the United States, the land of its origin, Pfeffer and Fong (2002) have gone as far as suggesting that the actual future of the business school is in doubt because both its research and teaching missions are compromised, perhaps fatally. Others accuse the business school of a moral failure and suggest that recent corporate failings and scandals – Long-Term Capital Management, Enron, WorldCom, to name the most visible – throw into question the reduction of management to an exercise in shareholder value and invite us to reflect more broadly about what constitutes value.

While we have great sympathy with Pfeffer and Fong's argument and consider the issue of the future of the business school to be of crucial importance for the future constitution and character of management elites, we do think that the discussion of this future should be considered in a broad perspective that links the business school to discussion of the future of the university. This is an absence in the literature that our chapter seeks to fill. It is our contention that the future of the business school and the future of the university are symbiotically linked and that in considering the role of the business school we have to raise fundamental questions about the role of the university.

The university has historically been a major site for connecting knowledge, culture and society (Delanty, 2001). However, the university itself, at least the modern idea of the university, is increasingly called into question. It has even been suggested that the growth and the undoubted success of the business school is one symptom of this idea's decline. Our chapter takes its title from Readings' (1996) study of the decline of the university, *The University in Ruins*, which argues that the university is an institution which has been forced to abandon its historical *raison d'être* and identity as it desperately seeks to respond to the ever more demanding consumers of its services.

According to its critics, social and economic forces have 'instrumental-ized the university' to the extent that it is now in danger of becoming irrel-evant as a prime site of knowledge production (Delanty, 2001, pp. 5–6). In Readings' (1996, pp. 19, 27) graphic phrase, the university is a '*ruined* institution, one that has lost its historical *raison d'être . . .* Henceforth, the question of the University is only the question of relative value-for-money, the question posed to a student who is situated entirely as a *consumer*, rather than as someone who wants to think'. The only unique role retained by the university is its power to offer credentials for student learning, and even this is not guaranteed to last.

Space constraints dictate that we cannot consider the full range of history in our discussion nor the great variety of types of university. We gloss over the differences of national trajectories in the development of higher education institutions to focus upon what we perceive as key trends and tensions in the development of contemporary debates about the devel-opment of the university. We examine the significance of these debates to the business school. In doing this, we rely, for pragmatic reasons, upon a number of 'ideal' types in our analysis, namely the 'modern university' (which we associate historically with Germany and Humboldt in the early nineteenth century, our historical starting point), the 'postmodern univer-sity' (emerging in the latter decades of the twentieth century), the 'US model of the elite business school' (starting to form in the early twentieth century and coming to full fruition in the second half of the century) and the 'European model of the business school' (yet to emerge).

UNIVERSITY IDEALS THROUGH TIME

The modern idea of the university emerged at the end of the eighteenth century. According to this emergent idea, the university was seen as 'a knowledge producer, serving the nation state with professional elites and as a codifier of national culture' (Delanty, 2001, pp. 22–4). Universities have long had the role of developing elites. Many of the early Oxford colleges were founded to guarantee the education and supply of an administrative cadre for the state and for the church. (There was even a term for the early medieval equivalent of MBA knowledge, *scientiae lucrativae*)[1]. What changes in the context of the modern university is the emphasis upon the university's role of new knowledge creation.

The plan outlined by Humboldt for the University of Berlin (prototype for the modern university) was premised upon a refocusing of the university's social role in serving the state – 'that of simultaneous search for its objective cultural meaning as a historical entity and the subjective moral training of its subjects as potential bearers of that identity' (Readings, 1996, pp. 68–9). In Humboldt's scheme, the educational mission of the university is defined as an interaction between research and teaching. Humboldt's project 'consists not only in the acquisition of learning by individuals, but also in the training of a fully legitimated subject of knowledge and society' (Lyotard, 1984, p. 33), the formation of no less than the modern self. The knowledge developed in the university is to be differentiated from that developed in other sites because, in theory anyway, it is not subject to the dictates of outside agencies but represents the outcome of the disinterested search for truth.

In the twentieth century this ideal was challenged. We see a schism slowly developing between the idea of professional training, which is increasingly desired by student and society but seen as increasingly divorced from the core university function, the transmission of knowledge based upon research that seeks as its main function to advance knowledge rather than practice. Nisbet (1971), for example, writes critically of professionalism supplanting scholarship. Should the university's prime role be that of autonomous defender of knowledge or should the quest for knowledge be subsumed in society's need for professional training? Indeed, will the university remain a major knowledge player?

Gibbons et al. (1994), in their influential study, argue that a new model of knowledge is replacing the old in which universities played a central role. The new production of knowledge takes place in a growing variety of sites outside the university and has as a prime characteristic the co-production of knowledge by many knowledge workers addressing problems in the context of application. As a result the university is, at least in part, de-legitimized as a privileged site of knowledge production, not least because of a growing dissatisfaction with, and suspicion of, experts. Delanty (2001, p. 5), following Beck (1992), talks of a 'wide-spread loss of scientific legitimacy and growing public calls for the accountability of science and technology'.

In this context the academic claim of neutrality, universality and objectivity is difficult to sustain.

The postmodern view is that the university has reached the end of its particular road, that '[i]ts founding cognitive ideas – the universality of knowledge, the quest for truth, the unity of culture – are becoming irrelevant and the social and economic reality has instrumentalized the university to a point that has made its autonomy neither possible nor desirable' (Delanty, 2001, pp. 5–6). Corporate 'bureaucratization' has led to 'the strong homogenization of the University as an institution' (Readings, 1996, pp. 19, 12). In the process, the university has lost its cultural function, enmeshed in the pressures for accountability and the aspiration to excellence in its dealings with its 'customers'. The search for this form of excellence runs the risk of creating a closed system without any objective external referents of the sense of absolute values that the university previously had been engaged in producing.

Kirp (2003) argues that the most powerful force for change in university life is the increasing dominance of business values, practical utility and the marketplace. Since the 1970s, students have shifted in 'massive' numbers from liberal arts courses to the 'practical arts'. Kirp's study examines a world in transition, perhaps inexorably, with some nostalgia for the world we might well be losing:

> This is how the world seems naturally to work when, as now, the zeitgeist is the market. If health care, museums, even churches have been caught up in, and reshaped by, intense competitive pressures, why should higher education be any different? . . . Still, embedded in the very idea of the university [. . .] are the values that the market does not honor: the belief in a community of scholars and not a confederacy of self-seekers; in the idea of openness and not ownership; in the professor as a pursuer of truth and not an entrepreneur; in the student as an acolyte whose preferences are to be formed, not a consumer whose preferences are to be satisfied' (Kirp, 2003, p. 7).

Many of Kirp's narratives of the commodification and marketing of higher education recall the bargain Doctor Faustus struck with the devil. We particularly like the story of the rebellion at Duke when the University increased its demands on undergraduates. The students rebelled, wearing a T-shirt with the slogan 'You can lead me to college but you can't force me to think' (Kirp, 2003, p. 47).

THE BUSINESS SCHOOL

The business school has pursued a chequered 'career' in the university context. In its earlier days it was closely associated with vocational training.

Indeed the business school was, from the start, criticized for not exhibiting the characteristics of the 'proper' university school. This came to a head in the post-World War II period when business schools were identified as lacking in a strong scientific foundation which led to weakness of their research. In essence, business schools were perceived as being little more than 'trade schools'. The reaction to this critique set the business school on a more mainstream academic trajectory in its struggle to establish its academic legitimacy, particularly in the research-led university.

The investment in research in the 1950s, particularly by the Ford and Carnegie Foundations, was motivated by the desire to counter the drift in business education and to provide clarity and direction about issues such as who should teach what to whom. The business school rallied and raised its research game and reputation. At the same time, the business school was perceived as fulfilling its practical role. A report commissioned in 1983 by the Futures Committee of the AACSB (Porter and McKibbin, 1988) concluded that higher education for business was serving the needs of the business community (McKenna and Yeider, 1991), thus accomplishing the desire expressed by President Eliot when he addressed the general education board at Harvard in 1907 in the attempt to obtain funds for establishing a business school, that such a school 'would soon demonstrate a great capacity for public usefulness' (Harris, 1970, p. 491).

But the emphasis upon academic integrity, ironically, opened the door to later criticism. Pursuing its academic agenda was perceived by many to lead eventually to a distancing from the ability to cater to the public demand for usefulness: 'adopting the ways of other academic social science departments has produced a new set of problems including concerns about the relevance and centrality of business schools and business education to the world of management' (Pfeffer and Fong, 2002, pp. 79–80). As demand for its teaching rose – particularly for the MBA – it was argued that the business school curriculum had little to offer to managers struggling with the realities of complex organizational issues. As a result, the business school was criticized for its 'overemphasis on analysis at the expense of both integration and developing wisdom as well as leadership and interpersonal skills, or teaching the wrong things in the wrong ways to the wrong people or at least at the wrong time in their careers' (Pfeffer and Fong, 2001, pp. 79–80).

This growing dissatisfaction with the business school's educational performance led to a consumer backlash, embodied in *Business Week* inaugurating its (in)famous ranking system. The rankings, together with a new social ethos of consumerism, have transformed purchasers of business school services, students and employers, into customers, and have given rise to ever more frenetic competition between schools desperate to remain in

or to leapfrog into the top ten elite division (Zell, 2001). Rankings also lead
to pressure for conformity to the narrow criteria used to define success.
The danger of the search for popularity is that it drives out diversity and
profundity.

REPOSITIONING OF THE UNIVERSITY
AND THE BUSINESS SCHOOL IN A NEW
KNOWLEDGE LANDSCAPE

For us, the major issue facing both the university and the business school
is the question of knowledge. Critical to the future of the business school,
and the issue that will determine whether it is fast approaching ruin or will
go from strength to strength, is the issue of purpose which is intimately
linked to the issue of the purpose of the university itself.

The prime purpose of the university historically concerns the generation
and diffusion of knowledge. The business school, like the university, will
have to re-define the legitimacy upon which it grounds its privileged knowledge claims. We accept that the contours of knowledge production are
changing but this does not necessarily mean that the university and business school will not or could not have key roles to play in a new knowledge
landscape. The business school faces a major challenge in the current
reconfiguration of knowledge spaces (Nowotny et al., 2001). Major opportunities exist – in knowledge production and in the role of knowledge
arbiter and broker in a more complex and differentiated knowledge production process. What is at stake here is a redefinition of purpose in the
light of the emerging reconfiguration of knowledge production. The challenge concerns the whole university, not just the business school.

> Today knowledge has become more important and at the same time no longer
> emanates from any particular source. This restructuring in the mode of know-
> ledge implies not the end of the university but its reconfiguration. The great
> significance of the institution of the university today is that it can be the most
> important site of interconnectivity in what is now a knowledge society. There is
> a proliferation of so many kinds of knowledge that no particular one can unify
> all the others. The university cannot re-establish the broken unity of knowledge
> but it can open up avenues of communication between these different kinds
> of knowledge, in particular knowledge as science and knowledge as culture
> (Delanty, 2001, p. 6).

This particular way of framing the knowledge challenge reminds us that
one area in which business schools have been judged deficient is in the lack
of an orientation to knowledge as culture. Indeed critics of the business

school and its increasingly central role, judged at least by demand for its courses, in the university system, argue that the business school's view of knowledge is both parochial and pernicious. For Allan Bloom (1987), what is particularly problematic about business school education is that it prioritizes one form of knowledge at the expense of the more general formation of the mind.

> The specific effect of the MBA has been an explosion of enrollments in economics, the prebusiness major. Economics overwhelms the rest of the social sciences and skews the students' perception of them – their purpose and their relative weight with regard to the knowledge of human beings. . . . the prebusiness economics major . . . not only does not take an interest in sociology, anthropology or political sciences but is also persuaded that what he is learning can handle all that belongs to those studies. Moreover, he is not motivated by love of the science of economics but by love of what it is concerned with – money. . . . there is nothing else quite like this perfect coincidence between science and cupidity elsewhere in the university. The only true parallel would be if there were a science of sexology, with earnest and truly scholarly professors, which would ensure its students lavish sexual satisfactions! (Bloom, 1987, pp. 370–71).

And this was before the wave of corporate scandals, such as Enron, in which the MBA was specifically implicated, and in the light of which business schools have been accused of producing business leaders who are not 'true professionals with true character' (Salbu, 2002). These kinds of criticism raise important questions about the business school's mission in a society in which individualism, consumerism and a particular variant of corporatism are rampant. Is the business school, in part, responsible for these qualities, a key engine of a particular *zeitgeist*, or is it merely a symptom? This question raises important questions about the business school's educational role. Bloom (1987, p. 20) defines the role of university teaching in traditional and liberal terms. 'No real teacher can doubt that his task is to assist his pupil to fulfill human nature against all the deforming forces of convention and prejudice'. The criticism of the MBA is that it is precisely an instrument of convention and possibly prejudice, in that it is based upon a particularly limited view of business, managers and, even, human nature.

As Gagliardi says, in his introduction to this volume, 'the basic conception of the manager's role and of how it is learnt continues to be – in substance and in almost all case – the conception adopted and disseminated fifty years ago by the first European business schools and consultancy companies that imported it from North America'. Management is viewed as a technical, quasi-scientific activity. The research that supports this view is itself rooted in an increasingly narrow empiricist, a-historical and a-cultural frame. We agree, again with the view expressed by Gagliardi in his introduction, that this makes it difficult, if not impossible, to develop managers as 'statespersons' and that one way of fostering such development is through exposure to 'humanistic culture, a thorough knowledge of history, philosophy, of art, of the heritage of knowledge and sensibility that humankind has constructed in its history on this continent and which can be an inexhaustible source of inspiration'.

We would suggest, though, that to understand why we find ourselves faced with our current dilemmas confronting business schools and how we might imagine new, more humanistic modes of management education we need particularly to develop our knowledge of history and politics if we are to understand and to counter the inexorable trend to Americanization in our field. This is a highly political arena. There is as yet no viable alternative, in the sense of strong countervailing force, to the US management education juggernaut, just as there is, as yet, no credible alternative to the MBA that commands any significant consumer interest.

We are also sensitive to the danger that the appeal to a humanistic alternative can be presented as an 'either/or', as in Bloom's swinging criticism referred to above. The strong form of this appeal is to suggest that society would be better if we closed down business schools and re-invested in the liberal arts. This is unrealistic. It seems to us that a more practical way forward is to consider how the business school might engage with the liberal arts in a more open, embracing and mutually sustaining way. We also suggest that this might offer particular opportunities for developing a European variant of the business school, drawing on the best of European and US traditions. This is a question of the construction of an alternative European identity.

One justification for a possible humanist turn is developed in the argument for critical management education (CME). In Christopher Grey's (2004) useful argument, CME takes as its starting point the recognition that to engage in management is to commit to a set of particular values, political and moral, and that these need surfacing and examination. Reflexivity about what we do in business schools means that we have to examine, and engage managers in the examination of philosophical, ethical and even aesthetic judgements. The CME 'answer' is 'to reconfigure management education in terms of an attention to values and to context' so as to create 'a capacity for ethical and contextual sensitivity' (Grey, 2004, p. 182).

Grey's critical position is somewhat more measured than more extreme critical management researchers who see the business school as one of the ruins of the capitalist system and symbol, no doubt, of the system's imminent (but strangely prolonged) demise. He calls – no small thing in itself – for 'a degree of honesty', noting that 'in any case, the failure of business schools to live up to their promises will eventually force them to make more modest claims anyway' (Grey, 2004, p. 184). Others are more strident and more apocalyptic: 'when the B-schools become empty, when the corridors contain dead leaves and the roofs leak, then they will be converted to sociology departments or housing for the elderly and CMS [Critical Management Studies] will have done its job' (Parker, 2002, p. 132). The 'ruins' scenario is here made explicit. It is an intriguing idea to imagine business schools reconfigured as housing for elderly sociologists. There are those who are critical of critical management research who think that some business schools already have been!

We agree with Grey's (2004, p. 184) argument that business schools should be places 'where complex ideas and complex practices can meet for the general good'. The agenda then is to design business schools to accommodate the requisite variety of knowledge types that would make them adequate to deal with this complexity and here the liberal arts, and sociology, have their parts to play. Grey argues that the business school can never be a professional school. We do not agree and, indeed, are not convinced that the business school can justify the legitimacy of its existence unless it engages with the formation of management professionals. Otherwise, liberal arts, sociology, psychology economics and a whole panoply of other departments have stronger claims to be teaching the issues that CME focuses upon.

The basic design principle of the professional school was identified by Simon (1967, p. 2) in an article that still has huge relevance for the challenges facing the business school: 'the professional school must have effective access to information and skills within the several sciences that are relevant to and contributing to the improvement of professional practice'. It seems to us that it is the desire for the improvement of management practice that motivates the CME agenda, at least in the way that it is developed by Grey. Simon (1967) argues that the business school needs to bring together knowledge from economics, psychology, sociology, applied mathematics and computing science. Culture is strangely absent here and it is this that the liberal arts would bring into the business school. Quite how this might be done is an issue for future debate, when the need to pursue this agenda is more widely recognized and accepted.

CONCLUSION

In conclusion, we return to our starting point, the role of the university. It is our contention that the business school idea and ideal are symbiotically linked to the idea, the ideal and the identity of the university. Indeed, one defence of the current role of the business school – not the major one by any means, but an important one – is that its 'commercial' success in attracting paying customers allows the university as a whole to invest in areas which are not as commercially viable. Many universities' finances are significantly dependent upon business school income. Some arts and humanities departments, for example language departments, are dependent on joint degrees with business and management to secure new students. Of course, this is not, by any stretch of the imagination, enough to guarantee the long-term viability of the business school or of the university itself. We do not champion the business school merely as the cash cow in the university portfolio.

The long-term viability of the business school, as of the university, will depend upon the vigorous defence of its identity and its social utility which will require that it engages with the issues we have raised in this chapter and with concepts that might, currently, seem alien to its mission – character, culture and the opening of the mind to more than the mere economic. 'Character' and its corrosion is one of the casualties of the new capitalism identified by Sennett (1998) as he addresses forces for fragmentation in the current business and social landscape. In brief, the business school has to reflect upon its history and its future mission to arrive at a new definition of its purpose, particularly with respect to knowledge production and diffusion, that commands the respect of those it serves in ways that they themselves are perhaps only dimly aware of. Its role as knowledge mediator, between pure science, applied science, social science, and, hopefully, liberal arts, will enable it to contribute to a new definition of culture and character appropriate to the perplexing challenges of our time. The European social science and liberal arts traditions have much to contribute here. Out of this contribution, we would hope for the creation of a new European identity for the business school, working towards the integration of knowledge as science and knowledge as culture.

The European business school finds itself faced with different dilemmas, one might suggest, more profound dilemmas, than those identified by Pfeffer and Fong (2001). The gold standard for the business school has tended to be the US elite schools and those European schools, such as INSEAD and London Business School, that have set out to adopt the elite American school model in a process of imitation. Other European schools are not as far down this road and there is now the suggestion, emanating from the US, that this might not be the best road to follow.

It will require a breadth of vision to address these issues, a vision informed by more than what are conventionally defined as the business disciplines and encapsulated in the typical business school curriculum. The quintessential philosophical question is: what is a good life? This links to Readings' (1996, p. 121) challenge, that universities need to rethink their contribution to the reshaping of 'the social bond' in a society faced with significant pressures towards fragmentation. Business has a crucial role to play in determining the parameters of the good life available to us. Business schools, too, have a crucial role to play in addressing this question and in clarifying their purpose and the kinds of knowledge we need as we face the uncertainties of the new millennium.

Finally, we would like to offer one more reflection on the relationship between the business school and its host, the university. We have argued that both institutions are faced with a new knowledge landscape. In our view the business school is potentially better placed than many other parts of the university to capitalize upon the opportunities this new landscape offers. Other parts of the university are already wrestling with it. For example, Nowotny et al. (2001) discuss the environmental sciences as a prototypical example where the interactions of different disciplines, drawn from different parts of the Academy and beyond, is leading to a rethinking of science. Other parts of the university remain behind their closed doors, trying to ignore the clamouring of the world beyond their gates. Some business schools, particularly in older universities, have adopted a similar position. We doubt whether this is a defensible position longer-term. The future, we suggest, will lie with those schools that can create new opportunities for knowledge production and knowledge brokering that can lead to new forms of value creation, economic, social and cultural.

NOTE

1. Anthony Hopwood, personal communication.

REFERENCES

Beck, Ulrich (1992), *The Risk Society*, London: Sage.
Bloom, Allan (1987), *The Closing of the American Mind: How Higher Education has Failed Democracy and Impoverished the Souls of Today's Students*, New York: Simon & Schuster.
Delanty, Gerard (2001), *Challenging Knowledge. The University in the Knowledge Society*, Buckingham: The Society for Research into Higher Education & Open University Press.
Gibbons, Michael, Camille Limoges, Helga Nowotny et al. (1994), *The New Production of Knowledge*, London: Sage.
Grey, Christopher (2004), 'Reinventing business schools: The contribution of critical management education', *Academy of Management Learning and Education*, **3** (2), 178–86.
Harris, Seymour E. (1970), *Economics of Harvard*, New York: McGraw-Hill.

Kirp, David L. (2003), *Shakespeare, Einstein, and the Bottom Line. The Marketing of Higher Education*, Cambridge, Mass: Harvard University Press.

Leavitt, Harold (1989), 'Educating our MBAs: On teaching what we haven't taught', *California Management Review*, **31** (3), 38–50.

Lyotard, Jean-François (1984), *The Postmodern Condition: A Report on Knowledge*, Manchester: Manchester University Press.

McKenna, John F. and Richard A. Yeider (1991), 'Business education and regional variation: An administrative perspective', *Journal of Education for Business*, **67** (1), 50–56.

Nisbet, Robert (1971), *The Degradation of the Academic Dogma: The University in America 1945–70*, London: Heinemann.

Nowotny, Helga, Peter Scott and Michael Gibbons (2001), *Rethinking Science. Knowledge and the Public in an Age of Uncertainty*, Cambridge: Polity Press.

Parker, Martin (2002), *Against Management*, Cambridge: Polity Press.

Pfeffer, Jeffrey and Christina T. Fong (2002), 'The end of business schools? Less success than meets the eye', *Academy of Management Learning and Education*, **1**, 78–95.

Porter, Lyman W. and Lawrence McKibbin (1988), *Management Education and Development: Drift or Thrust into the 21ˢᵗ Century*, New York: McGraw-Hill.

Readings, Bill (1996), *The University in Ruins*, Cambridge, Mass.: Harvard University Press.

Salbu, Steve (2002), Foreword to *Anatomy of Greed. The Unshredded Truth from an Enron Insider*, London: Hutchinson.

Sennett, Richard (1998), *The Corrosion of Character. The Personal Consequences of Work in the New Capitalism*, New York: W.W. Norton & Company.

Simon, Herbert (1967), 'The business school. A problem in organizational design', *Journal of Management Studies*, **4**, 1–16.

Zell, Deone (2001), 'The market-driven business school: Has the pendulum swung too far?', *Journal of Management Inquiry*, **10**, 324–38.

8. Problematizing and enlarging the notion of humanistic education

Daniel Arenas

TWO SEPARATE WORLDS

In a lecture given in 1959, called 'The two cultures', Charles P. Snow complained about the split between what he called the traditional literary culture and the progressive scientific culture. Today, a much more visible abyss seems to separate the culture of the humanities from the culture of management. Many of the presuppositions and arguments used in Snow's lecture and in the ensuing debate seem outdated. As Stefan Collini (1998) reminds us in his introduction to the new edition of Snow's book, the map of the disciplines has changed significantly, and continues to change. On the one hand, historians and sociologists of science have altered the way we understand scientific progress, and physics (the model for all modern sciences) has introduced unpredictability and randomness into its core. On the other hand, most scholars in the humanities are today much less interested in the preservation of a great tradition; they are more concerned about their specialization in a narrower and manageable body of literature than about 'literary culture' in general, and they write research projects[1] imitating their colleagues from the natural sciences. To some people's consternation, the humanities have become just another professional academic enterprise and have lost the cultural pre-eminence they might still have had when C.P. Snow read his lecture. In addition, the social sciences, which occupy a space between the literary and the scientific cultures, have become much more influential than they were back then. Finally, thinkers like Michel Serres have made efforts to demonstrate the connections between science and the humanities in order to found a new humanism based precisely on the new scientific discoveries.[2] Thus, the division between the sciences and the humanities might seem less strong today.

Nonetheless, the other divide, the divide between management and the humanities, continues to be as firmly entrenched in our mentality as it has always been, from Aristotle to Heidegger.[3] Despite some noble attempts, the business world and the humanities seem to ignore and even despise each other. The business manager still sees the intellectual as an unproductive dilettante; the intellectual and the artist still see the manager as narrowly concerned with maximizing profits and incapable of having higher concerns and aspirations. It might seem that these two activities have nothing to do with each other and that any attempt to put them in contact with each other is like trying to mix oil and water. Furthermore, perhaps something would be lost if the tension between the two domains were eliminated completely or covered up.

At bottom, there is an important point in common between this division and the one denounced by C.P. Snow, for in both cases what is called into question is the capacity of humanistic studies to contribute to the development of human welfare. If the humanities are unable to offer something to society, they are destined to be considered only as a relic from the past, which can be studied by a few specialists as one studies museum pieces. The humanities need, then, to make an effort to explain better their role in society, their contribution and their methods.

Yet, the same question can have a boomerang effect and be asked to the domain of business and management. Just as there is an urgent debate about the role of the humanities, the mixed results of economic globalization, the advent of what is called the knowledge society and the series of well-known business scandals have opened a debate about the role and legitimacy of corporations in society.[4] Until recently, it was uncontested that the sole role of corporations was to create wealth and jobs. Today, according to some analysts,[5] society at large asks from managers a greater awareness and sensitivity to the rapidly changing social context and to the consequences of their decisions, a greater commitment with the well-being of their communities and with the preservation of the environment, and the ability to listen to and communicate with the diverse groups of stakeholders. Some innovative organizations have started to realize that managers with an exclusively technical training have difficulties dealing with all these new demands.

Business schools have been at the centre of this debate. There is the well-founded suspicion, coming also from professors in these schools, that they have 'promulgated a series of theories with regard to business that are based on . . . the worst possible assumptions about human nature' (Mitroff, 2004) and that they have taught that what is 'rational' is to seek one's self-interest, understood in a very limited sense, through any means possible (Etzioni, 2002). Their MBA programmes have been said, by people like Henry Mintzberg, to 'distort managerial practice', which today 'is going off the rails with dysfunctional consequences for society' (Mintzberg, 2004). If this is to change, future managers should, among other things, be exposed to other dimensions of human nature, that is they should be encouraged to expand their vision, to develop their sensitivity and their sense of responsibility, and to improve their capacity to communicate with others. It is here that it becomes more plausible to think that managers can learn something from the humanities, if we understand the humanities correctly.

However, one should not rush enthusiastically to raise a toast to the humanities as if they were able to offer new solutions to organizational problems, as if they were the new tool needed to improve the quality of our management and the efficiency of our organizations. Before doing that, it is pertinent to become more aware about what the humanities are and how they have been used.

THE HUMANITIES: A BROAD DEFINITION

Indeed, what are we referring to when we talk about the humanities? Traditionally it meant the study of classical authors and of foreign and dead languages. At other points it seemed to refer to 'that without which no one can be an educated person'. How do we understand it today? In a somewhat reckless act I will sketch in three steps a way to understand what one means by the humanities today in discussions like the one I am engaging in here. The first step is given by the etymology of the word. Although later it came to acquire other connotations, something has been preserved of its original meaning: initially the Latin word *humanitas* appears to have been a translation of the Greek word *philanthropia*, which means 'love of the human condition' (there is controversy even about this, because some scholars link it to the word *paideia*, another broad Greek term which has been translated as 'civilization', 'culture', 'tradition' or 'education' and which, according to Werner Jaeger, refers to all those things at the same time but also to the ideal or aspiration of what it means to be human (Jaeger [1933] 1986). *Philanthropia* is the word Aeschylus used to describe what Prometheus had done when he stole the fire from the gods and gave it to the humans. In this sense, science and technology as well as literature and philosophy could clearly form part of the humanities. In this sense also, the humanities would later come to be contrasted with theology, the study that puts God and not man at the centre of its discourse. At any rate, in Greek and Roman antiquity, this love of the human condition was not merely altruistic: it implied both civic commitment and a striving for personal virtue or excellence.

The humanities also study what human beings have thought and expressed (and continue to think and express) about the meaning they give to life. This is contrasted with the study of what human beings have done (and do) to secure and improve their material survival and to secure a peaceful and harmonious life with each other. Even if traditionally expressions about the meaning of life have been studied by disciplines such as the study of literature, of art and music, of religions and philosophy, other disciplines are also indispensable to throw some light on these issues, among them history, anthropology, sociology and political science. And, in fact, natural sciences like astrophysics and biology raise as many questions about the meaning of life as painting and literature. In this sense, also, the humanities would include the inquiry into and discussion about the ultimate values underlying our decisions, ways of life, attitudes and beliefs. Such values, incidentally, often enter into conflict with one another, such as equality and liberty, liberty and security, justice and efficiency, production and distribution, the individual and the collective, the natural environment and human progress.

Another characteristic of the humanities, and this is the third step, is their non-instrumentality. This resistance to immediate utility is something in which people in the humanities might take pride, and it is precisely what C.P. Snow criticized and what gets on the nerves of many managers and businesspeople. If they have any practical use, it is on such a long time scale and so diluted that it is impossible to plan it or predict it. If nothing else, the schism between people of business and people of letters is a question of pace. Who can wait for long term, uncertain and vague results? But the charge against the humanities is even more serious than this: what can the humanities do to alleviate misery and pain? This uselessness was also the reason why the humanities used to be seen as the occupation of the members of the wealthy classes, who did not need to worry about more practical issues. All this is made worse because one sense of the word 'humanities' refers to the study of the classics and the preservation of a tradition. While this view of the humanities is much too narrow, it is true that strictly one cannot speak about progress when we talk about works of art, literature and philosophical ideas.

Thus, according to this loose characterization, what is meant by humanities today are those studies that do not have any clear, immediate utility, based on a love of the human condition, which inquire about what human beings have felt, thought and expressed concerning the meaning they give to their lives. These studies can be found in the disciplines that traditionally come under the label of the humanities (in the academic division called 'humanities') but can also be found in the social sciences and the natural sciences.

No doubt this attempt at a definition could start a controversy, either because it is too vague or because it leaves out something important. One advantage is, in my view, that it does not try to avoid the problems and ambiguities presented by the humanities, while it also shows how they can be interesting to citizens at large, and managers in particular, in so far as they foster curiosity about human issues and promote discussion of the values underlying human actions. Yet for me it is not essential for this definition to be completely satisfactory. For my point will be that controversy about the meaning and role of the humanities is an essential part of the very process of teaching the humanities. As we shall see later, a great deal of the interest of the humanities lies in their conflicts and controversies, which are also the conflicts and controversies we find in our society. As John Gray (2002) reminds us, modern liberal democratic societies are characterized by value plurality, that is by differences and controversy about some fundamental issues, and it would be a disservice to any student, and even more to managers, to pretend that there is a settled consensus on issues such as what the humanities are.

TWO WAYS TO CONNECT MANAGEMENT AND THE HUMANITIES

Before jumping to conclusions, it might be convenient to clarify the two ways in which one can understand the use of the humanities for management. One way which has proved to be very promising is the use of resources from disciplines such as literary theory and anthropology to study organizations and their cultures. The narrative approach to organizations developed, among others, by Barbara Czarniawska (1997) and the importance attached to symbolic and aesthetic resources in different areas of management would be excellent examples of this. This seems to be a translation to the organizational level of an increasing awareness that cultural questions (including questions concerning identity, values, religion, language and ethnicity) are relevant for understanding the social transformations of today's world, which does not necessarily imply that technological, economic, political and social aspects are irrelevant. The same 'cultural turn' (Jameson, 1998) that took place in social theory or the shift from 'redistribution' towards 'recognition' (Taylor, 1992; Fraser and Honneth, 2003) in political philosophy would also apply to organizational theory. There is a 'cultural' aspect that has to do with the identity, the values and the traditions of an organization and is important to analyse experiences such as mergers and takeovers among companies, their rapid growth and faster turnover of employees, their expansion to other countries and cultural contexts, and even the incorporation of information technologies. Thus, we have come to realize that understanding the functioning of organizations and societies depends also on understanding their cultural, symbolic and emotional elements.

A different approach to the question about the use of the humanities for management is concerned with their role in the training and education of organizational and social leaders. One could say that the first approach is that of scholars who are doing research on a particular object of study: in this case, organizations and companies. The second approach, in contrast, is that of practitioners who need to make decisions and assume responsibilities. My intention in this text is to focus on the latter. It is true that the two approaches are not incompatible. Furthermore, it is important for a practitioner to be acquainted with new ways to understand organizations and for the researcher to understand how the practitioner experiences her daily life in the organization. Nonetheless, there is a difference in emphasis one should not ignore, at least at the beginning of the analysis.

BUSINESSMEN READING GREAT BOOKS: AMERICAN EXAMPLES

The use of the humanities for the education of managers is not a new idea. It was not uncommon in 19th-century Europe to find managers and senior civil servants with a sound cultural background based on the readings of the works of Plutarch, Cicero and the like, often in their original languages. It is not clear whether that made them better managers or better citizens. Moreover, before one sinks into nostalgia, it is worth pointing out that in 1872 (130 years ago!) Nietzsche was already complaining about the 'utilitarian instinct' of his age, the weakening of culture and its transformation into journalism (Nietzsche [1872], 1956).

But, instead of talking about the 19th century, I want to start with a revival of the interest in humanistic education during the 20th century in the United States. This revival presented itself as a reaction against excessive professionalization and specialization, and against a narrow utilitarian approach. It is noteworthy that it took place on the other side of the Atlantic, although the stereotype (promulgated as early as Alexis de Tocqueville) says that the United States is a society that looks towards the future and is mainly interested in practical issues. I will briefly refer to three American examples that have a great deal in common: the concern for liberal education in colleges and universities, the 'Great Books Movement' and the Aspen Institute. Interesting lessons about the role of the humanities can be learned from these initiatives, not because they should become the models to imitate, but in part precisely because they seem to have become controversial models and this controversy cannot be neglected in the debate about the humanities today.

The first example dates from the 1920s and 1930s, when the colleges of Columbia University in New York[6] and of the University of Chicago underwent reforms in order to include a core curriculum in their undergraduate programmes. This consisted of a set of compulsory courses devoted to the humanities and social sciences, in which small groups of students in close interaction with professors would get first-hand knowledge of the most important works of literature, philosophy, history and other subjects. They would be acquainted with what Matthew Arnold had described much earlier as 'the best which has been thought and said in the world'. This model spread to other institutions and served to revitalize the 'distinctly American' small liberal arts colleges, which were able to maintain part of their original character after the major changes in higher education after World War II. Despite being less well-known internationally than the big research universities, today residential liberal arts colleges are considered to offer some of the best undergraduate education in the US and 'produce' a disproportionate share of leaders of that country (Koblik, 1999).

The ideal of this model of education underwent many threats and transformations, some of which will be broached later, and it took many different forms, but it shared a belief in the inadequacy or insufficiency of an education based on facts and the need to develop also the capacity of judgement, the capacity to evaluate the facts, to decide what to do with them and to justify one's decision. Rather than focusing on specific vocational preparation, expanding the power of the mind, promoting critical capacities, and emphasizing civic duty were the elements typically mentioned as part of the ideal of the liberal arts (Hawkins, 1999).

As a second example, in 1943, the same president of the University of Chicago who started the reforms in the college of that institution, Robert Hutchins, together with the public intellectual Mortimer Adler, started a discussion group with well-established businessmen in Chicago that came to be known as the 'Fat Men's Great Books Course' and had a great deal in common with the ideal of liberal arts. Out of that experience emerged the Great Books Foundation, which still today organizes meetings all over the US with people of all kinds (and not only managers of big corporations) to discuss books of literature, history and philosophy. According to one of its founding documents, the Great Books Foundation is committed 'to provide opportunities for all Americans to participate in the "Great Conversation" with the most probing minds of the Western tradition. The animating principle [is] the belief in the capacity and inner need of all people to question, seek understanding, and better themselves.'[7]

Finally, the third example: two of the illustrious participants of the 'Fat Men's Great Books Course' were Walter and Elizabeth Paepcke, who in 1950 founded the Aspen Institute. One of the core seminars of the Aspen Institute – the Executive Seminar, which they still recommend to first-time participants – is inspired in the Great Books programme. For in these seminars the participants 'examine the writings of philosophers such as Aristotle and Confucius, social theorists such as Adam Smith and John

Locke, etc.' In the documents of the Aspen Institute, we read that accord-ing to its founder: 'the Executive Seminar was not intended to make a cor-porate treasurer a more skilled corporate treasurer, but to help a leader gain access to his or her own humanity by becoming more self-aware, more self-correcting, and more self-fulfilling'.[8]

Behind these initiatives we find the conviction that, even if they have been written in other historical circumstances, the great works of literature, philosophy, religion, history, and sociology of the past express in a more original, more provocative, and fresher way the ideas that rule over con-temporary life. According to this approach, to become acquainted with and discuss these works is part of a comprehensive lifelong learning; they should not be left only in the hands of professional academics, because apart from their scholarly interest, they also speak to ordinary educated readers of today, they have the ability to inspire our thoughts or to clarify our own view in so far as, in some cases, they awake our desire to refute them.

Now, first, there is the question whether this kind of broad education in liberal arts or humanities (I will not make a distinction in this discussion) helps develop skills that later prove to be useful in a business career or a career in management. In short, whether it is a sound investment in time and money. And, second, there is the concern about whether this careerism endangers the very idea this type of education is supposed to be committed to, which probably goes against a view of the world in terms of personal costs and benefits. Yet, whatever the answers to these concerns, it is undeni-able that, today, initiatives like those we have seen above run into a number of difficulties: they go against the accelerated pace of our lives, against the general contempt for anything coming from the past, against the fascina-tion for trends and image, against the need to acquire professional skills or diplomas highly valued in the job market, against a narrow view regarding what is useful and what is useless, and against the use of leisure (if there is any left) almost exclusively for entertainment rather than self-improvement. Moreover, apart from the problem of their possibility, there is the question of their desirability. It is, then, necessary to become aware of the more sub-stantial criticisms of these attempts to recover the dialogue with the human-istic tradition. For we have to admit that the humanities in general, and these initiatives in particular, came under suspicion.

THE HUMANITIES UNDER SUSPICION

The challenges to the humanities did not come from the field of the natural sciences or from the business world, but from inside the world of the humanities. This is important because the question about the utility of the humanities for managers or their social function in general cannot be answered before understanding what happens inside the humanities themselves. I will mention only four of these criticisms.

One of the criticisms is the charge of Eurocentrism or West-centrism. The emphasis in humanistic studies had been on the cultural products of the West, assuming that they had superior value to those of other cultures or that they formed a separate, detachable tradition from other traditions. Indeed, it is possible that the whole movement in the United States that took place in the 1940s and 1950s had an ideological component given the particular historical context in which it took place: the fear of communism and of fascism, World War II and later the Cold War. In that context, some people might have felt that the fate of the world depended in part on the preservation of the Western cultural heritage and the tradition represented by the Great Books. However, since the 1980s the debates about feminism, multiculturalism and postcolonialism have dominated departments of literature, and the Western canon has been called into question.[9] The outcome of these debates or 'culture wars' (as they came to be known in America, where issues often take a rare sharpness that is not so common in Europe) is not that one should not read classical Western authors any more, but it would be naive to read them today as if nothing had happened.[10] Yet, overall, confidence was lost not just in the utility but also in the goodness of reading the Great Books. It became less clear which books one should read to be 'an educated person' or, indeed, what it meant to be 'an educated person', and whether it consisted in feeling part of a tradition of knowledge, values and attitudes that could be called 'Western civilization' or, indeed, whether there was such an identifiable tradition. In the educational curriculum this meant the proliferation of elective courses and the reduction or elimination of a common core. Some deplored this 'supermarket curriculum', seeing it as a way to encourage students to take easier, more entertaining or more career-oriented courses, while others celebrated it as a liberation.

In addition to that, it was also asserted that liberal and humanistic education was elitist, anti-modern and authoritarian.[11] What seemed particularly anti-modern and authoritarian was an education that prescribed a fixed set of questions and texts for all undergraduates to read and discuss (as was the case in the medieval university). What seemed elitist was that this education was not within the reach of everyone, but only of those who could leave aside more practical concerns (that is a more vocational training). This would probably be confirmed by a study of the socio-economic background of the students of the best liberal arts colleges and universities in the United States (Neely, 1999). A liberal and humanistic education might, then, be criticized because it endangers social cohesion and leads to a divorce between the elites and the rest of society, which in turn may also lead to a backlash, a suspicion against the elites. In short, this view of education seems to go against the two main modern ideals: freedom and equality. It is true that this criticism could be avoided by being open and flexible about the books and the content taught, by using an open teaching style and by making efforts to make this type of education accessible to people from different social backgrounds (there are examples of that). Moreover, one should recall here that there are predecessors of the Great Books movement in 19th-century Britain put forward mostly by socialists who understood reading Great Books as a way for the working classes to educate themselves and overcome their disenfranchisement. Nonetheless, the main point is that one cannot teach the humanities any more without making these concerns explicit.

A third criticism challenges what seems to be an essential presupposition of the humanities courses based on the Great Books: that the problems concerning human existence and social coexistence are permanent and timeless. If this is so, the best way to learn about these fundamental questions is by reading the greatest minds of our tradition, that is classical authors such as Aristotle, Dante or Rousseau. The critics object that it is misleading to take authors out of their historical context and they are sceptical about the existence of a common and constant human nature and about a limited and permanent set of fundamental questions. In fact, this criticism goes back to thinkers like Ortega y Gasset, who asserted that 'Man has no nature; what he has is history' (Ortega y Gasset, 1962). As a result, a humanities education today should incorporate this important debate within its curriculum, it should incorporate voices contrary to the view that human questions are timeless, voices saying that our worries and ideas are always dependent on historical and social circumstances and have little to do with those of the ancient Greeks, the Italians of the Renaissance or the French of the Enlightenment, and also voices advising us to look towards the future and forget about the past. In other words, a true humanistic education would include points of view that are against the humanistic tradition.

The fourth criticism I want to present here is perhaps the most forceful of all. The literary critic George Steiner articulates it very clearly in his book *In Bluebeard's Castle* when he affirms that today we cannot think about culture and the humanities without thinking about the Holocaust (Steiner, 1974).[12] Everything changed after we learned about the existence of a concentration camp next to Weimar – the town where Goethe and Schiller produced some of the great works of Western culture – and after we realize that this fact did not stop scientific and humanistic activities in German universities, as if they were impermeable to everything that happened around them. It has become clear that the Western cultural tradition was not a barrier against brutality and cruelty, that there can be a human-istic culture in authoritarian regimes and also that intellectuals (artists, writers, and so on) are able to welcome inhumanity or look the other way. In other words, the great atrocities committed in the 20th century in the heart of Europe were not the fruit of the invasion of some ignorant foreign tribes, but seemed to grow out of European culture itself. With this, the difference between the barbarians and the civilized, an essential difference for those who defend the humanities and liberal education, was abolished: as Steiner puts it, madness and barbarism were seen not as the fruit of ignorance but as the result of civilization.

These four criticisms raise serious challenges to the humanities: are we sure that the cultivation of our intellect and our taste, that the familiarity with 'the best which has been thought and said in the world' (be that of a small leading elite or the great majority of a population) leads to a more rational conduct, improves our association with others and makes society better? For it is precisely this relationship between the improvement of the individual spirit and the improvement of our association with others (and our sensitivity to their needs) that appears to have been broken. And this was also one of the principles of a liberal and humanistic education. In short, we are not sure any more that the humanities can make us more human. And with this what appears to have shattered is the link between the humanities and the ancient *philanthropia*.

If all this is so, should we conclude that the best one can do is to forget about the humanities, that both their usefulness and their intrinsic good-ness were nothing but dreams? Not necessarily; what it means is that one cannot be naive and must become aware that today, in our culture, the dis-tinctions between civilized and uncivilized, superior and inferior, cultivated and ignorant, the elite and the masses, have been called into question, and that European or Western culture and its tradition has lost the privileged position of superiority that it claimed to have. My intention here is not so much to demonstrate the truth of these assertions, but to suggest that they open a debate that should be part of the subject matter of humanities courses, that it would be futile to think about the use of the humanities for managers or to offer humanities courses to undergraduates or businessmen as if these controversies did not exist.

OVERCOMING THE NOSTALGIA FOR THE LOST COMMON GROUND

We need to overcome the view that the humanities can be the provider of a common ground that will make society more decent and more humane.

In fact, a concern that underlies the lecture by C.P. Snow, Steiner's book and the US experiences in liberal education is that, in contemporary societies, individuals and groups might no longer share a common language that would enable them to sustain a dialogue about the most polemical questions and to participate in public affairs. Specialization and expertise, which are so necessary both for material and scientific progress and for artistic activity, can lead to the incapacity to discuss and decide about issues that concern us all. This concern often transforms itself into nostalgia for a time in which there were common cultural references, beliefs, attitudes or values that worked as cement for society. Traditionally the study of the humanities was thought to be essential in the diffusion of the shared set of symbols and feelings that made it possible to have a cohesive society and culture. However, apart from the question of whether this was really so in the past or whether it is an illusion projected into the past, the important question is whether it is possible today.

As the University of Chicago professor Wayne Booth puts it in his article 'What knowledge, if any, should everyone pursue?' (Booth, 1995), the question is not simply about the importance of everyone in a society sharing the some kind of knowledge, whatever that might be. This aspiration could be satisfied today through football, pop music, TV shows or Hollywood movies. The question is rather whether there is some kind of knowledge *worth* having in itself. Today most people will claim that agreement on this point is impossible beyond the basic acquaintance with mathematics and one's native language: what is important for some will be unimportant for others, especially when we come to the domain of the humanities. Thus, the polemics about what curricula should be implemented in schools and colleges, what courses should be taught, what books should be read and included in the canon, and so on, is not likely to stop. Moreover, this polemics about what is worth knowing and what is worth reading is, at least, as old as modernity itself (remember the Battle of the Books in the 17th century over the superiority of modern or ancient writers). But, more importantly, contrary to most opinions, this lack of consensus could be interpreted as a sign of vitality rather than as a sign of decay and disintegration.

There might be much more agreement if, instead of asking about what knowledge is worth in itself, we ask whether there is anything that all citizens in a democracy should *try* to *pursue*. As Wayne Booth describes it, the emphasis is on *trying to pursue*, not on *having* or even on *trying to have*. The difference between pursuing and having is not trivial. In my view, it shifts the emphasis from the object to the subject, from knowledge and information to ideals and attitudes. Thus, perhaps when we are speaking about the humanities, it is not a fixed body of common knowledge one should expect all citizens (and managers) to aspire to, but a set of attitudes, predispositions and capacities.

If this is so, the humanities should not present themselves as the protector of the cultural common ground which makes social cohesion possible, but rather as what it really is (and probably always has been): a field of conflict between different ideological and aesthetic positions. Instead of trying to avoid conflict, instead of feeling nostalgia for a (probably fictional) golden age when we all shared a common cultural context (a time before multicultural, feminist and ethnic studies came on the scene), we should use these controversies to exercise the capacities that we want to promote in a humanistic education (Graff, 1992). What we need, then, is not to eliminate the differences in points of view, but to foster shared attitudes to live with these differences.

UNCERTAIN GOALS OF A HUMANITIES EDUCATION

The humanities become much more interesting if humanities courses include the controversies about what knowledge is worth having, the criticisms of particular humanities curricula and the general doubt whether the humanities can make us more human. But, more importantly, by including all this rather than hiding it, the humanities become a mirror of a society which is characterized by discrepancies and controversies.

How should we engage in this kind of education? Despite the criticisms we saw before and assuming a generous view of what counts as a 'Great Book', the teaching method espoused by the Great Books Foundation can accommodate these discrepancies and controversies very well, and can foster the exercise of certain desirable capacities and attitudes that help us live with them. They call it the method of 'shared inquiry' and it consists in the formation of small learning communities (15 to 20 people) 'to sustain an open dialogue, to form reasoned judgments and to build a common ground' for discussion. In these learning communities, the professor or group leader takes an almost amateurish stance, and assumes that he or she is not an expert on all the books that are read and discussed. The attitude of the professor is summarized in a radical way by the Great Books Foundation: 'Never Answer, Never Tell, Never Lecture, Never Sum Up – Never!'. Instead they advise: 'Start Arguments. Ask questions about which people will have different answers [. . .]', and pose questions that genuinely worry you and for which you do not have an answer. I would add here that it might be necessary and useful in some cases for the professor to show different ways to interpret the texts, if they do not come from the students themselves. But, by and large, it is easy to realize that this method is inspired by Socrates' *maieutic* pedagogy. It is more self-teaching than teaching. On their part, the participants should be predisposed to submit their opinions to the scrutiny of the others, for this method of liberal education requires that everyone's opinion be heard and explored and that every opinion be supported by argument and evidence. It is, then, an exercise in reasoning within communities of learning.

Yet, if we now go back to our starting question, how can all this be of any interest to people who devote (or will devote) themselves to making organizations work efficiently? Indeed, no one will claim that if there is any utility of the humanities, this is immediate or direct. In fact, any attempt to pinpoint the specific purpose of the humanities would amount to subordinating them to some other goal and this would stifle their creative, provocative, and critical potential. To ask about the utility of reading a poem, contemplating a painting or listening to a sonata seems to go against the very nature of these activities, for they appear to those who seriously engage in them as something worth pursuing in themselves, as a way of looking at the world that discards usefulness, efficiency, and cost–benefit analysis. Nonetheless, if one looks at what the institutions that promote liberal and humanistic education proclaim, one finds that they actually mention some results that they pursue. They might mention the instruction in a particular type of knowledge or the reading of particular authors, but often they put more emphasis on the capacities, skills and attitudes they want to foster. I shall give a few examples.

According to the Aspen Institute: 'The Executive Seminar experience enables participants to define and understand basic values that are at the heart of the most complex decisions leaders face.' This is related to something repeated several times by these initiatives: the objectives are not so much the Great Books in themselves, but to discover what they tell us. It is not an academic or historical discussion but a process whereby the participants get to know themselves better and to know the fundamental values and the value conflicts behind each option they prefer or each decision they take.

The Aspen Institute also says that, after its humanities seminars, 'leaders leave better prepared to manage relationships with diverse constituencies, conduct business in a global environment, and motivate followers through visions that unite and inspire'. There are three things in this package: first (changing the order), since the humanities courses should be based on an open dialogue from different points of view, a humanities training would improve one's capacity to argue for one's views and would accustom one to respect other points of view; second, it should help develop leadership abilities such as persuading and inspiring people to join a project, and understanding their needs and desires; and, thirdly, it should help develop a broader understanding of the world today.

Another common aspect in the documents of these institutions is that they define their goal as helping students or participants to learn how to learn on their own, independently from the tutelage of a professor. In other words, a humanities education should stimulate curiosity about any human and social issue. This is related to another intention, mentioned in some of these documents, of awakening in students in general, but also in those that (will) devote themselves to the world of business, an interest in civic issues. For one of the goals is that students become more 'conscious of their social and moral obligations', and that they become 'free and responsible citizens'.[13] There is no doubt that here one usually includes a deep concern for injustice, oppression and falsity.

Many of these institutions also emphasize the capacity to think critically and autonomously, which connects with one of the original senses of the term 'liberal' in the expression 'liberal education': to be free from prejudices, superstitions and dogmas. As some of these institutions claim critical thinking – together with reading and writing (which are tools to that end) – is better developed in meaningful contexts, discussing a particular story, rather than abstractly. This does not rule out the discussion about painting and literature, or other arts. One should remember here what George Steiner says, 'all serious art is a critical act' in so far as it is a selection and interaction between what is imagined and what comes as a constraint, and in so far as it is a reflection on the inheritance and the context to which it pertains (Steiner, 1989, p. 11).

Finally, some of them mention that an important element of the humanities is to awaken our sensitivity and our capacity to engage in discussion with each other about beauty and about our aesthetic experiences with works of art and with natural beauty. Art and beauty pose the main challenge in so far as they are something we cannot completely explain, predict or reduce to a particular function. As is sometimes said, they are a form of mystery (Steiner, 1989, p. 19). Perhaps what works of art do is to show us one way to face the uncontrollable. Furthermore, art can also be understood as an aspiration to transcendence, that is an aspiration to overcome death. The question of posterity and of our legacy is an important human dimension of which we can be reminded through the study of works that have survived their time.

According to this list of abilities taken from the documents of different institutions, the ideal of a humanities education would be one that (1) promotes the awareness of the ultimate values behind our decisions, (2) improves the capacity to argue, motivate and lead other people, (3) stimulates the curiosity and the commitment to the pursuit of knowledge, (4) awakens an interest in civic issues and a sense of responsibility, (5) helps develop critical thinking, and (6) nurtures sensitivity to beauty.

This is a very impressive and ambitious list of skills, capacities and attitudes. Probably too much to expect from a few courses or a few readings one can put under the label of the 'humanities'. And there is little empirical evidence of the success in achieving these goals. Moreover, as if all this were not enough, three warnings are in order here. First, nobody claims that the importance of cultivating aptitudes and abilities should amount to a negligence of content and knowledge. One could say that knowledge without attitudes and abilities is blind, but attitudes and aptitudes without any knowledge would be empty. In order to 'learn how to learn', one has to learn something. The subjective side of learning should not make us neglect the objective aspect of knowledge. Second, as mentioned earlier, a good way to exercise these abilities might be to become acquainted with the controversies about the humanities (for example, coming from the feminist, multiculturalist and postcolonialist perspectives) rather then neglecting them. For one of the contributions of a humanistic education might be to foster the abilities necessary to cope with conflict and difference. And, third, if one of the important goals of a humanistic education is a set of attitudes, predispositions, and values, these can at best be only indirect results. Although they are at the heart of a humanities education, they cannot be considered as its immediate objective, an objective that can be controlled and measured in a given amount of time. Ultimately, in education one is seldom sure of the results, and in a humanities education the results might be as unpredictable as the results of artistic creation.

DEMOCRACY AND CONFLICT

The question one needs to explore next is whether citizens need to develop and cultivate a certain set of abilities for a democratic society to function well or, as Benjamin Barber puts it, for a democracy to be strong (Barber, 1998); that is, to have a lively civil society, and a good balance between public administration, the economy and private non-profit associations. Beyond its particular use for organizations and for management, this is surely the ultimate horizon of any humanistic education. It is here that its use for society at large is at stake. My hypothesis is that these democratic attitudes and capacities would coincide to a large extent with those we described as being emphasized by a humanities education, especially because a democratic society is a society characterized by open discrepancies and controversies about important issues.

In fact, no matter how much one might disagree on other issues, the link between liberal education and democracy was clear in the US experiences mentioned above. Thus Robert Hutchins of the University of Chicago said in the 1940s: 'if democracy is going to function as it should, the man-in-the-street is going to have to think better'. St John's College, one of the most radical experiments in an undergraduate liberal education, claims that one of its goals is 'producing reflective participants in democratic self-government'.

It is not too contentious a claim to say that citizens of a strong democracy need to engage in some degree of critical analysis of society and in some reflection about human nature. This means that apart from being acquainted with the economic and technological reality in which they live, they should desire to know more about the different social, institutional, political and cultural initiatives, and should be willing to exercise their autonomous judgement and their critical abilities on them. One can think here about a broad variety of challenges such as genetically modified food, the degrees of inequality that one finds tolerable in a society or the need for a European Constitution.

In addition, democratic citizens need to have a predisposition for respectful dialogue with those holding different points of view and a predisposition to reach agreements on important social issues. Thirdly, they need to develop the capacity to argue convincingly and autonomously for their views. This means that they need to sharpen their argumentative skills and their capacity to persuade rhetorically. Finally, democratic citizens need to foster their capacity to care for the fate of their fellow citizens and feel that they are part of a community.

There is no doubt that citizens of today's democratic societies often fall short of this ideal, and the distance might even be getting bigger rather than smaller. This is not our concern here. The issue is that this ideal should be the hidden core of humanities courses. And it should also be the core of any humanistic element introduced in other courses of a curriculum. There will be disagreements about whether there is a group of canonical works or one literary tradition that can help towards this project more than others (whether one should read more Dostoyevsky, Thucydides or Shakespeare, whether one should read more female authors or more non-European authors or whether this is better achieved through the analysis of newspaper articles or the discussion of cases from the world of business). In fact, as we said, conflict about which texts and authors, and about which is the best way to read and discuss them, has become part of the subject matter of the humanities today and should not be avoided. Instead these conflicts should be treated openly in the classroom or in other meetings, without avoiding their political connotations (Graff, 1992). For to engage in these controversies not only shows that the humanities are a lively, interesting field, in which there are issues at stake, but also can be a way to stimulate the attitudes and capacities that we would like democratic citizens to have.

When one asks the question 'Can the humanities be useful for managers or future managers?', many would give an answer that would point to the usefulness for business organizations of people who possess analytical skills, are able to write legible reports and make oral presentations, and are equipped with a great deal of mental flexibility. However, if the purpose of the humanities is also to encourage the competencies, abilities and attitudes which are conducive to the ideal of a democratic citizen who knows how to live with conflicts, the question we should be asking in relation to the world of business and management is the following: are managers better when they are also good citizens? And the answer to this question depends, to a large extent, on one's expectations about what it means to be a successful organization and a successful manager. The broad notion of the humanities presented here could be useful for managers when one accepts, against what has become almost common wisdom, that personal improvement, organizational improvement and social improvement are not a zero-sum game.

However, I called this a *hidden* core of the humanities because we always need to remind ourselves that the capacities that the humanities aim to develop, the capacities that in our view can lead to a good and strong citizenship, are only a by-product of a liberal, humanistic education. Students join a college or managers become interested in the humanities to improve themselves as individuals and to learn about subjects for which they have curiosity, not to become better citizens. As mentioned earlier, if the college or the postgraduate programme is successful or not in making them better citizens in the broad sense indicated is an uncontrollable matter. It is something one needs to be very modest about, especially because the 20th century has taught us that the results of the humanistic tradition have not always been very democratic. The humanities should try, and might help, to teach people to become better or stronger citizens but they cannot brag about it; they need to be very discreet. This is why it is so difficult to make an open defence of them.

PUTTING THE IDEA OF LIBERAL EDUCATION INTO EUROPEAN PRACTICE

I have made a modest defence of the goodness and utility of the humanities understood not as the conservation of the classics or the preservation of a tradition, but as a type of studies at the core of which we find the intention to promote certain attitudes and capacities that are essential in a democratic society characterized by conflict, controversy and differences. As far as content is concerned, humanities courses need not be restricted to specific topics or to the Great Books of our tradition, although there is no doubt that these Great Books or classics continue to offer great opportunities to exercise these abilities, often because they make us want to argue against the view of society and human nature that they present. Yet, as Italo Calvino reminds us, reading the classics should not be exclusive, they should not be read at the cost of not reading any new novels, any newspapers or any new sociological studies. As Calvino puts it: 'To read the classics one has to establish *from where* one reads them' (Calvino, 2000). Furthermore, precisely because many of the best known examples of the Western tradition spring out of Europe or because Europeans already experience the weight of tradition more acutely, Europeans might feel less pressure to devote themselves to the preservation of a tradition or to establish lists of canonical works one should be acquainted with. This might make it easier for Europeans to adopt a broader view of the humanities or liberal arts.

If we take those attitudes and capacities to be at the heart of a programme in liberal education, it follows that this type of education cannot be limited to a particular period of an individual's life or to particular groups of people. For those attitudes and capacities need constant exercise; they are like muscles that can suffer atrophy. This question also affects business schools, and not only in their capacity to offer undergraduate degrees or MBAs. Given the fact that in many levels they train many of the leaders of today's society, they have acquired great social relevance and have also been the object of a great deal of distrust, precisely because they might be perceived as promoting a view of management that leaves aside (when it does not openly oppose) the view of democratic citizenship we have talked about above. Thus, it should not come as a surprise if business schools are asked to engage, in some way or another, in this type of liberal or humanistic education and to assume their share of responsibility for what business students do when they arrive at managing positions in business organizations. In part this is because business organizations can also be understood as communities where the habits, predispositions, attitudes and capacities of democratic citizenship can be either fostered or inhibited. In short, business schools will be asked to teach citizens as well as to train managers – or at least not to do one thing at the expense of the other.[14]

This is a view of the humanities and of their usefulness for managers and citizens at large that seeks to encompass all aspects of the human adventure and aims to awake an interest in all the topics that affect us as human beings: arts and literature, but also science and technology. For one of the main tasks of a humanities education is to awaken curiosity and deactivate indifference. This is a possible way to recover the etymological root of the term *humanitas*, which, as mentioned above, amounted to 'love of the human condition'. With the important addition that after the 20th century this love of the human condition should also include (especially in Europe) the study and debate of the darkest episodes in our common history and the possible dissolution of the common ground that the humanities tradition used to provide. Only by taking these tensions and controversies into account can the indirect connection between the study of the humanities and the development of a democratic citizenship – in organizations and society at large – be established.

NOTES

1. Though the claim that there is such a thing as research in the humanities is not uncontested; see Steiner (1989, p. 35).
2. See Michel Serres with Bruno Latour (1995).
3. Another classic example of this division can be found in some passages of Goethe's *Wilhelm Master's Years of Apprenticeship*.
4. Management studies and management education follow the other social sciences in taking the natural sciences as a model, and they have tried to find techniques that can be contrasted empirically. This has led to a rapid specialization, which is indispensable for any scientific progress. Nonetheless, as Max Weber already warned and Alasdair MacIntyre has reminded us, this led to an instrumental view of the management of organizations, which means that managers see themselves as both morally neutral and as strongly conditioned by some unquestioned premises (MacIntyre, 1984).
5. Peter F. Drucker, among others, has made such points with great emphasis (Drucker, 1993, pp. 97–111).
6. The promoter of this initiative was the professor of English, John Erskine, who established the General Honours Course in 1920.
7. Fiftieth Anniversary Brochure of the Great Books Foundation.
8. Webpage of the Aspen Institute: www.aspeninstitute.org (10/12/2004)
9. One reaction to these movements was Allan Bloom's best seller *The Closing of the American Mind* (1983). A defence of a multicultural liberal education can be found in Martha Nussbaum (1997).
10. An argument that is usually brought up to defend Western culture is that few cultures have shown to have a similar feeling of guilt and regret and a similar sense of self-criticism after the atrocities it has committed (colonialism, world wars, and so on). This may or may not be true, but in any case it is true that an education in the humanities should consist in trying to understand the errors committed in the past and to know better the links that unite us with that problematic past.
11. The philosopher and educator John Dewey, among others, raised this criticism of the college reforms of Robert Hutchins at the University of Chicago. But according to the Great Books Foundation, which admits it, the teaching methods they use are not unlike what John Dewey calls 'reflective thinking'.
12. As Steiner also notes, the suspicion against the humanistic tradition started earlier and it grew out of this tradition itself: artistic movements like Surrealism and Dadaism, and also psychoanalysis and existentialism, called into question the belief that culture can improve our social life.
13. This can be found among the documents of St John's College, one of the colleges in the United States that has embraced the ideal of liberal education most enthusiastically (www.sjcsf.edu, December 2003).
14. The broad view of the humanities presented here is what we try to apply at ESADE Business School in Barcelona. One of our initiatives is the introduction of elective courses on the humanities at the undergraduate level for our students of business administration and law. They are courses on a variety of topics such as cinema, Buddhism and

Islam, the classics of literature and a variety of political issues. We think that beyond the technical and professional training students receive they need a broader training, not necessarily to read Sophocles and Hobbes (which can also be helpful and has been done), but to understand better the contemporary world and its roots, and to acquire different ways of thinking about reality, ways of thinking that can be enriching, provide flexibility and promote a sense of responsibility. Another initiative is a programme called 'Leadership and Civic Commitment' that enrols 25 young managers between 30 and 35 years old, mostly from private business but a few also from the public administration and private non-profit organizations. These are managers who already have a well-established professional career and want to expand their understanding of today's social issues and to find ways to increase their level of commitment towards the community. In this course, the attention is focused on the economic, social, political and cultural environment in which organizations carry out their activity, an environment that is at the same time local and global. The material for reflection and debate does not come mainly from texts but from a series of lectures and debates led by experts in different fields. The guest speakers expound the main challenges in 24 areas: among them, the new scientific challenges, the welfare state, the new economy, multiculturalism, spirituality and contemporary art. In our view, although this might seem far removed from the traditional view of the humanities, it is also a way to promote a liberal and humanistic education.

REFERENCES

Arnold, Matthew (1869), 'Culture and anarchy', reprinted in M. Arnold (1993), *'Culture and Anarchy' and Other Writings*, ed. Stefan Collini, Cambridge: Cambridge University Press.

Barber, Benjamin (1998), *A Place for Us. How to Make Society Civil and Democracy Strong*, New York: Hill and Wang.

Bloom, Allan (1983), *The Closing of the American Mind: How Higher Education has Failed Democracy and Impoverished the Souls of Today's Students*, New York: Simon & Schuster.

Booth, Wayne (1995), 'What knowledge, if any, should everyone pursue?', in Philippe Desan (ed.), *Engaging the Humanities at the University of Chicago*, Chicago: University of Chicago Collegiate Division.

Calvino, Italo (2000), *Why Read the Classics?*, New York: Vintage.

Collini, Stefan (1998), 'Introduction', in C.P. Snow (1959/1998), *The Two Cultures*, Stefan Collini (ed.), Cambridge: Cambridge University Press.

Czarniawska, Barbara (1997), *Narrating the Organization: Dramas of Institutional Identity*, Chicago: University of Chicago Press.

Drucker, Peter F. (1993), *The Post-Capitalist Society*, New York: HarperCollins Publishers.

Etzioni, Amitai (2002), 'The education of business leaders', *The Responsive Community*, Fall 2002, 59–68.

Fraser, Nancy and Alex Honneth (2003), *Redistribution or Recognition?: A Political–Philosophical Exchange*, London: Verso.

Graff, Gerald (1992), *Beyond the Culture Wars: How Teaching Conflicts Can Revitalize American Education*, New York: Norton.

Gray, John (2002), *The Two Faces of Liberalism*, London: New Press.

Hawkins, Hugh (1999), 'The making of the liberal arts college identity' in 'Distinctively American: The residential liberal arts colleges', *Daedalus, the Journal of the American Academy of Arts and Sciences*, **128** (1), 1–25.

Jaeger, Werner [1933] (1986), *Paideia: The Ideals of Greek Culture. Volume I: Archaic Greece. The Mind of Athens*, second edition, Oxford: Oxford University Press.

Jameson, Fredric (1998), *The Cultural Turn. Selected Writings on the Postmodern, 1983–1998*, London: Verso.

Koblik, Steven (1999), 'Foreword' to 'Distinctively American: The residential liberal arts colleges', *Daedalus, the Journal of the American Academy of Arts and Sciences*, **128** (1), XIV.

MacIntyre, Alasdair (1984), *After Virtue*, second edition, Notre Dame, Ind.: University of Notre Dame Press.

Mintzberg, Henry (2004), *Managers Not MBAs. A Hard Look at the Soft Practice of Managing and Management Development*, San Francisco: Beret-Koehler Publishers.

Mitroff, Ian (2004), 'An open letter to the deans and the faculties of American business schools', *Journal of Business Ethics*, **54**, 185–9.

Neely, Paul (1999), 'The threats to liberal arts colleges' in 'Distinctively American: The residential liberal arts colleges', *Daedalus. Journal of the American Academy of Arts and Sciences*, **128** (1), 27–45.

Nietzsche, Friedrich (1872), 'Über die Zukunft unserer Bildungsanstalt' in F. Nietzsche (1956), *Werke in drei Bänden*, Karl Schlechta (ed.), Vol. 3, Munich: Carl Hanser.

Nussbaum, Martha (1997), *Cultivating Humanity: A Classical Defense of Reform in Liberal Education*, Cambridge, Mass.: Harvard University Press.

Ortega y Gasset, José (1962), *History as System and Other Essays Towards a Philosophy of History*, New York: W.W. Norton.

Sennett, Richard (1998), *The Corrosion of Character*, London: Norton.

Serres, Michel with Bruno Latour (1995), *Conversation on Science, Philosophy, and Time*, Ann Arbor, Mi.: University of Michigan Press.

Snow, Charles P. (1959), *The Two Cultures* in C.P. Snow (1998), *The Two Cultures*, Stefan Collini (ed.), Cambridge: Cambridge University Press.

Steiner, George (1974), *In Bluebeard's Castle: Some Notes Towards the Redefinition of Culture*, New Haven, Conn.: Yale University Press.

Steiner, George (1989), *Real Presences*, Chicago: The University of Chicago Press.

Taylor, Charles (1992), *Multiculturalism and 'The Politics of Recognition'*, Princeton, NJ: Princeton University Press.

9. Cultivation or civilization? Popular management concepts and their role in reshaping the way management is understood

Niels Dechow

Reasoning in terms of 'strategies', 'customers' and 'value-added' has become part of day-to-day language and often the idea is promoted that knowing tools equals knowing management (Armstrong, 2002). Apparently, some 5000 new book titles each year appear describing new management concepts (Collins, 2000). On this background, one would think that business schools are thriving in society with cohorts of students equally eager to learn about and to apply the latest results of research.

Paradoxically, this is not the situation. Business schools increasingly often find themselves under pressure. More and more often academia is faced with the experience that the customers want to hear about 'universal stories of organizing' (Czarniawska, 2003) and 'do-it-yourself' concepts that often appear to be out of touch with management practice and research related to this practice (Czarniawska and Genell, 2002; Saravanamuthu and Tinker, 2002).

This chapter suggests that the civilizing process into which Norbert Elias (1939/1994) inscribes European history provides a framework by which to understand academia as a distinct community – or as Elias phrases it, 'figuration' – in relation to surrounding society.

Having Elias as a starting point, the chapter moves on to the history of one popular management concept – the Balanced Scorecard (BSC). It has been selected from many other such concepts because it has changed properties quite dramatically over the course of 12 years of its existence. When introduced in 1992, the Balanced Scorecard was portrayed as a management practice which was about working with a 'dashboard' of both financial and non-financial performance measures. Most of the current research on the Balanced Scorecard takes its point of departure in this representation. In doing so the researchers neglect the fact that since the early appearance of the 1992 text occurred on the Balanced Scorecard, this concept has 'never quite been itself' from an epistemological point of view.

Next, the chapter illustrates how the later texts on this concept written by Robert Kaplan and David Norton increasingly portray the management of financial and non-financial performances as a project with a clear beginning and end. By 2004, the Balanced Scorecard is no longer about integrated dashboards. It is about a strategy mapping, a process that is detailed in terms of the description of project roles, responsibilities and tasks, but silent in terms of what it means to manage financial and/or non-financial performances as an ongoing practice. This transformation is interpreted in this chapter as meaning that the actual significance of the Balanced Scorecard is related to its emerging propositions about management as a project rather than as a practice.

Finally, the chapter revisits the observations mentioned in the introduction: that business schools are under pressure and that society mainly wants universal stories of organizing. Of special interest is that this quest for universal narratives does not mean that management research is no longer relevant. In my reading, this quest reflects a confusion following from the 'new competition for significance' between, on the one side, the old academic figuration that traditionally has never been trained to listen to society and, on the other side, different social groups outside academia that now articulate management on a scale ranging from projects to practice. In this competition, the relative significance of academia may appear to be weakening and business schools may find themselves under pressure. Yet, as argued at the end of this chapter, this situation could represent a rare opportunity for academia to show its relevance in at least two ways: firstly, by clarifying the socio-epistemological similarities and differences between consulting, practice and research as three different figurations of management theory; secondly, by explicating the intended, but especially unintended side-effects of management knowledge when it becomes contextualized to suit particular management figurations.

ELIAS ON EUROPEAN CIVILIZATION AND CULTURE

Elias argues that historically the feature making academia distinct was its concern with classification, reduction and purification of things society otherwise adopted and blended in order to assimilate the emerging bourgeoisie into the traditional rulings of the old court system. His argument is based on social transformation mainly in 18th century France and Germany, which he argues produced two significantly different discourses about society. The first was a traditional feudal discourse, nurtured by the court nobility, which focused on the maintenance and the adaptive *civilization* of distinguished behaviour suitable for the royal courts. The second was a new discourse, nurtured by an emerging middle class that focused on *cultivation* of spiritual and intellectual accomplishments.

> What legitimized this eighteenth-century middle class intelligentsia to itself, what supplied the foundation of its self-image and pride was situated beyond economics and politics. It existed in what was called for precisely this reason 'das rein Geistige' (the pure spiritual), in books, scholarships, religion, art, philosophy, in the inner enrichment, the intellectual formation (*Bildung*) of the individual primarily through the medium of books. (Elias, 1939/1994, p. 24).

Elias says that this new cultivating discourse emerged as protest to the civilizing discourse nurtured by the court system, which was mostly about appearance and form over content. 'Culture' in the German sense of the word was about intellectual, scientific or artistic *accomplishments*. Intellectuals mobilized it as a counter-position to the upper class that were seen to accomplish next to nothing, but for whom the shaping of its distinguished and distinctive *civilized behaviour* was central to its self-justification. The two most important representatives of the new intelligentsia were the 'clergyman' and the 'professor' who mobilized 'Bildung' (cultivation, as in von Humboldt's mantra '*Bildung durch Wissenschaft*, cultivation through science') to counter the exclusivity of the court system in which they could not take part (Elias, 1939/1994, p. 22).

Elias argues further that over time it was the civilizing process that overtook the cultivating stance in most European 'societies'. He argues that our notions of society have been shaped through a variety of actions permeating increasingly traditional boundaries and separations between social groups. Yet in 'science' it is the cultivating stance that continues to influence us, Elias continues. Even today it is common to see 'social achievement' as an accomplishment of self-sufficient, individual actors.

Elias's theory is based on the assumption that discursive developments are always situated in the context of agency. The important task thus is to explain actions and ideas within the framework of agency (see also Newton, 2001), which he refers to as 'figurations'. As Dopson (2001) argues:

> Elias developed the concept of figuration as a means of trying to overcome some difficulties associated with more conventional sociological terms and theories, in particular what he regarded as unhelpful dualisms and dichotomies such as between the individual and society, and also towards what he called process reduction, in which everything which is experienced and observed as dynamic and interdependent is represented in static, isolated categories. (p. 517).

Table 9.1   Cultivation and civilization as transformative processes

Cultivation	Transformation characteristics	Civilization
Science speaks to society through theory	Knowledge production	Society engages with theories as artefacts
Essence	Focus	Function
Self-referential	Reference	Cross-referential
Externally given	Constraints	Internally mobilized
Nursed adoption	Evolution	Emergent adaptation

Elias's interest in the figurations and their interdependencies makes his approach similar to actor-network theory (ANT) (for example Latour, 1987; 1999) in that they both stress that reality is best understood through a focus on the interdependencies and the networking activities happening. However, in contrast to ANT, Elias focuses primarily on the ways these figurations operate and eventually close in on themselves. Borrowing from Elias, this chapter focuses on networking between figurations inside and outside the university made possible by management concepts. It discusses how management academics as a 'research figuration' explore a popular conceptualization of performance management; and it shows how know-ledge producers in the 'consulting figuration' (outside academia) explicate this concept to prescribe performance management for practitioners, the latter being a third figuration of management knowledge. In setting science against society in this particular mode, the chapter focuses on the different ways in which research and consulting figurations operate (and define themselves), in order to clarify asymmetries between them. Extrapolating from Elias's historical account of the relation between acad-emia and society, characteristics of cultivation and civilization processes are used to discuss how popular management concepts – in their respec-tive mobilization by academic and consulting writers – reshape the way management is understood. The characteristics borrowed from Elias are listed in Table 9.1.

BUSINESS SCHOOLS STABILIZING THE BALANCED SCORECARD

The Balanced Scorecard is a concept introduced by Robert Kaplan and David Norton. It suggests that corporations should balance their traditional focus on financial performance with three additional foci – on customer, operations and innovation performance. The Balanced Scorecard is based on the assumption that financial performance depends on the ability of corporations to nurture performance in each of these three other areas.

The concept was introduced in the 1992 January issue of the *Harvard Business Review*, with the following analogy: 'Think of the Balanced Scorecard as the dials and indicators in an airplane cockpit. For the complex task of navigating and flying an airplane, pilots need detailed information about many aspects of the flight . . . Reliance on one instrument can be fatal.' (Kaplan and Norton, 1992, p. 71). As the quotation shows, the guiding metaphor was a 'dashboard' at that time. Since then the Balanced Scorecard has changed properties. By 2004, the programme is about building 'strategy maps', which requires organizations to mobilize value propositions in order to 'convert intangible assets into tangible outcomes' (Kaplan and Norton, 2004b).

The 2004 action programme is different from the 1992 action programme. Nevertheless, it is presented as being an integral part of the original Balanced Scorecard tool:

> A strategy map is a visual representation of the strategy. It provides a single-pane view of how objectives in the four BSC perspectives integrate and combine to describe the strategy. Each company must customize the strategy map to its particular set of strategic objectives. Typically, the objectives in the four perspectives of a strategy map lead to 20–30 measures being required in the associated Balanced Scorecard . . . The strategy map shows how the multiple measures on a properly constructed Balanced Scorecard provide the instrumentation for a single strategy. (Kaplan and Norton, 2004a, p. 35).

The 2004 action programme in several ways contradicts the 1992 programme. Thus a concept that started out as an intuitive performance management practice, over a period of 12 years has turned into a strategy project suggesting an implementation approach that emphasizes the articulation of value statements. (The details of the transformation from 1992 to 2004 are introduced in the next section.) This transformation, however, has been overlooked by the research figuration. The research on the Balanced Scorecard has predominantly been searching for its *essence* rather than effects – either intended or unintended.

Drawing loosely on Lukka and Granlund (2002), I show how different research publications on the Balanced Scorecard cultivate expectations in relation to it, instead of checking how this concept works in practice. The three research genres are reviewed to show how they construct notions of 'despair', 'gaps' and 'wants' in relation to a concept that is presumed to have stable properties. Lukka and Granlund have argued earlier (2002) that this leads to a fragmented communication structure within the management academy. I take their argument one step further: this fragmentation not only enables the cultivation of expectations and hype in relation to the Balanced Scorecard, but in doing so, reduces the perceived significance of the research figuration in terms of what it has to offer those who believe in the universal stories of organizing, and in the idea that knowing tools equals knowing management.

Critical Studies Articulating 'Despair'

Recent critical studies suggest that the Balanced Scorecard can never work (Nørreklit, 2003) or that, even if it works, it cannot do the right thing (Lawrence and Sharma, 2002). Common to these studies is that they produce their arguments based on philosophical reasoning. However, none of these studies reflect on the way the inscription of the Balanced Scorecard changes from a practice to a project, even though Nørreklit (2003) focuses her conclusion on the characteristics of the genre of management guru texts:

> the text is not so convincing as it is persuasive – a feature characteristic of the genre of management guru texts . . . Consequently, what the model offers is not particularly theoretically innovative and lacks a reliable theoretical base. The authors want to solve some problems that are commonly recognised, but they do not provide a valid model which can solve the problems they address. (pp. 591–2).

Nørreklit (2003) describes herself as a moderate social constructivist, and with reference to Umberto Eco, among others, she takes the stance that 'although we do not know what is absolutely right within a particular language game, we know what is absolutely wrong because a language has rules'. As she claims in the above quotation, the defining quality of a tool is whether it is theoretically innovative. Nørreklit (2003) argues that the Balanced Scorecard is not even based on reliable theory.

Lawrence and Sharma (2002) represent another example of the critical approach to popular management concepts. They adopt a Habermasian perspective to argue that the tool brings forward a theory of managing that jeopardizes the very essence of education. Their argument is based on what the authors describe as 'personal observations of the empirical organization as well as formal interviews with staff'. And while they argue that 'most questions were asked in an open-ended manner to help interviewees respond in their own ways' they also point out that 'the topics selected for interviews were mainly the adoption of managerial techniques such as the

BSC from the private sector', which after all settles the conversation with respondents as being about tools 'from a different political context'. While consistent with the Habermasian approach which calls for research on 'life-worlds as sets of regulative and constitutive steering mechanisms' (as quoted by Lawrence and Sharma), the result is that the actual embedding of the Balanced Scorecard is not an issue. Thus the readers learn how political conflicts and colonization can be mobilized in the name of systems, but they learn less about making a Balanced Scorecard work in public administration. From a political perspective on organizations, this is of course interesting. However, the struggles over the Balanced Scorecard as a political agenda overshadow – or even simply replace – the exploration of struggling to make the categories of the Balanced Scorecard meaningful in an organization, where customers happen to be students:

> The BSC is indeed a steering mechanism motivated by money and power that is designed as a means of bringing universities more in line with the needs of the interest groups currently in power. It is an attempt to subvert the educational and democratic process in favour of business interest. It is the silencing of the opposition to capitalist interest, which Habermas emphasizes in his theory of distorted communication. (Lawrence and Sharma, 2002, p. 675).

Nørreklit (2003) and Lawrence and Sharma (2002) produce critical accounts based on philosophical grounds and in this way they do bring management closer to the humanities. But is this a right way? They offer an a priori account of the Balanced Scorecard, that never accounts for the type of actions creating the critical effects discussed. Neither do they consider whether the effects identified are consequences of the implementation project, or of the ongoing mobilization of these measures in practice. They assume that BSC as an epistemic object has unchangeable and stable properties, and these properties make them despair.

Mainstream Studies: Measuring 'Gaps'

In what Lukka and Granlund (2002) refer to as the 'basic research genre', studies are designed with the objective to find empirical evidence to support the mechanism that Kaplan and Norton argue for in their texts. Some studies in this category are based on experimental design. Lipe and Salterio (2000) found out that managers (MBA students) relied more on common cause measures than on unique measures. Banker et al. (2004) suggest that evaluators, in order to rely on strategically linked measures, must understand the linkages between performance measures and strategy. None of these research designs discuss the Balanced Scorecard as such. BSC is inscribed as an object that promises to activate certain mechanisms; yet, these mechanisms are never discussed. Nevertheless, Banker et al. (2004) conclude that the Balanced Scorecard does not make much sense to managers, without explaining why.

Ittner et al. (2003a) produced a similar observation. They concluded that corporations often did not understand what the Balanced Scorecard meant. On average, firms claiming to use a Balanced Scorecard exhibited few differences in their emphasis on non-financial performance compared to the non-users. Ittner et al. (2003a) also discovered that although Kaplan and Norton (1996) claimed that the causal linking of performance measures is crucial to success, few companies related 'leading' and 'lagging' indicators into a model. However, the authors never explain what the Balanced Scorecard label signifies to its users. A simple conclusion states that the Balanced Scorecard is not what Kaplan and Norton claimed it to be.

Such results establish an image of 'gaps' between the Balanced Scorecard in principle and practice. For example Ittner and Larcker (2003) find that many corporations believe to have solved their performance management problems by adopting the BSC, thus 'mistaking it for an off-the-shelf checklist or procedure that is universally applicable and completely comprehensive' (p. 90). Although 'mistaking' suggests that a 'proper' or ostensive definition of the concept exists, their own observations do not supply it.

Ittner et al. (2003b) note that their data only show a significant positive association between scorecard use and satisfaction in the subset of their sample of corporations that have recently made changes in their measurement system. This leads to the speculation that the perceived benefits of the scorecard may be rather short-lived. As intriguing as these speculations are, they neither take into account that the Balanced Scorecard concept has continued to attract widespread attention for more than 10 years, nor do they explore the premises of their speculations in practice.

At any rate, the empirical and experimental studies suggest that it is not clear how the tool relates to practice – in particular to a successful practice. These studies content themselves with establishing the existence of 'gaps' but, like the critical researchers, they show no interest in the actions that produce those gaps.

Studies of Technology: Articulating Instrumental 'Wants'

The third category of texts published by the business academy subscribes to the instrumental vision suggested by Kaplan and Norton, and articulates 'wants' for this vision. Although most of this genre contains textbooks that seek to distribute existing knowledge, there are also some papers that attempt to explore new combinations and draw up scenarios where one technology comes to the help of another. Thus Hoque (2003) explored possible benefits of interfacing the Balanced Scorecard with total quality management (TQM), while Maiga and Jacobs (2003) examined the synergistic effects of combining the Balanced Scorecard with other management accounting systems on performance.

This genre approaches the Balanced Scorecard as a solution rather than as a theory, as illustrated in the following statements:

> In essence an organization can get 'back on track' by borrowing insights from the BSC approach. Such an approach provides new dimensions to the strategy-management control systems in several ways. The BSC approach helps an organization translate its vision and strategies into operational measures. Secondly, it communicates strategies to all levels of the organization. (Hoque, 2003, p. 556).

> The value of the BSC is that it assists the development of a consensus around the firm's vision and strategy, allowing managers to communicate the firm's strategy throughout the organization and forces managers to focus on the handful of measures that are most critical. (Maiga and Jacobs, 2003, p. 284).

These quotations articulate normative 'wants' on an instrumental basis, given their subscriptions to the idea of the scorecard as a tool. Implicit to this instrumentalism is an assumption that the Balanced Scorecard is an object with fixed properties. This makes it difficult to differentiate this genre from managerial textbook jargon:

> The Balanced Scorecard translates an organization's mission and strategy into a set of performance measures that provides the framework for implementing strategy. The balanced . . . also highlights nonfinancial objectives that an organization must achieve to meet its financial objectives (Horngren, Datar and Foster, 2002, p. 447).

> One of the advantages of the Balanced Scorecard is that it continually tests the theories underlying management's strategy. If a strategy is not working, it should become evident when some of the predicted effects (that is more car sales) don't work. (Garrison and Noreen, 2003, p. 450).

> The scorecard translates mission and strategy into goals and measures, organized into four different perspectives: financial, customer, internal business process, and learning and growth. (Simons, 2000, p. 187).

These quotations illustrate what Czarniawska (1999) refers to as the continuing reproduction of universal stories of organizing. While these texts do not explore how the Balanced Scorecard is translated into action, they mobilize 'wants' in relation to the BSC as technology and in this particular way they are reminiscent of Elias's claim – that 'real accomplishments' were seen as making of 'Wissenschaft' – or in this case 'technology'. What these texts articulate first and foremost is hope, especially in conjunction with what people would like to achieve with the Balanced Scorecard tool. Through their endless repetition that 'the right tools make things happen in the right ways', they establish for the reader what he or she should expect from the tool, no matter what organizational context.

Business Sciences: Providing Conceptual Stability

Current research on the Balanced Scorecard evokes the 18th-century Humboldtian preference for knowledge about, essence and content – over knowledge of, appearance and form. In the pursuit of measurable effects, the idea is reproduced that it is more important to know 'essence' than 'appearance' and more important to know 'content' than 'form'. Regardless of certain differences, all of these texts assume that the epistemological core of a Balanced Scorecard is given. Whether as critique or promotion, they see the Balanced Scorecard as a stable 'knowledge object' with a defined set of characteristics and properties. The 'despair', 'gaps' and 'wants' articulated by research and related educational texts teach the readers what to expect in relation to this tool. It is paradoxical that even the texts that are most critical of the Balanced Scorecard contribute to its stabilization. However, this accomplishment represents but a cultivation of the research figuration itself above the objects it studies. The research texts inscribe to this concept a certainty that even the original texts on the Balanced Scorecard were not able to provide. They formalize readers' expectations in relation to a tool that we know only through a fragmented account of 'despair', 'gaps' and 'wants'. These fragments stabilize certain modes of thinking in relation to a concept that by a consulting figuration has been labelled and marketed as a 'Balanced Scorecard'. But they neither broaden our knowledge of the practice of this tool nor contribute to new understandings of how organizations struggle to balance performance measures and management. In pointing out that this tool fails to accomplish the objectives promised by its creators, the Balanced Scorecard is enriched with an association to performance management that is more robust than what the original texts on the Balanced Scorecard by Robert Kaplan and David Norton were able to provide.

Hopper and Powell (1985) point out that it is not difficult to notice that advanced accounting techniques have had little impact on practice. The problem is that very few research studies on accounting in action have been undertaken to support this conclusion:

> It is ironical given the managerialist bias of so much accounting research and its reflection in leading textbooks, that 'advanced' techniques have had so little

impact on practice. Not unrelated to this is the growing realization that there are few close research studies of accounting in action. (p. 455).

With this statement as a starting point, the following section introduces an analysis of the Balanced Scorecard texts by Robert Kaplan and David Norton (1992, 1996, 2001, 2004). The section illustrates that the Balanced Scorecard concept has never been as stable as the business sciences have wanted to cultivate it.

THE BALANCED SCORECARD – FROM DASHBOARD PRACTICE TO STRATEGY PROJECT

Overview: 1992–2004

Robert Kaplan and David Norton (1992) introduced the concept called the Balanced Scorecard in the 1992 January issue of *Harvard Business Review*, with the following argument:

> managers should not have to choose between financial and operational measures. In observing and working with many companies, we have found that senior executives do not rely on one set of measures to the exclusion of the other. They realize that no single measure can provide a clear performance target or focus attention on the critical areas of the business . . . During a year-long research project with 12 companies . . . we devised a 'Balanced Scorecard' – a set of measures that gives top managers a fast but comprehensive view of the business. (p. 71).

Initially, the concept was defined by four relatively open-ended and equally important questions (Kaplan and Norton, 1992, p. 72): How do customers see us? What must we excel at? Can we continue to improve and create value? How do we look to shareholders? At the time, these questions were seen only as heuristics – a checklist, which according to Kaplan and Norton (1992) was always subordinate to making managerial sense:

> Even an excellent set of Balanced Scorecard measures does not guarantee a winning strategy . . . As one example, disappointing financial measures sometimes occur because companies don't follow up their operational improvements with another round of actions. Quality and cycle time improvements can create excess capacity. Managers should be prepared to either put the excess capacity to work or else get rid of it. (p. 77).

The second publication, in 1996, launched the idea that performance measures should be designed from a 'cause and effect' perspective. From this point onward, a repositioning of the Balanced Scorecard concept began, moving from an on-going practice mode to a project mode of organizing. By 1996 the narrative suspense was created in BSC through the idea that it is possible to 'tell the story of strategy' through a set of performance drivers (leading indicators) and outcome measures (lag indicators):

> A properly constructed scorecard should tell the story of the business unit's strategy through a sequence of cause-and-effect relationships'. (Kaplan and Norton, 1996, p. 149).

From 1996 onwards, the text becomes more and more prescriptive. For example, to the reader, it introduces a sequence of activities that managers must go through to create a scorecard:

> The first new process – translating the vision – helps managers build a consensus around the organization's vision and strategy . . . The second process – communicating and linking – lets managers communicate their strategy up and down the organization and link it to department and individual objectives . . . The third process – business planning – enables companies to integrate their business and financial plans . . . The fourth process – feedback and learning – gives companies the capacity for what we call strategic learning. (Kaplan and Norton, 1996, pp. 75–7).

The book, published in 2001, introduced multiple write-ups of successful implementation projects. It opens with the following words:

> Several years ago, we introduced the Balanced Scorecard. At the time we thought the Balanced Scorecard was about measurement, not about strategy. We began with the premise that an exclusive reliance on financial measures in a management system was causing organization to do the wrong things . . . Although we may not have appreciated the implications at the time, the Balanced Scorecard soon became a tool for managing strategy – a tool for dealing with the 90 percent failure rates. (Kaplan and Norton, 2001, p. 3).

And it continues:

> We have now analyzed the hundreds of strategy scorecards built since that time and have mapped the patterns into a framework that we call a strategy map. A strategy map for a Balanced Scorecard makes explicit the strategy's hypotheses. Each measure of a Balanced Scorecard becomes embedded in a chain of cause-and-effect logic that connects the desired outcomes from the strategy with the drivers that will lead to the strategic outcomes. (p. 69).

As mentioned, in 2004 Kaplan and Norton published a book that introduces the notion of 'strategy maps' as a 'guided process through which to convert intangible assets into tangible outcomes'. In contrast to the 1992 programme, the 2004 action programme is for higher-level managers, with a different perspective on the corporation. After 12 years, the concept turned from a practice mode to a project mode of organizing, while still being referred to as the same object of practice. However, while all texts continue to refer to the Balanced Scorecard, the latest text focuses much more on 'roles', 'responsibilities' and 'tasks' – that organizations must handle in order to venture with the object. It means that the problem that Kaplan and Norton offer to solve in 2004 is different from the one in 1992.

An Emergent Action Programme

The various texts on the Balanced Scorecard provide for the concept a variety of texts to draw upon, each of them making the Balanced Scorecard a plausible solution to a variety of problems that appear natural, realistic and perhaps even good (on the rhetoric of solutions, see Perelman and Olbrechts-Tyteca 1969). But whereas the audience in 1992 included those who managed performances, by 2004 the audience is top management, those who are making strategy. Strategy maps are designed to 'put all the pieces together' for the explorers in an organization, who are responsible for articulating its 'value propositions', that is, top management. Thus, when management in 1992 was about creating a system through which to ensure a balanced performance, by 2004 management has become a matter of defining the system through which strategy is to be measured. The 1992 Balanced Scorecard texts were short on the prescriptions and long on the descriptions of what they had seen competent managers do. The prescriptive part of the Balanced Scorecard was limited to the point that it is important to use a variety of performance measures, otherwise the text left things open-ended.

By 1996 prescriptions had been developed. The concept had also been supplied with a graphical user interface. It was described as a tool through which to translate into action. The metaphor of an airplane cockpit was used. Managers were introduced to the idea that they should seek to create a hierarchy of measures, rather than simply having multiple measures. The idea of having a dual set of leading and lagging measures was coined and it was prescribed that they were supposed to relate as cause and effect.

When the 2001 book appeared, it was primarily made up of case studies suggesting that these ideas could work in practice if only approached correctly. The book described how corporations had mapped their strategies, an illustration of the prescriptions offered earlier. But the 2001 publication offered also a 'trailer' for the 2004 concept of 'strategy maps'. The cases reported in 2001 are (of course) all cases of success. They 'prove' that it can be done and they seek to motivate the reader by suggesting that the corporations who have mapped their strategy and created a Balanced Scorecard 'thrive in the new business environment', as the book itself suggests.

Success and failure are now terms that are rarely applied to everyday practice, but often articulated in relation to working in a project mode. Kaplan (1998) acknowledged this change in the following reflections:

> the momentum from the early implementations, published articles, videos and speaking engagements, led to additional assignments with new companies. The implementation process was accelerated as Norton's consulting group . . . helped companies . . . We now had a team of knowledgeable consultants working with skilled creative managers at several companies. This led to new advance in both theory and implementation. We learned how to make the Balanced Scorecard the centerpiece of an organization's strategic management system . . . I believe that the reasons for the more rapid advance of knowledge was the leverage from Norton's consulting company, for which the Balanced Scorecard represented a major deliverable (and differentiator). (pp. 108–109).

Compared to earlier texts, the one from 2004 is the most elaborate in terms of the number and types of inscriptions it offers. Here Kaplan and Norton introduce how 'strategy maps' describe the logic of strategy. Yet, the most significant feature is how clear the text has become on a project mode of organizing. From the perspective of the 2004 publication, corporate leaders should see themselves as 'project managers', who constantly launch what Kaplan and Norton refer to as 'strategic initiatives' and 'action programs'. Strategy mapping is no longer an on-going practice (2004a) like it was in 1992:

> The strategy map describes the logic of the strategy, clearly showing the objectives for the critical internal processes that create value and the intangible assets that are required to support them. The Balanced Scorecard translates the strategy map objectives into measures and targets. But objectives and targets won't be achieved simply because they have been identified. The organization must launch a set of action programs (strategic initiatives) that will enable the targets for all the measures to be achieved, and it must supply scarce resources – people, funding and capacity for every program . . . (Kaplan and Norton, 2004a, p. 34).

We can see a new type of conceptualization that designs a different type of problem to be solved. The 2004 strategy maps define the problem as a question of how to measure strategy – or as specified in the book title: 'Converting intangible assets into tangible outcomes'. The 1992 text defined the problem as managing performance. For sure, the texts relate these problems to one another, but they differ in the sense that the first conceptualization created a heuristic for organizing practice, whereas the latter explicitly refers to itself as a model – an algorithm – for organizing projects.

The implication is that the things to manage differ in the two types of texts. Whereas the practice mode nurtured a performative mode, making practice reproducible, the project mode of organizing features a normative mode of organizing roles, responsibilities and tasks. The way in which the later text is put together – with its focus on roles, responsibilities and tasks – suggests that it belongs to a consulting context much more than a practitioner context. In the 2004 text, the manager's role is inscribed by activities such as finding resources – people, funding and capacity – for various strategic initiatives. Unlike in the 1992 text, their responsibility is no longer to routinize a balanced performance evaluation into a reproducible practice, but to bundle projects under a strategic theme; to construct the corporation as a business case:

> The action plan that define and provide resources for the strategic initiatives can be aligned around strategic themes that enable the initiatives to be viewed as an integrated bundle of investments instead of as a group of stand-alone projects'. (Kaplan and Norton 2004a, p. 34).

Regardless of whether we look at this as 'stand-alone projects' or 'business cases' that are both 'aligned' and 'integrated', what springs to mind is that this rhetoric addresses management as a project, which is about creating one-to-one solutions matching specific problems – as opposed to the incremental development of routines and practice. For the project manager in action, it is important to be able to bundle projects in order to facilitate resources and meet project deadlines. But these activities – or tasks – do not necessarily have anything to do with 'knowing processes' (Armstrong, 2002) and meeting the reproducibility criteria of sustainable routines as called for in times when managers were still compared to a cabin crew and the Balanced Scorecard was represented as a cockpit dashboard.

Knowing Management through the Balanced Scorecard

The development that the previous section introduces is not trivial, precisely because, as Latour (1999) reminds us, the circulation of reference takes management from one ontological status to the next. The introduction of an artefact – the strategy map – changes both the 'realm in which to understand' and the 'context of the understood'. From being a question of how performances are managed in practice, the 'strategy maps' want us to focus on ways of measuring strategy in a project-based mode of organizing. Regardless of how we evaluate this shift, it is a displacement with implications for what it means to know management in action. Yet this shift has not gained any attention from the research figuration, which instead – as illustrated previously – continues to classify, reduce and discuss the

Balanced Scorecard as if the concept was a stable phenomenon – a practice in and by itself.

As the various quotations from the official texts from 1996 to 2004 illustrate, the Balanced Scorecard is constantly changing properties in order to remain socially robust – or managerially hip. In the process of unfolding a project based management epistemology, binding mechanisms between human and non-human actors are introduced that change both the setting in which to manage and the objects to manage.

Whereas the early texts focused on creating a reproducible practice – routines without beginning and end, the later texts focus on rendering the mapping project controllable, giving it a clear beginning and a definitive end. In its present day version the Balanced Scorecard thus inscribes a different domain of the company; it gives voice to top managers rather than the line functions.

Together, the various texts allow management to be a variety of things – but it is not clear how one thing (the project) might lead to another (the practice). But, when creating 'a strategy map', the managers busy themselves with designing a beginning as well as an end to management. The 2004 Balanced Scorecard conceptualizes management through a number of texts that create binding mechanisms between roles, responsibilities and tasks that have to be fulfilled to get from point A to point B – precisely as a project needs to do. On a conceptual basis the Balanced Scorecard engages with the notions of a 'client' (who needs help in clarifying 'corporate value propositions'); and a 'consultant' (who knows how to 'road-map' the 'process'). In consequence the Balanced Scorecard no longer speaks about the practice of performance management. This may not change the fact that the Balanced Scorecard represents a way of knowing management. But it changes the means of knowing by confining knowledge of management within straightforward boundaries of a project. Yet, to the research figuration these changes have so far gone unnoticed.

DOES THE POPULARITY OF CONCEPTS RELATE TO THE CRISIS OF BUSINESS SCHOOLS?

Texts on popular management concepts such as the Balanced Scorecard remind us that production of management knowledge is by no means limited to the sciences. Outside the universities, knowledge producers continually invent new concepts that make a great variety of promises, but equally often these promises are often only loosely connected to the cultivating ideals of science. Nevertheless, as we have seen with the Balanced Scorecard, popular management concepts often profit from an epistemological 'blueprinting' granted by academia. Even when academia is critical, the current research contributes to the strengthening of an association between the Balanced Scorecard concept and the wider practice of performance management, for example.

This (self-)critique does not fit the traditional picture and expectations of academic inquiry. Traditionally, knowledge producers outside the university – consultants, for example – have been thought to blackbox the tools they sell in order to be able to implement them. Surprisingly enough, it appears that recent academic explorations do not open the Balanced Scorecard concept in order to explore its consequences, either. On the contrary, in the continuing production of path-dependent and self-cultivating studies, academia is struggling against the backdrop of its own shadow as it continues to isolate objects and purify them in order to study essences.

The Eliasian perspective used in this chapter serves as a reminder that knowledge production, whether inside or outside the university, is always self-centred. Whereas management researchers remain consistent with their traditional focus on cultivating the essence of popular concepts, management consultants focus on developing conceptual functionalities at arm's-length distance from academic tradition. Furthermore, the distinction between cultivation and civilization reveals the ways that the premises for knowledge production are changing. In the cultivating mode, knowledge production and knowledge transformation are grounded in an assumption that science speaks to society through theories. In the civilizing mode, knowledge production and transformation are emergent. Here society engages with theoretical artefacts to the extent that they provide functionality. As the Balanced Scorecard example illustrates, the result is that these concepts are constantly on the move.

This does not yet make the contributions from the research figuration less relevant. However, as the Balanced Scorecard epistemology is increasingly tied in with an ontological (project) worldview of consulting figurations, it becomes less and less clear how cultivated knowledge about Balanced Scorecards is contributing to a societal discourse about performance management that is currently dominated by Robert Kaplan's and David Norton's texts on the Balanced Scorecard.

In this sense, the crisis of the management sciences is related to the popularity of consultants' concepts. However, from an Eliasian perspective, both of these movements are affected by the way in which discourse about management has increasingly become a part of a general public discourse (Abrahamson, 1997). Elias would probably say here that the civilizing process – once more – strikes back at academia. In a civilized management environment, academic contributions are no less relevant than before. However, the increasingly civilized production of management knowledge makes it more difficult to position the cultivated viewpoints produced by the research figuration. This challenge is particularly relevant with regard to the ways in which the current discourse on performance management appears to be dominated by a consulting narrative.

The civilizing transformation discussed here in relation to the production of management knowledge contributes to a better understanding of the pressure exerted recently on universities (Czarniawska and Genell, 2002; Saravanamuthu and Tinker, 2002). Whereas it used to be the case that knowledge about management was monopolized by the universities, this is no longer the case. The response from knowledge producers outside the university results in the shift of the discourse into a conversation about 'potentialities' (Novotny et al., 2001) – things people would like to do. It is difficult to place the current research in this space, especially as it 'only' points out things people can't do or don't do well when working with the Balanced Scorecard. Instead, a consulting narrative prescribes how to do things with a Balanced Scorecard and therefore appears as practical and usable knowledge. Driven by its prescriptive focus, the consulting narrative organizes hopes, gaps and despair in relation to a linear project epistemology and thus promises both a clear beginning and a proper end. While appearing useful and perhaps even universal, the epistemology of this narrative is first and foremost socio-centric – by consultants for consulting. The 2004 Balanced Scorecard is not about performance management, it is about reality as the opportunity for consulting projects. Yet, in the ongoing conversation this point remains hidden – not least because the research figuration in trying to classify and distil what the Balanced Scorecard is and/or is not, remains as self-centred as the consulting figuration.

Researchers continue their search for ultimate truths behind the popularity of a concept that by itself is only a mundane graphic: four arrows loosely connecting four boxes labelled to list the performances of finance, customers, operations and R&D, respectively. That students react by asking for 'useful knowledge' is not surprising; it is surprising that academia continues to search for 'universal stories of organizing' instead of seeing popular concepts as tools through which to recreate its own role in relation to management consulting and management practice. The role is vacant for management research to act as moderator and interpreter of an increasingly civilized discourse on management.

Moderating the ways Management is Understood

The tool-driven development in the field of management suggests a need for post-humanist theory that – *pace* Elias – is focused on recognizing how human and material agency constitute each other across figurations of management research, consulting and practice.

If, as Armstrong (2002) suggests, there is a tendency to believe that 'knowing tools equals knowing management', the moderation needs to focus on the different ways various figurations inscribe the notion-pair of theory and practice. An important effect of the transition of management from a cultivated to a civilized knowledge production space is that the sciences no longer define theory in relation to practice. As this chapter suggests, the research and consulting figurations differ with regard to their respective views on theory.

Given the civilization of knowledge production in management it would appear that a significant role for the research figuration would be to moderate the civilization process by deconstructing the different perspectives feeding into this process. Each popular concept by itself may be insignificant for the practice of management – at least if we are to believe the current research. What these results suggest, however, is that the relevant question to study is not *if*, but *how* popular concepts work.

As Iterson et al. (2001) emphasize, with help from Elias's theory, a significant consequence of the shift from cultivation to civilization is a new level of informalization in knowledge production. In relation to the production of management knowledge, the consequences of this informalization are seen, for example, in the ways universal stories of organizing promise 'integration' and 'opportunity' rather than 'choice' and 'limitations'. With their promises of integration and opportunity universal stories of organizing reshape management – at least in terms of its rhetoric.

This development can be seen as a threat to management; alternatively, this development could be seen as promising for management research as a figuration. In a space for knowledge production that is increasingly civilized, there is a need for interpretive capacity that can both point out the choices and limitations often hidden within the 'new grand narratives' of integration and opportunity. It yet needs to be explored how these choices become transacted in local spaces. The research figuration can fulfil a role in countering the standardized narrative of 'best-practices' in management by studies of local practices.

CONCLUSIONS

Popular concepts reshape the way management is understood by bringing knowledge production into a civilized space. In this space the sciences no longer define theory in relation to practice. Popular concepts such as the Balanced Scorecard are often not sophisticated from an epistemological point of view. What makes these concepts both fascinating and problematic is the ways in which they carry forward specific theories about practice. The Balanced Scorecard introduces a way of working with performance management as a project – consistent with the consultants' work style. Largely, current research has ignored this development, as it is still situated in a cultivating mode of thought, according to which the role of research is to bring forward and speak to society through theories. It is therefore not surprising that most of current research sees it as their objective (and right?) to dismiss the Balanced Scorecard. It represents a phenomenon from the civilized knowledge production space outside universities. This stance serves, paradoxically, to stabilize the association between the concept and performance management far better than the Balanced Scorecard texts themselves. This chapter points out that there is a significant gap between the way a theory–practice relation is cultivated by the sciences and the new theory–practice constellations produced in the increasingly civilized knowledge production space of society that is at arm's-length with the sciences.

Business schools find themselves under pressure partly because of the gap between the ways science and society understand management practice and theory. In business schools, academia continues a long tradition of the cultivation of practice into theory. Society, in contrast, has civilized the production space for management knowledge. The outcome is a much closer, much narrower and therefore less robust association of practice and theory. What is important about the Balanced Scorecard is not that it carries the message about the integration of financial and non-financial performance management. The important point is that it provides a heuristic for the management of performance measures, which carries forward a theory of practice according to which management is about a linear project. This approach is consistent with the ways consultants work.

Because of the increasingly civilized production of management knowledge it is becoming less and less clear how cultivated research fits with the evolving and contextually fragmented discourse. Even though this situation does not make the outcomes of traditional management research less relevant than before, it does necessitate a new approach to research which takes into account the situation that knowledge production is no longer limited to the sciences. Academia is no longer the hob for theory building on surrounding practices. Relevance in management research does not come from the separation of theory from practice and from the removal of science from society. Relevance comes from the ability to moderate and interpret an increasingly civilized – albeit not always sophisticated – discourse on management.

REFERENCES

Abrahamson, Eric (1997), 'The emergence and prevalence of employee management rhetorics: The effects of long waves, labor unions, and turnover, 1875–1992', *Academy of Management Journal*, **40** (3), 491–533.

Armstrong, Peter (2002), 'Management, image and management accounting', *Critical Perspectives on Accounting*, **13** (3), 281–95.

Banker, Rajiv D., Hsihui Chang and Mina J. Pizzini (2004), 'The Balanced Scorecard: Judgemental effects of performance measures linked to strategy', *The Accounting Review*, **79** (1), 1–23.

Collins, David (2000), *Management Fads and Buzzwords. Critical-Practical Perspectives*, London: Routledge.

Czarniawska, Barbara (1999), *Writing Management – Organization Theory as Literary Genre*, Oxford University Press.

Czarniawska, Barbara (2003), 'Forbidden knowledge – organization theory in times of transition', *Management Learning*, **34** (3), 353–65.

Czarniawska, Barbara and Kristina Genell (2002), 'Gone shopping? Universities on their way to the market', *Scandinavian Journal of Management*, **18**, 455–74.

Dopson, Sue (2001), 'Applying an Eliasian approach to organizational analysis', *Organization*, **8** (3), 515–35.

Elias, Norbert (1939/1994), *The Civilizing Process*, Oxford: Blackwell Publishers.

Garrison, Ray H. and Eric W. Noreen (2003), *Managerial Accounting*, 10th edition, Irvin: McGraw-Hill .

Hopper, Trevor and Andrew Powell (1985), 'Making sense of research into the organizational and social aspects of management accounting: a review of its underlying assumptions', *Journal of Management Studies*, **22** (5), 429–65.

Hoque, Zahirul (2003), 'Total quality management and the Balanced Scorecard approach: A critical analysis of their potential relationships and directions for research', *Critical Perspectives on Accounting*, **14**, 553–66.

Horngren, Charles T., Srikant M. Datar and George M. Foster (2002), *Cost Accounting – A Managerial Emphasis*, London: Prentice Hall.

Iterson, Ad van, Willem Mastenbrook and Joseph Soeters (2001), 'Civilizing and informalizing: organizations in an Eliasian context', *Organization*, **8** (3), 497–514.

Ittner, Christopher D. and David F. Larcker (1997a), 'Coming up short on nonfinancial performance measurement', *Harvard Business Review*, November, pp. 88–95.

Ittner, Christopher D. and David F. Larcker (1997b), 'Quality strategy, strategic control systems and organizational performance', *Accounting, Organizations and Society*, **22** (3/4), 293–314.

Ittner, Christopher D. and David F. Larcker (1998), 'Innovation in performance measurement: trends and research implications', *Journal of Management Accounting Research*, **10**, 205–38.

Ittner, Christopher D., David F. Larcker and Marshall W. Meyer (2003a), 'Subjectivity and the weighting of performance measures: evidence from a Balanced Scorecard', *The Accounting Review*, **78** (3), 725–58.

Ittner, Christopher D., David F. Larcker and Taylor Randall (2003b), 'Performance implications of strategic performance measurement in financial services firms', *Accounting, Organizations and Society*, **28**, 715–41.

Kaplan, R.S. (1998), 'Innovation action research: creating new management theory and practice', *Journal of Management Accounting Research*, **10**, pp. 89–118.

Kaplan, Robert and David Norton (1992), 'The Balanced Scorecard: measures that drive performance', *Harvard Business Review*, 71–80.

Kaplan, Robert and David Norton (1996), *The Balanced Scorecard: Translating strategy into action*, Boston, MA: Harvard Business School Press.

Kaplan, Robert and David Norton (2001), *The strategy focused organization: How Balanced Scorecard companies thrive in the new environment*, Boston, MA: Harvard Business School Press.

Kaplan, Robert and David Norton (2004a), 'Strategy Maps – They show how to describe, measure and align your intangible assets to achieve superior performance and become more profitable', *Strategic Finance*, March, pp. 27–35.

Kaplan, Robert and David Norton (2004b), 'Strategy Maps – Converting intangible assets into tangible outcomes', Boston, MA: Harvard Business School Press.

Latour, Bruno (1987), *Science in Action*, Cambridge, MA: Harvard University Press.

Latour, Bruno (1992), 'Where are the missing masses ? The sociology of a few mundane artifacts', chapter 8 in Wiebe Bijker and John Law (eds), *Shaping Technology / Building Society: Studies in Sociotechnical Change*, Cambridge, Mass: MIT Press, pp. 225–58.

Latour, Bruno (1999), *Pandora's Hope – Essays on the Reality of Science Studies*, Cambridge, MA: Harvard University Press.

Lawrence, Stewart and Umesh Sharma (2002), 'Commodification of education and academic labour – Using the Balanced Scorecard in a university setting', *Critical Perspectives on Accounting*, **13**, 661–77.

Lipe, Marlys G. and Steve Salterio (2000), 'The Balanced Scorecard: Judgmental effects of common and unique performance measures', *The Accounting Review*, **75** (3), 283–98.

Lukka, Kari and Markus Granlund (2002), 'The fragmented communication structure within the accounting academia: the case of activity-based costing research genres', *Accounting, Organizations and Society*, **27**, 165–950.

Maiga, Adam S. and Fred A. Jacobs (2003), 'Balanced Scorecard, activity-based costing and company performance: an empirical analysis', *Journal of Managerial Issues*, **XV** (3), 283–301.

Newton, Tim (2001), 'Organization: the relevance and limitations of Elias', *Organization*, **8** (3), 467–95.

Nørreklit, Hanne (2003), 'The Balanced Scorecard: what is the score? A rhetorical analysis of the Balanced Scorecard', *Accounting, Organizations and Society*, **28**, 591–619.

Novotny, Helga, Peter Scott and Martin Gibbons (2001), *Rethinking Science – Knowledge and the Public in an Age of Uncertainty*, Cambridge, UK: Polity Press.

Perelman, Chaïm and Lucie Olbrechts-Tyteca (1969), *The new rhetoric: a treatise on argumentation*, Notre Dame, IN: University of Notre Dame Press.

Saravanamuthu, Kala and Tony Tinker (2002), 'The university in the new corporate world', *Critical Perspectives on Accounting*, **13**, 545–54.

Simons, Richard (2000), *Performance Measurement & Control Systems for Implementing Strategy, Text & Cases*, New Jersey: Prentice Hall.

PART 3

Bringing humanities into the
heart of management

10. Management as product of the European knowledge tradition: A modern form of ancient *paideia*?

Keith Hoskin

MANAGEMENT AS POWERFUL KNOWLEDGE

The starting point for this reflection is that management, although manifestly a means of exercising power, always does so through being a form of knowledge. From its first materialization, I shall suggest, management has always been a knowledge-based approach to exercising power. Today, given its success and ubiquity in the running of modern economic and governmental worlds, it has additionally shown itself to be an extremely powerful form of knowledge. I therefore want to reflect here upon what kind of knowledge management is – and has always been – and thereby to locate management as knowledge form within the European knowledge tradition.

I do so, not as some antiquarian gesture towards the glories of the European past, nor as some oppositional reaction against the contemporary dominance within management of American models of best practice, or the influence of American gurus and research paradigms. On the contrary, I feel it is important to recognize and celebrate that American success, not least because it is a key part of my reflection to acknowledge that management is very much an American breakthrough, and indeed an American 'invention'.

At the same time, I do not want to rest content with celebrating the American provenance of management, and the subsequent dominance of American thinking in and around management. For while it is essential to have a realistic recognition of that achievement and its magnitude, it is essential too, I shall argue, to understand where it has come from, and where potentially it may lead. For, in so far as management is a knowledge-based form of exercising power, we need to have an informed understanding of the nature of that knowledge, in its strengths and its weaknesses, and of how its past may condition, but does not therefore totally determine, its future. If that may at this point appear a somewhat enigmatic observation,

I hope what I mean will become clearer once I have gone more deeply into the history of management as knowledge-form, and also, in this phrase I advisedly choose, 'invention'. In particular, I hope it may become clear, from the historical analysis developed here, how management is not simply an American breakthrough, but carries within it a significant but perhaps not fully appreciated residue of the European knowledge tradition.

What I have in mind here is a two-fold or two-part set of influences. First, I would support the view that others have made (for example Locke, 1984), that management as modern knowledge form draws upon and forms part of the elite modern knowledge system of academic disciplines. In this regard I would further want to recognize that disciplinary knowledge system as a significant development in its own right, and as a discontinuity even in the Western knowledge tradition, with a genesis in the institutional world of Enlightenment learning in 18th-century Europe (Hoskin, 1993a). But further, I want to argue that we can only understand management as knowledge form, and how and why it materialized as a knowledge invention in the United States, by locating management within that much longer European knowledge tradition, out of which the Enlightenment breakthrough emerged. So if there is an important discontinuity out of which management as such emerges as a distinctive modern knowledge form, there is also a continuity to be acknowledged with that older knowledge tradition, which stretches back to the beginnings of alphabetic culture in ancient Greece – that tradition which has been variously known as that of Western Reason, Humanism, the culture of the *Logos*, logocentrism, and finally and perhaps most informatively in this context, *paideia*.

That older knowledge tradition is not something upon which we typically spend much time or thought today. Typically, even if the historical or diachronic dimension of the modern knowledge world of the disciplines is raised as an issue at all, serious analysis of such modern knowledge as management will begin at the latest with the Enlightenment. Now in one respect that is eminently reasonable, given that so many of our successful modern disciplines and sub-disciplines are post-Enlightenment fields of study, with no prior history to speak of, either in terms of theoretical provenance or practical application. So many key modern fields of vital significance to the running of the modern world and the formation of our modern selves are in this category. All the forms of big science, experimental and applied, all the great social sciences, economics, statistics, psychology, political science, and even most of the fields of literary and historical scholarship and all the personal sciences of the mind, soul and body (from psychoanalysis to health and sports science) are creations of the 19th century, with either no, or only vestigial, real precedent as knowledge fields before the Enlightenment (Berlin, 1976).

And yet . . . to ignore that older tradition, and to overlook how far these modern knowledge fields embody and reproduce aspects of that older Western knowledge tradition is to truncate our understanding and to fail to understand the dynamics of modern knowledge and its power. Or so I shall argue here. Most particularly, I shall argue that this is true of that extraordinary and extraordinarily powerful knowledge-form, management. So I do not intend to ignore or devalue the modern history of management as knowledge form, but I shall consider only its initial genesis as a feature of the modern knowledge world of the disciplines, and then only as a means to then considering how it has become a particularly powerful knowledge discipline, with all the pluses and minuses that entails. For my prior and greater concern or thesis here is that both the development of management to date and its potential lines of future development going forward need consideration within the wider knowledge framework that is the tradition of *paideia*.

RESUSCITATING *PAIDEIA*: OR TOWARDS ACKNOWLEDGING THE ROLE OF CONTINUITY IN THE EUROPEAN KNOWLEDGE TRADITION

What is *paideia*? It is, literally, a Greek term designating the development of the child (in ancient Greek, *pais*), a noun-form that can be applied to both male and female, even if *paideia* as cultural phenomenon was for most of European history largely the preserve of males. It is, however, a term that had become, by the fourth century BCE, a key cultural sign, denoting that educational development of the child who becomes the elite but also rounded human being. *Paideia* becomes the sign designating and announcing true education; it is what makes people fully human. It also becomes, as Greek alphabetic culture and imperium extend beyond the Greek-speaking world (as they already do with the rise to power, first in Greece and then beyond, of the non-Greek Macedonians, father and son, Philip and Alexander) what makes even non-Greeks truly Greek and human. As that happens, *paideia* becomes the term for the culture shared by all those who are numbered within the population of the 'truly educated', regardless of ethnic or socio-cultural provenance, and *paideia* as practice becomes the cultural cement of first the Greek and then the Greco-Roman worlds, the means through which imperium and the alphabetically literate culture that it supports (or which supports it) is produced and reproduced.

In the latter case, as Rome becomes the second great alphabetically literate imperial power, and so, as Eric Havelock observed, the world's first 'copying culture' (Havelock, 1975, p. 67), *paideia* is joined as key cultural and educational term by a Latin corollary, *humanitas*, as signalling that quality which renders humans most human, a quality which is also produced by undergoing a proper form of literary and cultured education, but is now (as in the vision of Cicero and Quintilian) to be obtained by being eloquent in both the alphabetically written languages of literacy and literature, Greek and Latin. With these twin terms henceforward in play, later ages in the Latin west of Europe derive reformulations of the educational ideal from the Latin term, as with humanism and the humanities. *Paideia*, along with *humanitas*, therefore becomes a watchword of the European knowledge tradition, with resonance across the various eras of European history, wherever the production of an educated and cultured elite remains a core feature of culture and imperium, which is effectively in every country and culture that is a beneficiary (if beneficiary is the appropriate term) of the subsequent alphabetic diaspora, first in Europe and then beyond.

For instance, as the Latin alphabet (like Cyrillic but interestingly not Greek) becomes a vehicle for the writing of vernacular languages (something that appears to begin around 1000 CE), the culture of *paideia/ humanitas* becomes acquirable by study in the vernacular as well as in Greek and Latin. Today of course that culture will typically be developed in alphabetic cultures where the study of Greek and Latin has virtually disappeared. But this, in itself, does not stop or divert the process of becoming 'fully human' through becoming educated in the *paideia* tradition. It simply supplements the original Greco-Roman practice with new knowledge demands, including the demand to be numerate in the arabic numeral sign system (something that first joined the alphabetic system in the 13th century and is now a basic requirement for becoming educated at all).

This *paideia* may also (but today does not necessarily) have a religious dimension, as memorably articulated for the Judaeo-Christian tradition by Saint Augustine and disseminated into the Latin Middle Ages and beyond. But it may also have a more secular emphasis, as in the various forms of Renaissance humanism, both southern and northern. Today it is not enough even to prove competent in the use of alphanumeric sign systems, the exponent of *paideia* must also be fluent in working with semiotic systems too. And since the 19th century, it has, in one of the great reversals of literate history, become open to, and expected of, females as well as males to become such exponents.

In short, the tradition of *paideia* arguably lives on, even today, in the image of the well-educated person who is competent to succeed in what often gets designated as the knowledge or learning society. At the same time, one of the strange or intriguing developments of the past fifty years is the virtual collapse of any awareness of the term *paideia* and its potential ongoing significance. That is something that can best be brought out by invoking perhaps the most significant and evocative deployment of *paideia* in our recent past, its use as the title of a once-lauded but now largely forgotten work by the German scholar, Werner Jaeger.

THE RISE AND FALL OF PHILOLOGY: THE HIGH-WATER-MARK OF *PAIDEIA*?

Jaeger produced, in the 1930s and 40s, a monumental three-volume work entitled, in its English version, *Paideia: the Ideals of Greek Culture*. It opens as follows:

> *Paideia*, the title of this work, is not merely a symbolic name, but the only exact designation of the actual historical subject presented in it. Indeed it is a difficult thing to define; like other broad comprehensive concepts (*philosophy*, for instance, or *culture*) it refuses to be confined within an abstract formula. Its full content and meaning become clear to us only when we read its history and follow its attempts to realize itself. By using a Greek word for a Greek thing, I intend to imply that it is seen with the eyes, not of modern men, but of the Greeks. It is impossible to avoid bringing in modern expressions like *civilization*, *culture*, *tradition*, *literature* or *education*. But none of them really covers what the Greeks meant by *paideia*. Each of them is confined to one aspect of it: they cannot take in the same field as the Greek concept unless we employ them all together. Yet the very essence of scholarship and scholarly activity is based on the original unity of all these aspects – the unity which is expressed in the Greek word, not the diversity emphasized and completed by modern developments. The ancients were persuaded that education and culture are not a formal art or an abstract theory, distinct from the objective historical structure of a nation's spiritual life. They held them to be embodied in literature, which is the real expression of all higher culture. That is how we must interpret the definition of the cultured man given by Phrynichus:
> > *Philologos ho philōn logous and spoudazōn peri paideian.* (Jaeger, 1947)

These words form (or more precisely do so in their English translation) the proëm to what is arguably one of the great achievements of philological scholarship of the twentieth century. First published in Germany in 1933, and meant, as the Preface pointedly says (p. ix), 'not only for scholars, but for all who seek to rediscover the approach to Greece during our present struggles to maintain our millennial civilization', it went into a second German edition in 1935, a first English one in 1939 and a second in 1947, by which time Jaeger had long left Germany for Harvard. It is of course dated in certain ways, for instance in its juxtaposition of the constructs 'nation', 'spiritual life' and the possibility of their having an 'objective historical structure': or in the belief in an 'essence of scholarship and scholarly activity' that should obtain across all fields of specialist endeavour, despite all their diversity; and last but not least, in the almost disarming assumption that there could be a general readership for a work that ends its proëm (and then indeed bestrews its text) with Greek quotations, plain and unadorned.[1]

At the same time, this is a text which can and should still very much speak from its past to our present, particularly to a contemporary consideration of management as a feature of elite formation and elite culture, and more generally, perhaps, for the valuable and different light it throws on the usage of the term 'culture'. It can do so, I suggest, in two distinguishable but ultimately connected ways.

First, Jaeger's is one of the most significant evocations of the long-term significance of *paideia*, as a key feature both of our past and our present. His three volumes may ostensibly concern themselves only with the ancient Greek and Roman worlds, but even if they are read as having that compass, they develop a theme with an important contemporary resonance. For Jaeger brings home how far *paideia*, as this construct that constantly exceeds easy or reductionist definition or translation, will not be constrained into being just, or primarily, either a social or alternatively an individual phenomenon.

Instead *paideia* exists only by inhabiting and shaping the individual as such, and simultaneously disseminating itself across the whole population of its exponents and devotees. To bring this home, after an introductory volume on Archaic Greece and 'The Mind of Athens', the whole of Volume Two is devoted to how *paideia* is developed into such a significant construct through the learning and thinking of one individual, Plato, before the social and cultural implications of this are worked out in Volume Three, and we see how *paideia* then becomes not just the intellectual adornment of the literate elite, but the administrative and cultural cement for the successive edifices of Greek and Roman imperium, however wide the multi-lingual and multi-cultural domains they commanded (and as already implied, they were, from Alexander's time on, always wide).

That, I suggest, is an important insight to hold onto in looking to envisage possible future ways of thinking about management as knowledge-form and its potential development. We need a way of understanding how this knowledge, now so powerful, operates simultaneously at so many levels: as a socio-cultural phenomenon which now colonizes public-sector and not-for-profit entities as well as businesses, as organizational phenomenon, which operates across a given entity and within each of the cells within it, as well as the means of connecting those cells into what Barbara Czarniawska has described as an 'action net' (for example Czarniawska, 2004): and as an increasingly widespread mode of self-development and self-care. We cannot remain content with even a residually sociologistic or psychologistic approach to understanding this knowledge. For we will then fail to understand its power as knowledge form. We also need a way of understanding it that adequately respects the way in which there is continuity in our knowledge tradition while also properly acknowledging what is new and different. In addressing both these issues, there is, I suggest, much that we may take from Jaeger, and indeed from a whole series of other distinguished philologists and historians of the same era.

Some of the landmark works bringing this home would include Eric Auerbach's *Mimesis: the Representation of Reality in Western Literature* (1953, original German publication, 1946), Henri-Irenée Marrou's *History of Education in Antiquity* (1956, original French publication, 1948), Ernst Curtius' *European Literature and the Latin Middle Ages* (1953, original German publication, 1948) and Robert Bolgar's *The Classical Heritage and its Beneficiaries: from the Carolingian Age to Today* (1954). All in their way maintain the same double focus on the individual and the socio-cultural. All, in the richness of their studies, are sensitive to institutional, linguistic and cultural difference, but also to individual difference and uniqueness too.[2] But additionally the very fact that such authors could generate these works in different European (and not just European) countries and intellectual cultures, as their original dates and places of publication underline, should bring home just how far *paideia* has until recently been both with and within us, across Europe, and beyond.

In that respect, Jaeger's work, along with the other texts just cited, is itself a manifestation of the continued and continuing operation of *paideia*, an exemplary demonstration also of the double action of philology, or how an individual can demonstrate the highest quality of detailed philological and historical scholarship but then combine it with a broad concern for, or love of, *logos*, of a kind that is a million miles from a misguidedly slavish devotion to 'the glories that were Greece'. The concern to allow *paideia* to be seen 'with the eyes . . . of the Greeks' marks his recognition that this may be our past but it is also of its own time, and 'other'. It is also the basis from which I want to develop a proposal for resuscitating our engagement with the construct of *paideia*, building on this too readily forgotten tradition of work, and showing how it may be relevant to considering management knowledge, and management as knowledge, going forward from here.

RE-THINKING *PAIDEIA* IN AND FOR THE KNOWLEDGE WORLD OF 'LATE DISCIPLINARITY'

If there has been one theoretical development which has a particular pertinence to resuscitating or reinvigorating the construct of *paideia*, it is the emergent theoretical concern with practices. For *paideia* has always required a deep and extensive engagement with educational practice, in all its different manifestations from ancient Greece on. But although the great works just noted all in various ways tell us much about the details of the practices involved in producing and reproducing the culture of *paideia*, they were all written in an era when practice was not theorized in the way that has become common since. So let me offer a brief analysis of how one may conceptualize the production and reproduction of *paideia* in its various manifestations and forms from ancient Greece on via a history of practices. That history may then form the basis for re-thinking management as knowledge form within the latest era of *paideia*, the world of modern disciplinarity.

In such a history there is necessarily a focus on two kinds of phenomena: the kinds of sign system available for the articulation of knowledge by those who are learned and those who are learners, and the forms of pedagogic practice through which they encounter those sign systems. The everyday practice of becoming adept, at any given time and place, in the ways of *paideia* will involve first learning to read and write those sign-systems, and then learning the dominant knowledge discourses purveyed in those sign-systems. But becoming adept at the same time involves successfully learning via the pedagogy through which, at the given time, those sign systems and knowledge discourses are purveyed.

What we learn from the great philologists, supplemented by more recent work (for example Havelock, 1975; Ong, 1982) is how crucial to the success of *paideia* was the invention of the alphabetic sign system, and we can add, its subsequent supplementing from around 1200 CE by the arabic numeral system.[3] But one of the insights generated by a focus on practices, including pedagogic practices, is that a technical breakthrough at the level of a sign system, while necessary to generating new modes of knowledge discourse, is not sufficient. Havelock developed one of the more forceful articulations of this conclusion, through reflecting on why it is that the alphabetic system is developed by 700 BCE at the latest, but the culture of Greek 'reason', the logos, as epitomized in the work of Plato to which Jaeger devotes so much of his work, does not materialize till around 400 BCE. Interestingly Havelock himself indicates precisely how a shift in pedagogic practice is the difference that makes the difference, when he observes (as had Marrou before him) that learning to read and write using this sign system is not very high status in the early centuries of the alphabetic era. It tends to be used for record-keeping while true education continues to reflect the earlier oral tradition of elite culture, stressing the memorizing of poetry, the oral delivery of verse and prose and musical performance, in an elite education known as *mousike*. This is difficult, as he observes, for us to understand in our world where 'the maximum of education is identified with the maximum of literacy' (Havelock, 1982, p. 189).

But where Havelock goes beyond the earlier scholarship is in paying attention to what he calls the 'nuts and bolts of Greek education' (1982, p. 205, n.4) so that he makes visible in a new way how pedagogic practice can transform both the use and status of a sign system, and generate in the process a new way of seeing or understanding what learning is. Havelock notes that there is a change in how learning to read was taught, with the development of a first rigorous method for teaching the child to read (and also thereby setting up a set of assumptions about what 'language' is that is with us still). That method is the forerunner of phonics, the alphabetic method, which Havelock concludes from the fact that references to this method do not appear until around 400 BCE in Athens, probably began in Athens no earlier than 430 BCE. That method first taught children the letters of the alphabet in 'order' (that is the order that is now standardized for Greek, and in its separate but related ordering, also for the Latin alphabet). It then taught them the possible syllabic combinations of those letters, then taught them nonsense strings of such syllables, then individual words, then finally sentences. It is the ultimate in meaningless but analytically rigorous technique. It also promotes the assumption in the learner (before the learner is even able to realize that an assumption is being made at all) that the perfect deciphering of letters and syllables leads to perfect (and meaningful) reading. It also turns out that this way of learning promoted within at least one learner in the first generation of those who learned under this method in Athens (assuming Havelock's dating is right) a new way of thinking about the nature of knowledge and knowing. That learner was Plato, born around 430 BCE and clearly one who learned under this method as he recalls both in the *Politicus* (278) and *Theaetetus* (206) how difficult the process was. But it then becomes the template for understanding the nature of the world in the theory of Forms or Ideas. For Plato's whole approach is based on the assumption that the physical world and the noetic world are both made up of entities which are constructed from supposedly basic elements into syllables and then meaningful wholes, and further that humans come to understand the world and its entities through learning to decipher below the surface of the whole its elements, through the process of analysis of wholes into parts and basic elements, and then, moving in the other direction, through learning to create new synthetic understandings through the reverse process of seeing how basic elements can be made, through their proper combination into syllables, into various new meaningful wholes.

There is not space to go through a full analysis of all the passages where Plato has recourse to the letters of the alphabet and their combination into syllables and wholes as his means of explaining the nature of the world of ideas (see further, Hoskin, 1993b). But for instance, in the famous passage in the *Phaedrus* (274–7) where Socrates warns against a trust in writing, the passage ends with Plato arguing (276A-B) that mistrust must only be reserved for visible texts, while the genuine Logos is that which exists as the purified invisible writing of the Ideas, and which is 'written with understanding in the soul of the learner'. In the *Philebus* (15ff) and the *Politicus* (278ff) the letters of the alphabet are the 'example' explaining how the soul recognizes the elements of everything, physical or noetic. For this continued invocation of the alphabet as a system made up from elements to syllables to the meaningful wholes of the *Logos*, Ong has suggested that 'perhaps Plato's ideas were the first grammatology' (1982, p. 168).

Whether that is the case or not, Plato, that central figure in Jaeger's analysis of *paideia*, turns out to be the man who does not only initiate logocentrism, but also launches a link between writing, pedagogy and the constitution of knowledge forms within the Western knowledge tradition. And that is something that becomes clear once one re-reads the analyses made by the great philologists via a theory of practices.

The same can be done for the later moments where there is significant sign-system change within the alphabetic tradition. At that medieval moment when arabic numerals came together with alphabetic writing to constitute a new kind of alphanumeric sign world (see note 3), we also find in the Latin west the emergence of the universities around 1200 CE, as those educational institutions that first, in the West, initiated the practice of oral examining of students (and the award of degrees on the basis of performance in those examinations). Work with Richard Macve (Hoskin and Macve, 1986) has reviewed the significance of that conjunction of sign-system and pedagogy for the development of new forms of textual lay-out (paragraphing, punctuation, indices) and for the development of new forms of knowledge that combine the qualities of information collection and retrieval made possible by such lay-out and a commitment to constant (oral) examination. Such new knowledge forms include the practices of confession and inquisition developed by the university graduates within the Catholic church from around 1200 CE on, and of course the practice of keeping accounts in double-entry book-keeping. But from our viewpoint here, the more significant such conjunction is that around 1800 when the alphanumeric system is supplemented by a new kind of pedagogic practice, wherein students in elite institutions of higher learning are required not just to undertake oral examination but are required to write and be examined, and are also subject to the new practice, apparently unprecedented in any educational culture, of numerical grading of their performance.

MANAGEMENT AS KNOWLEDGE FORM WITHIN THE TRADITION OF *PAIDEIA*

I have investigated elsewhere the way in which this new set of pedagogic practices impacted on the way in which humans learn and the learning that they produce (Hoskin, 1993a). That analysis traces how the students who first learn under the combined practices of writing, examining and numerical grading are in European institutions from the 1760s on. In Germany they have to prepare written work and are examined in the space of the seminar, in France they have to do practicals and are graded on them in the space of the laboratory, in England they have to take maths exams in the space of the examination hall. But not only do they learn in a new way, they produce new learning. For the students in France become the pioneers of the new laboratory-based scientific approach, and men such as Bichat develop new knowledge fields such as biology, while those in Germany, such as Wolf, become the founders, ironically, of the modern study of philology of which Jaeger would be such a distinguished exponent. The fields of biology and philology are two of the first new and modern 'knowledge disciplines'. The consequent development of an open-ended network of disciplines then follows, whose truths are all developed by men, and now women, who learn under constant writing, examining and grading and then largely generate their new truths via methods that demonstrate the virtue of putting those practices to work to generate new knowledge.

This analysis of practices has then been put to use in my work with Richard Macve to argue for a direct link from this European development to the development of management as a knowledge invention. We accept the thesis that Alfred Chandler first proposed in *The Visible Hand* (1977), that management develops in the USA in the early 19th century, and there became the means to developing the modern business enterprise, that unprecedented business entity where managers manage other managers, via a system that he describes as 'administrative coordination'. What we add (for example Hoskin and Macve, 1988) is a new analysis of who develops the first forms of management identified by Chandler as appearing in the US Armory at Springfield and on the US railroads. In our conclusion, the men who 'invent' management are all graduates of the US Military Academy at West Point, and they are able to do so because they in turn have learned under constant writing, examining and grading and can now put those practices to use to solve the practical and age-old human problem of 'getting people to get things done'. Their invention consists in putting those practices to work in ways that successfully produce that administrative coordination of which Chandler speaks. In particular the introduction of these practices produces a new kind of writing-intensive process for coordinating activity, but a writing that constantly examines and puts numbers not just on products but processes, not just financial performance but non-financial human performance. It simultaneously produces a new centripetal way of getting hierarchical structures to work, a way of making the link-points in action nets strong rather than weak, by the constant exercise of surveillance and judgement by writing, examining and grading. Getting this new system right was an invention, in the sense that the structuring and the processing had to be aligned right. It was not self-evident, but a work of creative technical innovation.

But of course if that was the start of management as knowledge form, that was not its end. For the wider disciplinary impetus that had already in Europe begun to generate new knowledge disciplines would do the same to management. And that is the start of the apparently distinctive and new American knowledge juggernaut that is management research. Such research and the teaching institutions that nurture and showcase that research are largely American breakthroughs from the later 19th century into the mid-20th century. We see the proliferation of research areas that do not previously exist but begin to acquire their now-familiar names from the late 19th century on – operations management, financial management, human resources management, organizational psychology, strategy, marketing, information technology and systems. But if management, like many other disciplinary fields, is in this respect peculiarly modern, at the same time, once one sees how it emerges within the more general growth of the new disciplinarity, one has two possible ways of deepening our understanding of management.

First, we may see how this knowledge form is still within the tradition of *paideia*, since the world of knowledge disciplinarity is itself just the latest manifestation of what began with *paideia*, understood as a particular conjunction of alphabetic/alphanumeric sign system with pedagogic practice. But second we may also see the weaknesses as well as strengths of management as knowledge form from this perspective.

One great weakness (which is now being seen as significant in much management discourse) is the direct consequence of being a disciplinary success story. Here management, as disciplinary knowledge form within a knowledge-world that embodies and lionizes disciplinarity, is condemned to constant change along disciplinary lines, in which the constant production of new acceptably disciplinary knowledge generates new disciplines and subdisciplines. So managers become condemned to having to learn (or be familiar with) ever more knowledge areas, each with its own (and often conflicting) assumptions about the nature of knowledge, its distinctive methods for 'being competent and knowledgeable' and its own cherished truths. And systemically, as many have realized, there is a fractioning of understanding and increasingly frequent dialogues of the deaf. But, as the *paideia* tradition may remind us, disciplinarity is not, as the latest manifestation of Western reason, not just about fractioning into sub-specialisms but about connectivity across knowledge areas. So we hear the increasing calls for synthesis, for critical understanding and for multi-disciplinary or trans-disciplinary ways of doing things. So we inhabit a world of changing management with contrary pulls, but both under the sign of disciplinarity. But changing management is therefore also an active possibility, so long as we have an adequate diagnosis where management originally comes from and so have an adequate way of thinking about the range of possible ways in which it can go forward, so long as we continue to live under the sign of disciplinarity . . .

CONCLUSION: *PAIDEIA* AS WATCHWORD FOR A NEW EUROPEAN OPPORTUNITY?

I say advisedly that 'we' live under the sign of disciplinarity. For just as much as managers deploy a knowledge and way of understanding that is disciplinary, so do all those who engage in management research. And there is, I suggest, a corollary or parallel to the dilemma that managers face in the field of management research. The great American success story there has been the development of more and better technical know-how, more quantified analyses of the positivist persuasion, knowing more and more about less and less. The gap that looms or potentially welcomes researchers in lies in the field of transdisciplinary connections.

We do not have to walk into that gap. We do not have to accept the potential welcome. But at the same time, if we are able to reflect upon the history of management as knowledge form, with the benefit of a longer time-frame than is conventional and with an understanding of just how far European traditions of *paideia* are still at work in the apparently most instrumental and positivist forms of disciplinary management knowing, then we can perhaps take the step beyond apparent determinism and launch a whole series of interventions that resuscitate the tradition of *paideia* in the way that Jaeger so thoughtfully yet passionately envisaged it.

NOTES

1. In fact I have made a concession to modern reading sensibilities, by transliterating the phrase, where Jaeger writes it using the Greek alphabet. Let me make one more – given that the era has definitively passed when an author might invoke the conceit that a

general, even an elite general, readership might be classically educated – by attempting to translate the ancient tragedian's words in something like the spirit of Jaeger's sentiments here. So one translation might be: 'the lover of *logos* is the one who loves words and strives after *paideia*'. But that arguably outdoes Jaeger, by not only preserving the supposed untranslatability of one Greek word but claiming the same status for another, much pored over in Jaeger's day and since: *logos*. So alternatively, the *philologos* might perhaps be read as the 'philologist' if by that term we mean that kind of scholar exemplified by Jaeger himself; and for *paideia*, we might still follow Jaeger's other line of thought, and substitute all of 'civilization, culture, tradition, literature or education'. All of which goes to show the authorial convenience afforded if one can only avoid having to translate in the first place, by assuming the reader will be competent to read the original . . .

2. Marrou's work for instance follows the identical pattern of analysis, only adding Isocrates to Plato, thus signalling how ancient *paideia* implicated rhetorical modes of knowing alongside the philosophical. Or again, Auerbach's concern with the differing ways developed in Western literature for 'the interpretation of reality through literary representation or "imitation"' (1953, p. 554) is articulated exclusively through the analysis of short excerpts from a few individual authors from each selected historical moment – for example Homer and the Old Testament in Chapter 1, Petronius, Tacitus and the New Testament in Chapter 2, Stendhal, Balzac and Flaubert in Chapter 18, Virginia Woolf and Proust in Chapter 20.

3. There is an important, if contentious, issue over the difference constituted by the so-called alphabetic breakthrough, and the extent to which that form of sign system contributes to the success of Greek, Roman and medieval forms of *paideia*. Before the alphabetic breakthrough (c. 750 BCE), syllabaries had from around 2000 BCE sought to trace a language's sound-*units*, that is to translate the signification carried on in the oral flow format of speech into visual format through developing a set of visually differentiated characters. But whereas syllabaries and the related consonantaries are made up of characters that operate at the level of the 'sound-unit as such', the alphabetic breakthrough consists in developing a set of signifiers that goes below that level, by turning some of what we now call the 'letters' (Greek *grammata*) into vowels (that is 'sounded signifiers' or in Greek '*phoneenta*') and the rest into 'sounded with' ones (consonants or *symphona*). All *alphabetic* notation systems comprise a set of letters of this type, with the consequence that 'instead of one symbol for the sound *ba*, you have two, *b* plus *a*' (Ong, 1982, p. 91), in a system where 'b' is unsoundable without the addition of some vowel sound (in English conventionally 'ee'). The alphabetic breakthrough in that respect resides not, as is sometimes thought, in the invention of vowels, but the invention of consonants, signifiers that have no existence except as writing – speech degree zero. Any language's phonemes can then be traced via a set of easily-learned (20–30) signifiers, with low residual ambiguity, and having such a sign system enables literacy to be more easily learned by individuals and disseminated culturally (Havelock, 1975). A similar argument can be made for the success of *alphanumeric* textuality from the Latin medieval world on, where arabic numerals are first inscribed using the signifiers in their familiar modern form, and incorporating '0' as a positive sign rather than just as a space or a dot (as in earlier Arabic texts). The arabic numeral code is analogous to the alphabet, not only in its ability to produce a whole population of easily calculable numerical expressions with a small number of signifiers, but through doing so, as the alphabet had with the consonant, by incorporating *absence*, in this case absence of number, into its set of numerical signifiers. Writerly discourse now constitutes speech double zero; it can also, relatively easily, render new ranges and numbers of people numerate as well as literate; it can also proliferate new kinds of alphanumeric code – for example, algebras using letter-forms alongside number-forms, logarithms, the differential calculus – and in the process enable new horizons to mathematical thinking.

REFERENCES

Auerbach, Eric (1953), *Mimesis: The Representation of Reality in Western Literature*, Princeton: Princeton University Press; orig. publ. 1946, Berne: A. Francke.

Berlin, Isaiah (1976), *Vico and Herder: Two Studies in the History of Ideas*, London: Hogarth Press.

Bernal, Martin (1987–91), *Black Athena: The Afroasiatic Roots of Classical Civilisation*, vol. I and II, New Brunswick, NJ: Rutgers University Press.

Bolgar, Robert (1954), *The Classical Heritage and its Beneficiaries: from the Carolingian Age to Today*, Cambridge: Cambridge University Press.

Chandler, Alfred (1977), *The Visible Hand*, Cambridge, MA: Harvard University Press.

Curtius, Ernst (1953), *European Literature and the Latin Middle Ages*, London: Routledge & Kegan Paul; orig. German publ. Franke, 1948.

Czarniawska, Barbara (2004), 'On time, space, and action nets', *Organization*, **11** (6), 773–91.

Havelock, Erik (1975), *Origins of Western Literacy*, Toronto: Ontario Institute for Studies in Education.

Havelock, Erik (1982), 'The preliteracy of the Greeks', in E. Havelock, *The Literate Revolution in Greece and its Cultural Consequences*, Princeton: Princeton University Press, pp. 185–207.

Hoskin, Keith (1993a), 'Education and the genesis of disciplinarity: the unexpected reversal', in Elaine Messer-Davidow, David Shumway and David Sylvan (eds), *Knowledges: Historical and Critical Studies in Disciplinarity*, Charlottesville: University Press of Virginia, pp. 271–304.

Hoskin, Keith (1993b), 'Technologies of learning and alphabetic culture', in Bill Green (ed.), *The Insistence of the Letter: Literacy Studies and Curriculum Theorizing*, London: The Falmer Press, pp. 27–45.

Hoskin, Keith and Richard Macve (1986), 'Accounting and the examination: a genealogy of disciplinary power,' *Accounting, Organizations and Society*, **11** (2), 105–36.

Hoskin, Keith and Richard Macve (1988), 'The genesis of accountability: the West Point connections,' *Accounting, Organizations and Society*, **13** (1), 37–73.

Jaeger, Werner (1947), *Paideia: the Ideals of Greek Culture*, Oxford: Blackwell, 2nd edition: 1st English Edition, 1939, orig. German publ., 1933.

Locke, Robert (1984), *The End of the Practical Man: Entrepreneurship and Higher Education in Germany, France and Britain, 1880–1940*, Greenwich, CT: Jai Press.

Marrou, Henri-Irenée (1956), *A History of Education in Antiquity*, London: Sheed & Ward, orig. publ. Paris, 1948.

Ong, Walter (1982), *Orality and Literacy*, London: Routledge.

11. A journey beyond institutional knowledge: Dante's reading of the *Odyssey*

Silvia Gherardi

When we reflect on the role of humanities in the education and formation of future elites we should recall the changed status of knowledge in contemporary society. This has been summed up in the considerations that Jean-François Lyotard put forward, in 1979, in *The Postmodern Condition*, a report on knowledge in the more developed societies prepared for the University Council of the Quebec government. The thesis of Lyotard's book is that knowledge changes when societies enter the postindustrial era and cultures the postmodern age.

According to Lyotard, the ancient principle that the acquisition of knowledge is inseparable from the formation of the spirit and the personality is lapsing into disuse in postindustrial society and postmodern cultures. This is because knowledge is considered like any other good: it is produced to be sold and consumed in order to be valorized in a new type of production. The impact of technological changes on knowledge will principally affect research and the transmission of knowledge. Knowledge has become the driving force of production; it has altered the composition of the active populations of the more developed countries; and it is the main constraint on the growth of the developing countries. Knowledge is already one of the main commodities at stake in the competition sustained by the legitimating power of technical and scientific knowledge. But scientific knowledge, Lyotard argues, does not comprise the entirety of knowledge.

Knowledge does not consist solely of a set of denotative statements. It also comprises the ideas of knowing how to do, live and listen. It therefore concerns a competence which goes beyond the determination and application of the sole criterion of truth to include those of efficiency (technical qualification), justice and/or happiness (ethical wisdom), sonorous or chromatic beauty (auditory, visual sensitivity), and so on. Understood thus, knowledge coincides with an extensive 'formation' of competencies. It is the unitary form embodied in a subject made up of different kinds of capabilities (Lyotard, 1979).

Myths and stories are the pre-eminent form of this knowledge, and narrative obeys rules which fix its pragmatics. For example, Lyotard argues, folk stories recount positive or negative formations – or in other words, the successes or failures of heroic endeavours – and these successes or failures legitimate particular social institutions (this is the social function of myths), or they represent positive or negative models of integration in consolidated institutions.

The valorization of narrative knowledge is also to be found in the work of the psychologist Jerome Bruner (1986), who in *Actual Minds, Possible Worlds*, describes two diverse and complementary cognitive modes: paradigmatic understanding and narrative understanding. What Bruner calls the paradigmatic mode of cognition is based on the narrative mode, but differs from it in that it seeks to specify the flow of experience, to distinguish, individualize, compare, calculate and make comparative judgements. Whilst the paradigmatic mode allows only one representation of reality at a time because its validation criterion is truth (true/false), the narrative mode yields a plurality of simultaneous reconstructions/representations of the world because its validation criterion is plausibility. It is through narrative, in fact, that a situation acquires meaning for the self and for others, because it is story-telling that constructs the categories that give names and meanings to the events narrated. The extraordinary power of narrative knowledge resides in the connections that people establish in their narratives between the exceptional and the ordinary as they attempt to explain, justify and interpret everyday facts.

In denouncing the way in which instrumental, paradigmatic and scientific knowledge has become 'knowledge *tout court*', both Lyotard and Bruner emphasize the marginalization of narrative knowledge and urge the assumption of a broader view of what knowledge is and how it is intrinsically bound up with formation of the mind and the personality.

In the field of managerial education, when we ask the question 'why do people and their organizations seek out knowledge?' the most frequent answers emphasize the instrumental use of knowledge. Managers need that knowledge that enables them to solve problems, to gain competitive advantages, to exploit innovation commercially, and to contribute to the well-being of future generations. The essential premise of managerial education has been, and largely still is, the instrumentality of knowledge to the solving of problems, or to use Lyotard's (1979) term, its performativity.

Several authors (Lyotard, 1979; Bruner, 1986; MacIntyre, 1990) have contraposed the dispassionate and paradigmatic form of knowledge with another: that of narrative knowledge. We only know the world through the

accounts that we and others give of it; and, according to ethnomethodologists, when we recount the world we create social bonds and the social
world itself. But besides the rationality and purposiveness of knowledge-
gathering, there is another aspect that is undervalued: that of a search for
knowledge driven by a love of knowledge for its own sake.

Against this background, when we consider the formation of the personality in the broad sense, the type of non-instrumental knowledge that
characterizes humanistic education assumes a particular sense. I shall
address this topic from a particular point of view, without claiming to treat
humanistic knowledge as a unitary corpus, and without claiming that all
humanistic knowledge is narrative knowledge. I shall consider humanistic
education as an antidote to analytical, paradigmatic and instrumental
knowledge in that it enhances narrative knowledge and mythical thinking
as a form of moral education and the ethical and aesthetic transmission of
knowledge. This will be the argument of the chapter, whose context of reference is management training and which assumes a myth widely current
in Italian culture as a paradigmatic example.

KNOWLEDGE CONVEYED THROUGH MYTHS

The popular use of the term 'myth' is pejorative: myths are erroneous
beliefs or fables. For anthropologists the chief characteristics of myth are
as follows (Cohen, 1969, p. 337):

> a myth is a narrative of events; the narrative has a sacred quality; the sacred
> communication is made in symbolic form; at least some of the events and
> objects that occur in the myth neither occur nor exist in the world other than
> that of myth itself; and the narrative refers in dramatic form to origins or
> transformation.

But what is a myth and how to define it is the object of several theories
of myth. Following Cohen (1969, p. 338), we can assume the existence of at
least seven types of theory: myth as a form of explanation; myth as a particular type of thought: mythopoetic; myth as an expression of the unconscious; myth as a means to create and maintain social solidarity; myth as a
means to legitimate social institutions and practices; myth as a symbolic
statement about the social structure; and finally the structuralist theory. As
an example that reduces the variety of theories to three large families of
explanation, Cohen proposes the Oedipus myth, which may be interpreted
in terms of sets of universal themes: autochthony, incest and descent – as
analysed by Lévi-Strauss – parricide, incest and fantasy – as in Freud – and

as succession to positions of power and authority in a sociological reading. The three interpretations are interlocked and their gist is that, by establishing a narrative, myth 'locks a set of circumstances in an original set of events. And the effect, and perhaps the unconscious motive for this, is to provide a point of reference in the past beyond which one need not to go' (Cohen, 1969, p. 350).

In organization studies, analyses of organizing as a narrative activity (Czarniawska, 1997), of the aesthetic knowledge of organizational life (Strati, 1999), of the emotional dimension of story telling (Gabriel et al., 2000; Gabriel, 2004) have made it possible to look at knowledge in organizations and in organizing practices in a broader sense, accepting Lyotard's (1979) warning that scientific knowledge has always existed in tension and competition with subjective and narrative knowledge. And, within organization studies, the organizational symbolism approach (Alvesson and Berg, 1992; Strati, 1998) has treated myth as a form of knowledge which not so much conveys factual knowledge as transmits a *forma mentis*: a perceptive grid used to interpret experience and which conditions the vision of the reality internal and external to both people and work communities.

Myth transmits a code which allows knowledge to be produced from the observation and interpretation of reality, from dismissal of the reason, from poetry based on the senses and the imagination. Mythical thinking contrasts Cartesian rationality and brings to light the aesthetic side of organizational life, for it relates to visual thinking and to poetic rather than rational forms of knowing (Strati, 1998, p. 1389). Mythical thinking, in contraposition to the notion of logos, opens the way to aesthetic understanding in organizational life. Strati (1999, p. 153) illustrates this thesis recalling the concept of myth in Vico ([1725] 1968, xix). For Vico, mythical thought is fantasy, metaphor and image, and those who seek to understand how individuals actually construct their social world should examine their mythical thought, since human behaviour does not obey the abstract principle of Cartesian logic; nor do feelings obey it, nor even thought. There are several reasons for paying attention to mythical thought:

> because no exact reasoning exists, only the metaphors, the images and the gestures with which individuals express themselves and communicate; because sacred and secret hieroglyphics constitute a large part of the language used by people to think, as well as to feel, and enable them to construct the civil world; because non-reasoned connections, writes Vico, based on 'robust sense and vigorous imagination', yield wisdom, and this form of knowledge is not rational but poetic (Strati, 1999, p. 153).

According to Strati (1999, p. 2), aesthetics in organizational life 'concerns a form of human knowledge, and specifically the knowledge yielded by the perceptive faculties of hearing, sight, touch, smell and taste, and by the capacity for aesthetic judgement'. In aesthetic knowledge, 'feeling', understanding and knowing are intermeshed, and they merge into their being-in-use within the organization (Strati, 1999, p. 92).

Myth, the knowledge embodied in stories and traditions, and mythical thinking, connects us to the humanity of the past and the future, thereby situating practical knowledge within the stock of knowledge that is our collective heritage. In this way we may have a broader view of what constitutes 'knowledge' which helps us to explore a less intentional, less instrumental, more reflexive aspect of knowledge: knowing in face of mystery.

I have already argued in discussion of learning in organizations and practical knowledge that we can explore not only knowing as problem-driven but knowing as mystery-driven as well (Gherardi, 1999). While knowing as problem solving – that is another way of labelling instrumental knowledge – represents the main form of understanding the relationship between people and their reason for searching knowledge while working, managing, and organizing, the concept of mystery encourages us to see our connections to humanity.

Under the first view, knowing is principally 'problem-driven': the need to solve a problem (an external stimulus) occasions learning. This can be flanked by another view: knowing as mystery-driven.

In Turner's (1991, p. 7) words:

> The distinction between problem and mystery was originally made by Gabriel Marcel, and transferred into organisational settings by Goodall (1991). To experience a problem, Marcel suggested, is to divide the narratives of 'us' from the narratives of 'them', and to see in this division a natural superiority of the observer, us, over the objects of observation, them. By contrast, mystery encourages us to see ourselves as integrally connected to others, as co-constructors of developing narratives of life which become entangled with our sense of being. To look at learning as a way of solving problems assumes the kind of dichotomy that Marcel refers to, assumes that good learning is that which produces a solution to a specified problem. Learning as a way of moving towards an understanding of mystery makes us ask questions about both our own lives as members or managers of organisations, and about the contribution which our organisations are making to the development of shared activities, in a world in which we realise that we are increasingly interdependent with each other, and dependent, too, upon the way in which we negotiate our relationships with the material world and its ecosystems.

Knowing in the face of mystery also conveys the idea that acquiring knowledge is not only an activity but is also passivity. Knowing in a passive mode – according to Polanyi (1958, pp. 127–8) – is like teaching a person to surrender himself/herself to works of art: 'this is neither to observe nor to handle them, but to live in them. Thus the satisfaction of gaining intellectual control over the external world is linked to a satisfaction of gaining control over ourselves' (Polanyi, 1958, p. 196). As in the arts, which are the best example of human non-instrumental activity, we commit ourselves to knowledge for its own sake. We engage in art and in knowing for the love of creation; both forms of activity may be seen as an endeavour without a specific purpose. The Greek term for this 'doing' as an end in itself is *poiesis*: an endeavour without a specific purpose. It does not claim to be useful; nor does it claim to contribute to some undertaking or to resolve some problem. We engage in art for the love of creation; we engage in a new experience for the love of adventure; we breach the boundaries between the known and the unknown in order to satisfy a desire for transgression. Poetry gives embodiments to forms of feelings and intangible objects of desire. Poetics – Brown (1977, p. 7) argues – provides a privileged vocabulary for the aesthetics consideration of forms.

I shall develop a line of argument that connects the role of humanities to managerial education on the assumption that it brings to the fore forms of knowing other than rational, instrumental, paradigmatic, problem-driven. For the sake of argument, I identify the humanities with mythical thought and maintain that they bring in light the aesthetic side of understanding organizational life and the positioning of managers within it. When knowing is not problem-driven, but mystery-driven, it relates to imagination, mythical thought, and to poetic rather than analytic forms of knowing.

Mythical thinking is opposed to that of science and philosophy because it is unconstrained by the requirement of comprehending real objects, and it is stimulated by the mind to invent their properties (Cassirer, 1955–7, pp. 94–6).

In what follows I shall provide an example of how mythic knowledge may operate by referring to the literary figure of the 'journey into the unknown', and to one of the greatest of all travellers: Ulisse.[1]

ULISSE AND THE FORBIDDEN KNOWLEDGE

I shall offer the myth of Ulisse,[2] who takes his crew on a 'journey into the unknown', and I shall do so drawing parallels with commonly occurring organizational situations in order to elicit in the reader the shared experience that myth is able to create between writer and reader.

Following Eco (1990, pp. 54–5) and Czarniawska (2004, vii) I propose a semiotic reading of the text. While a semantic interpretation is one that looks for the meaning of the text and answers to the question: what does this text say?, the semiotic interpretation wants to know how it is possible for the text to say what it does.

Homer's *Odyssey* represents one of the earliest forms of knowledge shared through myth and narrative. It has come to stand as a timeless reflection on humanity's journey into the unknown. Ulysses is the hero who 'far and wide roamed and saw the towns of many people and of many people he knew the mind (*Odyssey* 9.229). The Grecian hero 'who far and wide roamed' is the hero who suffered on his return voyage; he is an unwilling traveller, a traveller despite himself. The sea is everywhere, but it is an object of hatred that propels the sailors into peril and death. In modern times the Grecian hero has come to symbolize travel as transformation and transition: as in the poem *Ithaca* by Constantinos Kavafis (1992), where Ulysses expresses adventure and desire of discovery. But, as Leed (1992) and Hartog (1996) argue, in the classical world travel was pain and punishment, expiation of guilt, and desire to return. The *Odyssey* narrates a voyage decreed by the gods and it is a narrative of male power: the term carries the meaning of pain, and the verbs *to fare* and *to fear* have the same etymological root. It was only in the following centuries, and especially during the Renaissance, that the term 'voyage' assumed the connotations of discovery, exploration and personal transformation. Van Gennep (1909) stresses that the voyage is a terrain of global metaphors expressing every kind of transition and transformation.

Dante's description of Ulisse's voyage was the precursor to the change of meaning in the voyage. In fact, Dante furnishes a modern narrative of Ulisse as a hero who thirsts for knowledge and who is punished for being a pagan, but also as a modern who is excessively curious and seeks to know too much. As the poet Giorgio Séféris (1987, p. 264) wrote, the shipwreck of bodies and minds narrated by Dante is like a deep and indelible scar left by the disappearance of the ancient world.

The myth of Ulisse as reinterpreted by Dante symbolizes humanity in search of knowledge. For Dante the thirst for knowledge is what makes humanity human. It is a desiring process, a journey whose meaning lies in the travelling itself and not just in reaching the destination. As a matter of interest, in Dante's account Ulisse and his crew perished as they passed through the Pillars of Hercules. Contrary to the Greek and Latin traditions, in which Ulisse's adventures concluded in Ithaca and where we are told nothing about his death, accounts appeared during the Middle Ages of a second voyage by Ulisse from Ithaca. Dante therefore transposed the story of Ulisse. Evident from the relevant canto in *Inferno* is his admiration for the Greek hero and the implicit parallelism between the 'knowledge journey' undertaken by Dante through the nether regions of life and Ulisse's 'knowledge journey'. While Dante's journey is guided by Virgil, Ulisse's voyage is a 'pagan' journey in which the limits of knowledge are natural limits, and in which the Pillars of Hercules perform the same signifying function as the annotation 'hic sunt leones' on medieval maps.

Dante located Ulisse in the *Inferno*[3] among the fraudulent counsellors because he was guilty of various deceptions: he 'unmasked' Achilles (who had disguised himself as a woman and gone into hiding), forcing him to take part in the war in which he lost his life; he stole the statue of Minerva in Troy which protected the Trojans; he devised the deception of the Trojan Horse and won the war by deceit. I have chosen Dante's interpretation of Ulysses not as a symbol of deceiving intelligence but as a figure of 'the journey into the unknown' and because I consider it to be a myth deeply engrained in Italian culture. Most of the Italians of my generation know the few lines that follow by heart; they are so well known as to be used as the logo of the faculty of humanities in my University and I saw the first lines of the Canto used as advertising for inviting people to use public libraries in order to discover how the story will follow. Therefore I imagined it plausible that the poem could come to a manager's mind and act as an ethical and emotional spur. In Dante's interpretation Ulisse is the symbol of the desire to know and of the hero who challenges God's will. The thirst for knowing is the force behind every vicissitude that afflicts Ulisse and his crew. And the thirst for knowing is what attracts humanity to the unknown, to discovery, to exploration, and to creativity.

Dante recounts that Ulisse and his companions were old and slow when they came to the narrow passage where Hercules had set up landmarks to signal that no man should venture beyond. On the right hand they left Seville, and on the other they already had left Ceuta. That was the moment when Ulisse said:

'O brothers', who through a hundred thousand dangers have reached the west, to this so brief vigil of our senses that remains to us, choose not to deny experience, following the sun, of the world that has no people.

Consider your origin: you were not made to live as brutes, but to pursue virtue and knowledge.' (Dante Alighieri, *Inferno*, canto XXVI, pp. 112–20)

In the following sections I shall consider the rhetorical devices that Dante put in Ulisse's mouth to persuade his companions to do what he wanted: push forward into the unknown, transgress the limits of legitimate knowledge that the Pillars of Hercules represented for the humanity of his time. My intention in doing so is to elicit the reader's mythic knowledge in order to invite reflection on the role of desire in knowing.

'O BROTHERS WHO THROUGH A HUNDRED THOUSAND DANGERS HAVE REACHED THE WEST'

Ulisse wished to arouse a desire for knowledge and a passion in the breasts of his companions. To do so he appealed to their identity and to the pride that accompanies a collective identity. He accorded them the status of 'experts': they were men who had persisted onwards through a thousand perils, and their survival testified to their skill as mariners and to their worth as companions. Ulisse's exhortation emphasizes that their achievement was not a matter of luck but the result of mastery over specific expertise. The sailors had 'made their own way'; they had subjected events to their will, giving their voyage sense and a direction. They were men who had voluntarily undertaken a voyage to the West. Ulisse was therefore appealing to their expert knowledge, to their identity as 'masters' proven by survival of a thousand perils. His description of these men as brothers was therefore legitimated by the skill demonstrated in their mastery of difficult situations and in their ability to give deliberate direction to what they did and what they knew. They resembled Ulisse because they were joined to him by comradeship and because he shared a bond of brotherhood with them. They were like Ulisse and he was like them; together they reciprocally mirrored their attributes.

Mirroring in the other is a moment of fulfilment, a lull in the quest. Pleasure resides in moments of reciprocal mirroring as moments of fulfilment of desire. The collective celebration of skills and achievements within a community of practitioners not only contributes to the creation of a memory of community (Orr, 1993) but constitutes a ritual for the fulfilment of a desire for reciprocal mirroring.

To classify in organizational terms what Ulisse accomplished by enacting a discursive practice known as 'exhortation', I call it the 'transmission of passion in a community of practitioners'. The undertaking of long voyages westwards across the Mediterranean was certainly not a widespread social practice in Ulisse's time. It represents more the figure of an 'adventure' than that of a 'practice', but it enables us to see how the *topos* of a passion for adventure yields insight into the transmission of passion in daily organizing. In fact, work groups, occupational or professional communities which for more or less long periods of time, and with a more or less stable structure of social and organizational relations, give rise to shared practices, share a practical knowledge that is not solely instrumental, and they display not only mastery of practices but also a passion, a feeling that is emotion and aesthetic understanding. And aesthetic knowledge is another form of passionate knowledge. Passion about what one does, and about doing it well, is a sentiment that pertains to a community of practitioners and anchors its identity. However, if this sentiment is not kept alive, celebrated, and relived in memory and stories, if it is not transmitted to novices, it will fade into routine, into passionless activity. Transmitting passion for a profession, occupation or a skill, for the mastery of practical situations, is an organizational practice for managing expert, tacit and collective knowledge. It has to do with knowledge management.

In organizational practices, aesthetic judgements and the expression of emotions are subject to social negotiation, definition and re-definition which shape the community of practitioners' identity and define its boundaries. The knowledge of the expert consists of mastery over canonical and non-canonical practices, over a body of knowledge acquired through social and cognitive learning processes. But it is also made up of passion, shared experience, collective identity – and the pride that accompanies it – pleasure and fulfilment and their opposites, pain and frustration (Himanen, 2001). Inherent in the practice of mentoring – as a relation between two people with learning and development as its purpose – 'is the notion of desire: the desire to learn, to support, to challenge, to achieve, to understand, to influence, to manipulate, to dominate, and the desire of physical attraction' (Megginson and Garvey, 2001, p. 7). Learning, development, mastery are logical, emotional and social achievements situated in a personal and collective knowing trajectory at the conscious level and at the deeper psycho-analytical one (Antonacopoulou and Gabriel, 2001).

When knowledge is reduced to mere instrumentality, what is lost is knowledge as a desire that takes us far from the realm of necessity, structuring and cognition as expressions of mental activity, and brings us closer to pleasure, play and aesthetic knowledge. When studying the circulation and transmission of expert knowledge, one should investigate the transmission of passion, within the ludic spaces of work and the expression of passions in a professional identity formation.

Ulisse and his crew have at least two features in common with a contemporary project group working together: a myth which operates through the *topos* of the knowledge journey; and a shared practice which operates through the sharing of a repertoire of knowledge about the world and the place of that community in the world.

There are consequently numerous organizational situations in which, 'amid a thousand perils unto the West', work groups harbour and reproduce a practical 'knowing-how': a set of relations with instruments that enable and mediate work practices; a shared understanding of the meaning of what they do. The production of knowledge itself 'can be seen as desiring processes by which actors seduce (and select) new participants and meanings' (Bruni, 2001, p. 3).

TO THIS SO BRIEF VIGIL OF OUR SENSES THAT REMAINS TO US, CHOOSE NOT TO DENY EXPERIENCE . . .

As Ulisse exhorts his comrades, he reminds them of the finitude of life and of the time that separates them from the end of sensory experience.

What is the purpose of this insistence that the human condition is dominated by the certitude of its end? The sense of time – of the *hic et nunc* – emerges in relation to the span of an entire lifetime. Together with awareness of the dramatic force of the moment-now arises doubt over the volitional nature of human experience. As finite beings, do Ulisse's mariners follow a script that has been written for them by fate or previous experience, or do they have the power to decide their futures? Ulisse's reference to 'this so brief vigil' suggests that whatever answer is given to the question, the moment-now is decisive, and that in the perception of decisive moments, time becomes absolute because past and future implode into the present. The time of desire is not the future, as alleged by the analytic thought that projects desire onto the desired object and its absence. Rather, it is the perception of an absolute time that materializes the urgency and absoluteness of desire in the moment-now.

Consequently, whether Ulisse's mariners have come to live that moment through the inertia of history or as a consequence of their endeavour to find a route westwards, or whether they are by nature volitional beings able to control their destinies, they are faced with the drama of choice in the moment-now. In organizational terms, Ulisse directs a well-established social practice which holds that 'great decisions' become 'great' by virtue of a social ritual that dramatizes the present, builds tension towards the highest pitch of uncertainty, and foreshadows the moment of relief that comes with the resolution of doubt and the suspension of will.

But what is it that suspends the mariners' will and absolutizes their desire? The forbidden experience of passing beyond the Pillars of Hercules. Nevertheless Ulisse is not exhorting the mariners to action. Rather, he is emphasizing the experiential meaning that such action would hold for them. Experience is dense with significance, and it is this that differentiates it from events. An event becomes an experience when it is imbued with a particular meaning that locates it temporally and meaningfully in the flux of events.

Ulisse's exhortation kindles the mariners' desire for knowledge because it is expressed in negative form and absolutizes the present. Ulisse does not urge his men to engage in a hazardous experience, to throw themselves headlong into something that may prove fatal – as it subsequently did, in fact. He instead exhorts them not to deny themselves the chance of engaging in experience. He invites them to allows themselves to desire, to dare, to be protagonists.

It is common sense that experience enriches; that it contains lessons for those able and willing to learn. Much has been written on learning from experience, and also on how experiences can be artificially multiplied by augmenting the ability to appropriate knowledge. Thus, knowledge learned through experience is attributed a distinctiveness which abstract and decontextualized knowledge does not possess. Experience is made up of 'experiencing': that is, knowing through the senses, knowing through suffering, knowing through the creative act of appropriating a contextually produced meaning. The creative nature of learning is enhanced by knowledge through experience.

However, once the positive character of experience has been affirmed, what meaning attaches to the double negation of not denying oneself? There are experiences that lie beyond a limit; ones that we may decide to ignore or to forgo.

Ulisse's mariners were volitive beings able to choose whether or not to respect the limit, to deny themselves the experience of eating the forbidden fruit of knowledge. An invitation not to deny oneself experience is an exhortation to abandon oneself to the desire of knowing what lies beyond a limit imposed from within or without. Desire is transgressive. It subverts a social order (external and/or internalized). Creating new knowledge, experiencing unknown situations, is to go beyond a certain threshold and venture into the unknown and the forbidden.

Exploring the unknown therefore entails passage beyond the threshold that separates the known from the unfamiliar. At the same time, a desire to explore the unknown acts upon the structure of temporality: the force of the desire works through negation of the present. The feeling of transgression is in the message: at this specific moment, that thing is now possible.

The time of desire is an absolute time in which one looks towards the unknown and feels the allure of forbidden experience. This brings us to the theme of the negative as gratuitousness: the desire to know and to transgress the boundaries, not for functional reasons but for expressive, poetic ones.

The literature on knowledge management and knowing has insisted on knowledge as the sphere of learning, and it is obsessed with codifying and structuring knowledge, and with making tacit knowledge explicit. This implicit attention rule leads to undervaluation of the fact that the most fruitful knowledge management processes are those that involve the creation of knowledge through discovery, play and invention. These are the processes that abandon the safe havens of knowledge to explore the obscure region of non-knowledge. A poetic concern with knowledge-creation processes requires attention to be paid to the gratuitousness and purposelessness of the desire to know.

EXPERIENCE, FOLLOWING THE SUN, OF THE WORLD THAT HAS NO PEOPLE

The Pillars of Hercules marked the boundary of the known world for the ancients. Beyond them lay an unpopulated, or at any rate unknown, world forbidden to humans. Passing the Pillars of Hercules was therefore to disobey the gods, because beyond them was the end of the known world. Ulisse was therefore firing his men with the desire to know the unknown, and this desire for knowledge then became a transgressive force. Bataille (1957, p. 72) reminds us that a ban exists in order to be transgressed. In fact the nature of a ban is grounded not in reason but in sensibility. Desire is transgressive because it evades the reason and obeys the urges and passions. But it is not always blind. The desire drawing us to the unknown is a force which does not respect the limits of the known world. It therefore transgresses in the twofold sense of going beyond and of disobeying. It is a force that flouts conventions, which does not believe in common sense, and which appeals to direct experience as a source of knowledge. Venturing into the unknown is therefore a transgressive experience, for the realm of the 'known' is sustained by the institutions that enshrine what is legitimated as knowledge. These institutions and shared beliefs defend what a community deems worthy of being believed and transmitted because it has been subjected to the historic norms of knowledge validation. By contrast, the unknown is potentially dangerous and contaminated by false beliefs and magical thought.

The relation between knowledge and transgression has been largely ignored by the organizational literature, which legitimates the control and therefore the codification of knowledge in restricted and presumably certain settings, much more than it is willing to legitimate breaches of the rules, non-canonical practices, or the underground knowledge that circulates in every community of practitioners and is the source of discovery, invention and new knowledge.

The organizational dilemma between exploitation (of already acquired knowledge) and exploration (of new knowledge) has been analysed (March, 1996) in relation to the economic consequences of their respective strategic orientations. The dilemma has been less studied at the symbolic level. Exploratory behaviour does not recognize boundaries, which it regards as mobile. It arrogates to the explorer the right to recognize (or otherwise) the correctness of what is taken to be commonsensical (or assumed to be scientifically valid). It is therefore knowledge that can only be discovered by disobeying the institutions.

The relation between knowledge creation and boundary crossing has been recognized by studies on innovation (Robertson et al., 1996) and scientific discovery (Bijker et al., 1987). Practice has a logic that is not that of logic – argues Bourdieu (1994, p. 140) – and experts or specialists in practice have highly complex systems of classification which are never constituted as such, and which can only be so constituted with great effort. This is the problem that arises in the construction of expert systems, and with artificial intelligence or knowledge management. The relationship of experts with the given of their activity is not calculation as utilitarianism would have it, but habitus[4], practical reason and a specific form of libido. What makes people compete in the scientific arena is different from what makes them compete in the economic one. There are as many forms of libido as there are social domains. Knowledge management literature asserts the instrumentality of knowledge, an economic *nomos*. Ulisse proposed a libido of *poiesis*, a *nomos* where knowledge is the realization of the humanity within us.

CONSIDER YOUR ORIGIN: YOU WERE NOT MADE TO LIVE AS BRUTES, BUT TO PURSUE VIRTUE AND KNOWLEDGE

With these words Ulisse completes his definition of what distinguishes humans as human, and what makes human life worth living. It is the search for knowledge that differentiates human beings from animals. By exhorting his men to remember their essence and their descent (the word *semence* denotes both the seed as nucleus and original unit and seed as chain of descent), Ulisse rounds out the definition of their identity that he had begun by calling them experts, volitive beings, masters of their destiny. By now appealing to their most profound and existential humanity, he shifts them from the plane of necessity to that of freedom. In so doing, he justifies the search for knowledge for its own sake and implicitly asserts the superiority of the force that attracts humanity to the unknown, compared to the impulse of instrumental reason. The desire for knowledge for its own sake is not a desire directed at an object, but rather a force, a tension, an orientation to the future. This is a form of knowledge (knowing) which is not directed at the object (known object) but is a knowing in relation to an interior experience or a sentiment (Bataille, 1934). As Marcel Proust wrote, 'the voyage of discovery lies not in finding new landscapes, but in having new eyes'.

Ulisse defines the ultimate purpose of human existence as the pursuit of virtue and knowledge. He thus introduces an element which flanks the desire for knowledge as a force that drives human beings beyond the confines of what is known, and which may appear to contradict his exhortation to transgress. But the concept of virtue relates to a dimension of subjective responsibility that gainsays the common-sense belief that there is no human (populated) world beyond the Pillars of Hercules; it also clashes with the prohibition against crossing that threshold imposed by the gods. This is therefore not a matter of reprehensible disobedience. Ulisse's emphasis on an ethical dimension reinforces the central tenets of his argument: that it is the desire for knowledge which makes humanity human, and that the pursuit of knowledge is virtuous because it is an ethical imperative stronger than the dictates of the institutions, whether religious (the gods) or social (the institutionalized belief in an unpopulated world). And here the text inserts Ulisse's comment:

> With this little speech I made my companions
> so keen for the voyage that then I
> could hardly have held them back
> (*Inferno*, canto xxvi, pp. 121–3)

To follow virtue and knowledge is an ethical imperative for Ulysses but it is also an epistemological and methodological principle present in the concept of compassion used by Peter Frost (1999) to invite organizational scholars to build notions of empathy, of concern for the inhabitants of the world they study. Paying attention to compassion opens research to emotion as well as to intellect. To act with compassion requires a degree of courage in inventing new practices that embody empathy and love and a readiness to connect to others. In Frost's words 'compassion counts as a connection to the human spirit and to the human condition. In organizations there is suffering and pain, as there is joy and fulfilment' (p. 131). Concepts like virtue, compassion, empathy are not only orientations or feelings, but also competencies which if they are not used are lost. And we may now wonder whether Ulisse was a compassionate leader – who exhorted his crew to follow their inner nature – or an egoist who was only interested in his own desire to transgress boundaries.

The *Canto* ends with the image of the boat navigating the ocean ('five times the light beneath the moon had been rekindled and as many quenched, since we had entered on the passage of the deep') until a high mountain appeared and from the new land a whirlwind rose and struck the forepart of the ship:

> Three times it whirled her round with all the
> waters, and the fourth time it lifted the stern

aloft and plunged the prow below, as pleased
Another, till the sea closed over us.
(*Inferno*, xxvi, pp. 139–42)

DESIRING AND KNOWING: CONCLUDING REMARKS

Mythic knowledge operates by establishing social bonds among persons, generations and different contexts of use. The myth of Ulysses, reinterpreted by Dante, attributes particular symbolism to the journey as a journey in pursuit of knowledge. Following Cohen's (1969) three main interpretations of a myth (structuralist, psychoanalytic, and sociological) I shall briefly summarize the relationship between knowledge and desire starting from a structuralist reading of the knowledge journey.

The structure of the myth divided into four movements: (i) Ulisse affirms that men must distinguish themselves from beasts; (ii) he founds the essence of humanity on the pursuit of virtue and knowledge; (iii) the Pillars of Hercules represent the limits of knowledge; (iv) going beyond them is humanity's challenge against the gods. Also in this myth, as in the majority of those analysed by Lévi-Strauss, the principal narrative centres on the opposition between nature and culture. The pursuit of knowledge is intrinsic to human nature, but so too is the pursuit of virtue. The latter is the social elaboration of behavioural norms respectful of human society and divine will. What is to be done when conflict arises between the ethical imperative to pursue the ultimate end for which men are born and the limits imposed on that imperative? If Ulisse obeys the desire, his knowledge becomes transgressive.

In this the structure of the Ulisse myth reflects Lévi-Strauss's (1963) scheme: A:B = C:D (the first and second elements – human versus the non-human – found human nature, while the third and the fourth – the limited versus the unlimited – founds society) and answers his question: what is myth for? And his reply is: to mediate oppositions or contradictions.

The main function of myth – as Cohen (1969, p. 346) affirms – is to act as a device for mediating oppositions as experienced by men: 'the myth recounts certain events, but its significance for those who recite and attend to it lies not in the narrative description, but in the structure, in which significant "contradictions" are posed and "mediated" '. Myths are formative because they transmit a *forma mentis*. They educate into the existence of the contradictions present in human experience. In the formation of the mind of the contemporary generation, Ulisse is an anchor with the past and with the ever-present contradiction that the desire for new knowledge conflicts with conventions, and that conventions can and must be challenged even when punishment is certain. The core of this message is that the desire to know is what makes humanity human.

If we wish to interpret Ulisse's myth as the expression of the unconscious, we may refer to the psychoanalytic reading of the instinct to master and instinct to know. Freud discusses the instinct to master and instinct to know in the *Three Essays on the Theory of Sexuality* (1962): the instinct to master aims at knowing the world in order to master it, and the instinct to know stems directly from the instinct to master (which breaks the world in order to know it). This instinct to know and the elaboration of childhood theories seek to resolve the enigma of the origin of life: where do babies come from?

In an interesting discussion of the individual psyche, Sardas (2001, p. 19) presents a mix of the pleasure–knowledge and knowledge–pleasure combinations: the instinct to learn that will induce the pleasure of success, and the instinct to master which, when satisfied, will represent control of the relationship with others.

According to Sardas this pleasure of learning can serve:

- a desire for discovery of another world, hitherto 'forbidden'. This relates to the child's desire to know about parents' sexuality, and to the taboo on knowledge about the other gender's world;
- a desire to master, distinguished in two components: mastery for mastery's sake (understanding for the pleasure of understanding), related to the pleasure of thinking and to sublimation; and mastery for action which, unlike the previous case can give rise to real competence in either the mastery of artificial objects or the mastery of relations with others;
- a compulsive need to understand. Individuals who in their early childhood suffered a deficient relationship with a mother who provided insufficient care, and who will constantly try to understand the source of this deficiency in the world. It is clear that this compulsion to understand is a form of suffering.

A sociological reading of myth highlights the dialectic between the knowledge institutionalized at a particular time in history and protected by social or divine norms (in the text: 'as Another pleased') and the search for new knowledge, that is, innovation. To innovate is to go beyond constituted knowledge, to refuse to comply with conventions but instead challenge them and venture into the unknown. On the other hand, the codification of knowledge and its canonical transmission are functional to the conservation of knowledge and to the foundation of truth. Civil society is based on the sharing of beliefs and values, but creativity constantly subverts the rules of the *status quo*.

We entrust knowledge to myths in order to narrate contradictions, to make sense of experience and to convince ourselves and others of its meaning, not only in cognitive terms but in emotional and motivational ones as well. Rhetoric is a discursive practice intended to motivate, to arouse desire, to persuade, to create objects of desire, and to relate language to action and identity. Work practices are not mediated by linguistic artefacts like meanings, beliefs or schemata; it is discursive practices that create reality in the form of 'objects of desire', 'objects of knowledge'. Those who investigate discursive practices in work and organizing should pay attention to the transformative capacity of language and – as I have argued in this chapter – to the covert but linguistically expressed action of the power of desire. Language does not create meaning alone; it also fascinates, enthrals, seduces, produces pleasure, terror, horror, contempt, emotion and therefore passionate knowledge. Besides the dimensions of logos and ethos, also pathos acquires citizenship in organization studies (Gagliardi, 1996; Frost, 1999).

The desire to know therefore has a logic which is not that of formal logic (Bourdieu, 1994), and to understand it we must break with the intellectualist tradition of the *cogito* and venture into the terrain of desire as intentionality, as a form of libidic investment. Passionate knowledge holds the narrative, emotional, affective and aesthetic dimension of work together.

Discussion of desire in organizational studies shows that desire is significant in various ways to the proper understanding of organizational life. Gabriel et al. (2000, pp. 293–4) emphasize the usefulness of desire in providing an explanation for human motivation which differs from those based on need and incorporates 'a social and psycho-sexual dimension'. Desire differs from need, and also from instinct, by virtue of the meaning, fantasy, imagination and value that render it 'culturally constituted'. The importance of the cultures thrown into relief mainly by sociology is matched by the connection between desire and pleasure emphasized by depth psychologists, and of the discourse on 'things sexual as against things unsexual' carried forward by Michel Foucault and discourse theorists.

Strati (2001, p. 3) argues that 'luckily, no precise definition of desire has been formulated. Nor has it been possible to assess its exact influence on human action, despite the efforts of a large part of the human sciences, including the philosophy of mind' (Schueler, 1995). Hence, the concept of desire is ambiguous and imprecise and is unable to explain the motives for social action. And yet it provides us with a rare opportunity to refer action to the inner complexity of the human personality, beginning with – in my view – its ability to develop aesthetic knowledge and to construct symbolic systems. Considering desire as a force which drives a search for knowledge sheds light on the role of pleasure, fantasy and the imagination in the construction of practical knowledge and of knowledge management.

I have used the story of Ulisse to show how knowing in the face of mystery works. By appropriating the myth, the reader may insert him/herself in a narrative of the desire for knowledge that began many years ago but which can be actualized in many other stories of which s/he is the protagonist.

NOTES

1. I shall keep the Italian spelling of Ulisse to refer to Dante's interpretation of Ulysses myth so that I can differentiate between the two interpretations of the myth.
2. I discussed the myth of Ulisse in a previous article and in relation to the quest for knowledge (Gherardi, 2004). I am grateful to Yiannis Gabriel for the support he gave me in elaborating the theme of knowledge and desire.
3. I am indebted to Attila Bruni for drawing my attention to this detail and for providing me with bibliographical material.
4. Sociologists have usually relied on habits, dispositions, routines, customs and traditions to account for reproduction of practices. In particular Bourdieu's (1990) habitus maintains that actors' sense of the game sustains human activity and it is inscribed in the body, as a system of sense perception and taste. On the contrary Giddens (1984) claims that practical consciousness determines routine actions alone. The social character of habits can be better understood as the mode of engagement of people acting strategically in common situations. For a discussion of the notion of habitus see Héran (1987).

REFERENCES

Alighieri, Dante (1970), *The Divine Comedy*, London: Routledge & Kegan Paul.

Alvesson, Mats and Per O. Berg (1992), *Corporate Culture and Organizational Symbolism*, Berlin: De Gruyter.

Antonacopoulou, Elena and Yiannis Gabriel (2001), 'Emotion, learning and organizational change: towards an integration of psychoanalytic and other perspectives', *Journal of Organizational Change Management*, **14** (5), 435–51.

Bataille, Georges (1934), *L'Expérience Intérieure*, Paris: Gallimard.

Bataille, Georges (1957), *L' Erotisme*, Paris: Edition de Minuit.

Bijker, Weibe, Thomas P. Hughes and Trevor Pinch (eds) (1987), *The Social Construction of Technological Systems*, Cambridge, MA: The MIT Press.

Bourdieu, Pierre (1990), *The Logic of Practice*, Cambridge: Polity Press.

Bourdieu, Pierre (1994), *Raisons Pratiques. Sur la Théorie de l'Action*, Paris: Ed. du Seuil.

Brown, Richard (1977), *A Poetic for Sociology*, Cambridge: Cambridge University Press.

Bruner, Jerome (1986), *Actual Minds, Possible Worlds*, Cambridge, MA: Harvard University Press.

Bruni, Attila (2001), 'The knowledge era: the story of a research project', *Ephemera*, **1** (3).

Cassirer, E. (1955–7), *The Philosophy of Symbolic Forms I-II*, New Haven: Yale University Press.

Cohen, Percy (1969), 'Theories of myth', *Man*, **4** (3), 337–53.
Czarniawska, Barbara (1997), *Narrating the Organization: Dramas of Institutional Identity*, Chicago: The University of Chicago Press.
Czarniawska Barbara (2004), 'Foreword: a semiotic reading of strong plots', in Yiannis Gabriel (ed.), *Myth, Stories and Organizations*, Oxford: Oxford University Press.
Eco, Umberto (1990), *I Limiti dell'Interpretazione*, Milano: Bompiani.
Freud, Sigmund (1962), *Three Essays on the Theory of Sexuality*, London: Hogarth Press.
Frost, Peter (1999), 'Why compassion counts!', *Journal of Management Inquiry*, **8** (2), 127–33.
Gabriel, Yiannis (ed.) (2004), *Myths, Stories and Organizations: Premodern Narratives for Our Times*, Oxford: Oxford University Press.
Gabriel, Yiannis, Stephen Fineman and David Sims (2000), *Organizing & Organizations*, London: Sage (1st edn. 1993).
Gagliardi, Pasquale (1996), 'Exploring the aesthetic side of organizational life', in Stewart R. Clegg, Cynthia Hardy and Walter R. Nord (eds), *Handbook of Organization Studies*, London: Sage, pp. 565–80.
Gennep, Arnold van (1909), *Les Rites de Passage*, Paris: Nourry.
Gherardi, Silvia (1999), 'Learning as problem-driven or learning in the face of mystery?', *Organization Studies*, **20**, 101–24.
Gherardi, Silvia (2004), 'Knowing as desire', in Yiannis Gabriel (ed.), *Myth, Stories and Organizations*, Oxford: Oxford University Press.
Giddens, Anthony (1984), *The Constitution of Society*, Berkeley: University of California Press.
Goodall (Jr), Harold L. (1991), *Living in the Rock' n Roll Mystery: Reading Context, Self and Others as Clues*, Carbondale, Ill.: Southern Illinois University Press.
Hartog, François (1996), *Mémoire d'Ulysse. Récits sur la Frontière en Grèce Ancienne*, Paris: Gallimard.
Héran, François (1987), 'La second nature de l'habitus. Tradition philosophique et sens commun dans le langage sociologique', *Revue Française de Sociologie*, **XXXVIII**, 385–416.
Himanen, Pekka (2001), *The Hacker Ethic and the Spirit of Information Age*, New York: Random House Inc.
Homer, reprinted in (2004), *The Odissey*, London: Penguin Classics.
Kavafis, Constantinos (1992), *Oevres Poétiques*, Paris: Imprimerie Nationale.
Law, John (1999), 'After ANT: complexity, naming and topology', in John Law and John Hassard (eds), *Actor Network Theory and After*, Oxford: Blackwell, pp. 1–14.
Leed, Eric (1992), *The Mind of the Traveller. From Gilgamesh to Global Tourism*, New York: Basic Books.
Lévi-Strauss, C. (1963), *Structural Anthropology*, New York: Basic Books, pp. 202–12.
Lyotard, Jean-François (1979), *The Postmodern Condition*, Manchester, UK: Manchester University Press.
MacIntyre, Alasdair (1990), *After Virtue*, London: Duckworth Press.
March, J. Games G. (1996), 'Exploration and exploitation in organizational learning', in Michael Cohen and Lee Sproull (eds.), *Organizational Learning*, Thousand Oaks, CA: Sage, 101–23.

Megginson, David and Bob Garvey (2001), 'Odysseus, Telemachus and mentor: stumbling into, searching for and signposting the road to desire', paper presented at the 17th EGOS Colloquium, subgroup on 'Knowing as Desiring' Lyon, 5–7 July.

Orr, Julian (1993), 'Sharing knowledge, celebrating identity: war stories and community memory among service technicians', in D.S. Middleton and D. Edwards (eds), *Collective Remembering: Memory in Society*, Beverly Hills, CA: Sage, 169–89.

Pickering, Andrew (1992), *Science as Practice and Culture*, Chicago: University of Chicago Press.

Polanyi, Michel (1958), *Personal Knowledge*, London: Routledge.

Robertson, Maxime, Jackie Swan and Sue Newell (1996), 'The role of network in the diffusion of technological innovation', *Journal of Management Studies*, **33** (3), 335–61.

Sardas, Jean-Claude (2001), 'Desire for knowledge and identity dynamics: the case of multi-skills development', paper presented at the 17th EGOS Colloquium, subgroup on 'Knowing as Desiring' Lyon, 5–7 July.

Schueler, George F. (1995), *Desire. Its Role in Practical Reason and the Explanation of Action*, Cambridge, MA: The MIT Press.

Séféris, Giorgio (1987), *Essais, Hellénisme et Creation*, Paris: Mercure de France.

Strati, Antonio (1998), 'Organizational symbolism as a social construction: a perspective from the sociology of knowledge', *Human Relations*, **51** (11), 1379–402.

Strati, Antonio (1999), *Organization and Aesthetics*, London: Sage.

Strati, Antonio (2001), 'Aesthetics, tacit knowledge and symbolic understanding: Going beyond the pillars of cognitivism in organization studies' paper presented at the 17th EGOS Colloquium, The Odyssey of Organizing, subgroup on 'Knowing as Desiring' Lyon, 5–7 July.

Turner, Barry (1991), 'Rethinking organizations: organizational learning in the nineties', paper presented at the EFMD Research Conference, Isida, Palermo.

Vico, Giambattista ([1725] 1968), *Principi di una Scienza Nuova*, Naples: Mosca. (Eng.trans: *The New Science of Giambattista Vico*, ed. in 1968 by Thomas G. Bergin and Max H. Fisch, Ithaca, NY: Cornell University Press).

12. Strong plots: Popular culture in management practice and theory

Barbara Czarniawska and Carl Rhodes

It is generally assumed, not least by the contributors to this volume, that managers are trained to fulfill their professional roles in educational institutions: business schools, universities. What if their education has another source, or other sources, as well? In this chapter we explore the influence that culture, especially popular culture, exerts on practice and theory of management.

IN TIMES WHEN MANAGERS STILL *HAD* CHARACTERS . . .

'Social Character' and the Humanities

In 1981, Michael Maccoby, social psychologist, one of Eric Fromm's last collaborators, and the author of the 1976 management bestseller *The Gamesman*, published a new book. Its title was *The Leader*, and it shared its main thesis with its predecessor: successful managers understand, and often embody, the positive element of the contemporary 'social character', the attitudes and values dominant during a given era. 'The gamesman' was the successful manager of the 1970s, but the 1980s called for a new type, 'the leader', as described by Maccoby in a synthetic version of six in-depth interviews[1] with renowned managers of the era, two of them from outside the USA.

One of the non-US leaders interviewed by Maccoby was Per Gyllenhammar, at that time the CEO of Volvo, one of the largest Swedish corporations.[2] He and two US managers expressed the view 'that education for leadership should teach the ethical and humanist tradition of religion, philosophy and literature' (Maccoby, 1981, p. 231). Why?

> The study of Bible, comparative religion, ethical philosophy and psychology, and great literature leads one to explore the inner life, particularly the struggle

195

to develop the human heart against ignorance, convention, injustice, disappointment, betrayal, and irrational passion. Such education prepares one to grapple with his fear, envy, pride, and self-deception. It raises questions about the nature of human destructiveness and the legitimate use of force. Without it, a would-be leader tends to confuse his or her own character with human nature, guts with courage, worldly success with integrity, the thrill of winning with happiness (p. 232).

In other words, 'great literature' develops character. Maccoby presaged Richard Sennett's later (1998) preoccupations, and he worried about Sweden:

In Sweden, the failure of education in the humanities ill-equips managers and leaders to understand the malaise of a distorted notion of self-fulfillment. Well-educated in engineering, few of the managers I met at Volvo are familiar with either the Bible or Scandinavian classics such as *Peer Gynt*[3] . . . the progressive spirit has led Sweden in a direction of material progress and political democracy at the expense of the individual's spiritual, aesthetic, and intellectual development. In the march toward a consumer, both community and the inner life are being lost (p. 233).

There is a certain contradiction, or perhaps just a gap, in Maccoby's reasoning: the successful leader *expresses* or embodies the positive element of social character but, obviously, a leader whose character has been developed in contact with humanities is able to contribute to *shaping* or constructing this social character. Are leaders therefore the products or the producers? Effects or causes? This is a question of much interest to us.

Taking Up the Message

In 1989, the *Harvard Business Review* published an article called 'Reading fiction to the bottom line'. Its author, Benjamin DeMott (a professor of humanities at Baruch College, City University of New York) was invited by the Phillip Morris Foundation to deliver a series of lectures on business culture. Not quoting Maccoby, DeMott did his errand, showing how a story by Lionel Trilling from 1945, and another by Donald Barthelme from 1980, captured 'the social character' of their times and, what is more, this presaged metaphors and concepts that emerged in the social sciences only much later.[4] DeMott's conclusion was clear:

What matters is that people who think, regardless of their discipline or occupation, participate in a culture that has powerful, overreaching, all-embracing tides, and that creative thought, particularly as it surfaces in the literary arts, is an exceptionally valuable guide to the direction of those tides. (. . .) The truth is that all of us belong to the whole of the age we inhabit, not alone to the special sector called work, production, investment; none of us *can* live in a world apart (DeMott, 1989, p. 134).

It was in this spirit that one of us (BC: Barbara Czarniawska), together with Pierre Guillet de Monthoux, edited a collection called *Good Novels, Better Management* in 1994. Although the actual title was chosen by the publisher (who hoped, in vain, that the book will become a part of popular culture), it accurately expressed the attitude of the editors and the contributors. The first sentence of the Introduction says: 'The purpose of this book is to show how good novels can educate better managers' (Guillet de Monthoux and Czarniawska-Joerges, 1994, p. 1). The editors argued their point as follows:

> Fiction accomplishes the feat which organization theory often misses: it combines the subjective with the objective, the fate of the individuals with that of institutions, the micro events with the macro systems.
>   Novels also transmit *tacit knowledge*: they describe knowledge without analysing it, thus tapping on more than an explicit message characteristic for paradigmatic teaching. (p. 9)

The editors continued by saying that novels offer vicarious experience, and a sense of history and tradition in management, but they were firm on one point: it was *good* novels that counted. The novels read and interpreted from the managerial perspective by the contributors were classics in their countries: Conrad, Zola, Musil.

'High culture', however, has not been the only form of culture considered by those who have studied work, organizations and management. William H. Whyte dedicated two chapters of *The Organization Man* (1956) to 'the organization man in fiction'. There he traced representations of his eponymous organization man in fictional stories from the cinema, novels and popular magazines. Whyte believed that popular fiction could be read to gain 'an index of changes in popular belief' (p. 231). His point resonates with ours.

More recently the topic of the relationship between management and popular culture has been taken up by several authors,[5] and we take but one example. This is the book edited by John Hassard and Ruth Holliday, called *Organization-Representation* (1998). As the title indicates, it focuses on the matter of representation ('This book covers a variety of insights into the way in which organization is represented in the popular media', p. 1), but with an educational purpose: 'a pedagogical desire to use commonplace media representations in the classroom as an aid to teaching and learning how organizations work' (ibid.). The editors argued for their perspective in a way similar to their predecessors:

> While the stories of such [TV] dramas may be simple morality tales, the repre-
> sentations of organization within them are frequently different from conven-
> tional understanding of the workplace. Such programmes reject the image of the
> rational, disembodied, unemotional workplace, replacing it with representations
> of embodied, personal, emotional and frequently petty settings and interactions.
> (p. 7)

We agree with the statement above and we appreciate the importance of the emphasis the editors and the contributors to *Organization-Representation* put on popular culture. In this chapter, we would like to complement their insights with some observations of our own. Our interest is in the relationship between popular culture, and management theory and practice in terms of how they each work to emplot working life into particular narratives.

A PERSPECTIVE FOR THE TIMES WHEN MANAGERS *ARE* CHARACTERS . . .

There could be no doubt that the humanities can aid character development, and that high culture (great literature, art, philosophy) can express the ideals and describe the practices of its era. To these claims, we would like to add three more.

The first is that popular culture fulfills the same functions of high culture on a larger scale.[6] It does so not only in the sense that it reaches 'the people', but also in the sense that it can be a vehicle that *popularizes* high culture. One only need think of the almost endless re-use of the plot of Shakespeare's *Romeo and Juliet* as a model for the love story. In doing so, popular culture might caricature or flatten its 'high other'; alternatively it might question its elitism. Nevertheless, elite and popular cultures have more similarities than it seems at a first glance – especially in terms of their forms of emplotment. Much as the authors quoted in the first section of our chapter wished differently, culture – high and low – expresses, nay, constitutes the positive *and* the negative elements of the social character of an era. A key difference between the two is that popular culture reaches more people and with greater speed.

Our second claim is that popular culture, apart from portraying its own era, also perpetuates *strong plots*, known from mythologies (Greek and Judeo-Christian in case of western management), classic drama and folk tales. Emplotment, as Hayden White (1998) pointed out, is not only a question of the form; indeed, the form carries a content, or medium is the message. The re-use of strong plots might be a matter of convention, of lack of imagination, of literary conservatism, and so forth, but it still offers a blueprint for the management of meaning, so central to managerial practice.

'Simple morality tales', to quote Hassard and Holliday again, may be not so simple in this sense.

This leads us to our third thesis: that popular culture not only transmits ideals and furnishes descriptions, but also *teaches practices* and provides a means through which *practices might be understood*. Both Sicilian and US *mafiosi* took their cues from movies, first from *The Godfather* and then from *Scarface* (Varese, 2004). Abstract models do not teach you what to say or how to act during your first management meeting, a movie might. In short, the mirroring *and* the projection, the expression *and* the construction, the imitation *and* the creation are never separated. This stance locates us close to the so-called circuit model (Johnson, 1986–87), postulation that production, circulation and consumption of cultural products constitute a loop, not a line. Expression becomes control, as popular culture selects and reinforces certain wishes and anxieties of its audience (Traube, 1992, p. 99); control provokes further expression, both of submission and of resistance. Maccoby supposedly *described* the successful leaders of the 1980s but, by doing so, he also helped to *make* them successful. A manager might read a detective story or watch a western movie for amusement, might learn from them actual – or invented – practices, and might imitate those, not necessarily via explicit reflection. One can only speculate on the influence of John Wayne on a generation of baby-boom male managers.

Mixing up Maccoby, detective stories and westerns raises the question of what we mean by 'popular culture' in this chapter. As an attempt at a delineation (not definition), we might say that we include popular literature (novels that stand on the shelf called 'Fiction', and not 'Literature' in English bookstores), films, TV series, cartoons, journalists' tales, but also management bestsellers, magazines, videos, and so on.[7] Lines between high and low culture are judgmental, political and arbitrary (Street, 1997). As a result they can also be destabilized – both Maccoby and DeMott amply demonstrate this in the case of management. Additionally, contemporary mass culture has a tendency to appropriate 'high' cultural forms (Traube, 1992, p. 76); again, following the example where high culture appropriated many older folk culture forms (of which opera and folk tales are the best examples).

In what follows we illustrate our points with three examples. The first is an ethnographic account of the decline of a particular organization as it was re-told in interviews between one of us (BC) and Bruno – a manager in the organization. Here we explore how organizational practices actually follow strong plots and how detouring from expected forms of emplotted behavior can be rendered unacceptable. Secondly, we turn our attention to two novels – a detective story and a spy story – to see how popular literature mediates between classics and mundane practices. We examine how these novels perpetuate certain strong plots in relation to gendered practice of the financial service industry. Thirdly, we turn to examples of popular culture that appear to be more critical and subversive of strong plots. In reviewing the comic strip *Dilbert* and the television cartoon *The Simpsons* we suggest that popular culture not only reinforces strong plots but can also carry a sophisticated critique. We end the chapter with a reflection on the possible role of research vis-à-vis popular culture.

A DRAMA CALLED DECLINE, OR THE EMPLOTMENT OF MANAGERIAL PRACTICE

Bruno's Story

Our first example draws on the observations of 'Bruno', a first-level manager at 'Analog Pomerania', a division of a multinational electronic company, during 14 months in the late 1980s (Czarniawska-Joerges, 1989).[8] At the time, the electronic equipment market was contracting, and although Analog's profits were still satisfactory, growth was slowing down. The first diagnosis was as follows:

> it has been decided that too much fat has accumulated and it must be cut back. That must be the famous middle-management syndrome. The fat accumulates around the organizational waist and therefore it makes it difficult to bend. This is not unique to Analog. It is normal that middle-aged, prosperous organizations accumulate too much fat. But when you cannot reach your feet anymore, something must be done about it (Bruno 2, in Czarniawska-Joerges, 1989, p. 93).

'Keeping fit' is a strong plot in itself, and has its own (re)solutions. A ban on coffee and cakes at meetings was called for, then another ban on assignments abroad and travel in general. This was followed by a ban on promotion raises, which was topped by a ban on investments and on external recruitment.

It did not help; the plot wouldn't hold. It was pointed out that what used to be Analog's niche in the market had ceased to grow, whereas the growth areas were never addressed by Analog. 'Recession' became an official label. The ensuing decision was to change market orientation, and to strengthen the marketing function for that purpose. As external recruitment had been banned, an internal campaign started, resulting in 300–500 applications (those responsible for the campaign were too perplexed to count properly) for 50–60 marketing jobs. Chaos resulted – not only from the application process, but also from the realization that so many people (Analog Pomerania employed 4500) were displeased with their jobs. As the mobilization of marketing competencies depleted other departments of skills, rumors of a reorganization started.

The rumors proved to be right. A decision at the top was reached to restructure the whole of Analog – 'from functions to processes'. Decline, or recession, as it was euphemistically called, might have been behind the decision, but its contents were, said people at the Analog Pomerania, 'an idea whose time has come'. Many other traditional measures were also taken: letters to employees asking them to economize; an analysis of internal communication flows; voluntary early retirement, and so on. The message from the headquarters to the regional offices was: we count on your initiative, and we are going to take away the middle control level to give you more leeway. Appeals were made for the help and cooperation of first-level managers. The headquarters sent a videotape featuring the CEO of Analog:

> It was not so silly as one could expect. He is in his office, with his family pictures around and the whole thing, and he sits for a while, then he stands up, talks to somebody who remains out of view, then he talks some more. And what he says is, that a general approach for the constructive people – [the Americans] like very much to call themselves constructive – is to use this situation to turn it into something positive of course, and we cannot go on doing what we were doing before. We now have to stop and look critically at everything we have been doing before, maybe we were doing wrong things and maybe we were not doing things we should be doing, and this is positive, because it means, hopefully, changes for the better. That was the flair of it (Bruno 5, p.106).

While the video was a success, a film shown at a managers' meeting was a flop:

> . . . showing the mountain climbers on a particular steep piece of a high mountain [Bruno laughs into the phone]. You can imagine the rest.
>
> BC: No, you tell me.
>
> Bruno: I do not remember the details. I looked at the view – it was a beautiful film, really. And there was this large, safe male voice in the background, saying: 'Are you taking these challenges? Start another project today!' Then you will have to imagine how difficult it will be on the way to somewhere, and you will have to work very hard . . . And there are three people standing on the top of this mountain in the sunshine: success! That was the film.
>
> BC: But what was the point?
>
> Bruno: I do not really know. The idea is that it is very difficult to get there, and it is up to you to try (Bruno 8, pp. 106–107).

But the most shocking and most ambiguous occurrence happened later at the same meeting. The Head of Operations in Pomerania addressed the group:

> He talked a lot, but it became very clear that what he actually said was: 'We [top management] see all these problems, and we can see a lot of details of the

problems, but we have no solutions at all. And would you be kind enough to help us?' He was sort of standing there, poor chap, saying: 'Have you got any bright ideas?' Silence. Of course there was silence. They are not used to it.

There were some whispers around; my boss for example, he said: 'He [Head of Operations] is the one who is supposed to tell us! If you are supposed to change your behavior, you have to know which way! And to what effect! If we do not know how to change it, how can we do it?' (Bruno 8, pp. 107, 110.).

Bruno for one took the appeal seriously. At the first opportunity, he reconsidered the role of his group in the organization and came up with a concrete, if revolutionary, suggestion as to how this should be changed to the benefit of the company and the individuals involved.

So when I got back to the office, just before five, I went to talk to my boss who still happened to be there, in order to speak about something else, and then presented this idea. And he was utterly defensive. One has to bear in mind that he is the architect of what we have today in this (. . .) section, he made it from scratch – and that obviously is a problem when it comes to change. He is otherwise an open-minded person and very nice. So I argued and he argued back: to ignore all that, not to put on such a big hat, it does not work anyway, you won't get the resources, you know, the old stuff: 'You can't change things!' (Bruno 9, p. 107).

In time, Bruno accepted that 'the hat was too big' (in terms of emplotment, he was proposing things out of character) and that his idea was actually being realized by people introducing 'business processes'. Indeed, more and more changes were initiated from the top. After some more months Bruno came to the following conclusion:

So, using the contributions from the bottom – not so much bottom, as this appeal was addressed to managers, the lowest level but still managers – this appeal, which was originally formulated by HO was never followed up, neither by him, nor by anybody else. Maybe that was just a slip of the system, which now will be forgotten and repaired by coming to the normal procedure, which is to make decisions at the top and then inform people about them (Bruno 14, p. 108).

A month or two later, a big event took place, including all the employees of Operations. And, much to Bruno's surprise, Head of Operations repeated his message:

And this time it was for all the people, for the grass roots, not only for managers. And it was basically very similar. It was not 'Help! we do not know what to do', but more like 'This is all up to you.' (. . .) And people were utterly confused again. (Bruno 18, p. 108).

Later, Bruno came to hold the general opinion that the whole thing was due to peculiarities of Head of Operations. This opinion grew stronger in time:

I am uneasy about him, because I don't understand him. I don't understand how can he be where he is. So far, he has not shown any of the signs, or traditional aspects of what one would expect of a person who is a part of a team running a fairly large company. (Bruno 24, p.118).

What is expected of such a person? Bruno's description of the General Manager of Analog Pomerania might offer some clues:

He is a remarkable man. He has enormous knowledge of what is happening now. (. . .) He talked two hours, solid, asking questions and answering questions, but all that was job-related or short-term-goal related, problem-related. There was nothing about a vision. So that is a worry. (. . .) Because leaders must have this sort of constructions, these visions, if they are leaders. (Bruno 23, p. 118).

Maccoby would have agreed. At the same time, it was tempting to see the decline and reactions to it – those of leaders, followers, and audiences – as a kind of dramatic performance, where a given stage setting determines the genre, and then some variation of a well-known play belonging to the genre is performed by involved actors and critically observed by the audience outside.

Arriving at a Plot

Successful performance combines the live theater tradition – that of audience participation and actors improvising the play as it unfolds – with a ritual where all know the rules. The stage setting is done jointly, and as the play goes on, the leading actors perform their roles, and the rest of the cast take their cues accordingly. The play in this case runs as follows: the stage setting – a decline – demands a performance in which actors called 'the leaders' tighten control, and the actors called 'the followers' oppose it for a while and then join in and follow, and if all is played well the play soon ends on a more positive note, especially if applause from the audience is forthcoming. This particular plot, as Wildavsky (1984) pointed out, follows the story of Moses (up to the point that the leader often does not reach The Promised Land).

In problematic performances, the stage setting can provide immediate complications. A difference of opinion – among actors, or between actors and audience – as to what stage setting is appropriate, may ruin the performance from the start. Sometimes, however, an apodictic sponsor, director, or a leading star can prevail and force others to accept one given plot and genre in favor of another. Usually, however, as in Analog's case, the choice of the setting, and of the plot, is a continuous process, where there are several plots in the offing, and one wins as a result of negotiations, the reactions from the audience, persuasion to abandon deviant plots, and so on.

Why this plot? Why at this time? The 'social character of the era' (of which the Head of Operations was clearly ignorant) is one answer. Another answer might be formulated in Jungian terms, postulating that the attitude toward leadership is an enactment of archetypes, articulated in myths, our collective unconscious (Booker, 2004). Yet another interpretation, the one we favor, is that some plots are strong – or stronger than others – because they have been institutionalized, repeated through centuries, well rehearsed. The orthodoxy of the representation controls the possible meanings (Rhodes, 2001a). One should therefore speak of *conventional* rather than traditional plots, and of *dominant* rather than strong plots: they are strong in a given time and place. There are many mythologies and each of them contains many myths, many Greek dramas – some of which are more remembered in certain times than others – and a great many folk tales. Traditional plots are used because they belong to a common collective memory, from which they can be retrieved in order to be shared (we are evoking here Avishai Margalit's (2003) distinction between common and shared memory). What is more, they are chosen from among many on the grounds of present concerns. Greek mythology has had the periods of neglect and periods of concentrated attention, not least in Greece. The myths of Sisyphus and Oedipus, Yiannis Gabriel (2004) reminds us, were retrieved and made famous by Camus and Freud not so long ago.

Another question that comes to mind is whether the plot was put into this story by its actors or by the researcher. Although the possible answer to this innocent question marks the abysmal divide between structuralists and poststructuralists, we shall avoid drastic choices by pointing out a third possibility. The plot – a meaningful structure – was put there by the actors in their attempt to manage meaning, but it could be recognized (perhaps wrongly) by the researcher who had access to the same common repertoire of plots. This means that one of the important aspects of organizing is emplotment.

This also means that the dramaturgical metaphor could be seen as an analogy. Paul Ricoeur pointed out the analogy between action and text (Ricoeur, 1981; Czarniawska, 2004a): to emplot is to organize, to organize is to emplot – among other things. Stories are not just chronicles; they provide a logic to a narrative so that a multitude of events can be structured, and made sense of. A plot is active in its construction of meaning; it is not just a passive rendering of 'what happened'. This leads us to the question: how are plots retrieved from a common repertoire? Some managers might read the Bible (or Wildavsky on Moses), some might even watch Greek tragedies, or Shakespeare and Ibsen on the stage, but hardly all. Our answer is that it is popular culture that retrieves them, makes them simple, accessible and relevant, and in this way perpetuates them.

FALLEN WOMEN

The Beautiful and the Damned

We now turn to another study (Czarniawska, 2004b), which provides a close-reading of a detective story by the Swedish journalist David Lagercrantz, *Star Fall* (2001). This story revolves around the stock market crash and two murders that followed (or preceded) it. The second victim is a 'General Bank's' IT analyst, Elin Friman. Elin is not only a victim, but also a perpetrator, a tool in the hands of the Russian mafia, and related to it by her relationship with her former chess teacher. The mystery is resolved by Daniel Mill, an amateur detective whose moral sensibility made him end his analyst's career, and turned him into an astute critic of the world of finances (as well as making him rich and therefore independent).

Elin is perceived by her male colleagues primarily as a sex object: 'her smile, at the same time uncertain and cool, which sometimes seems to be an erotic promise', and so on, through various parts of her body. She listens to men and appears to admire them: 'She made him talk, made him elaborate long theories on economy, the company, love, human longing. Her presence intoxicated him (. . .) When he noticed that she looked in the same way at all the male bosses, he began to dislike her willingness to serve, her incessant cleverness' (p. 11, translations BC). As an employee of the General Bank, she tends to exaggerate all the desirable traits: 'He encouraged ambition and responsiveness to General Bank's corporate culture, but Elin went too far. The bank absorbed her totally, so that sometimes she seemed to lack a core. She could be anything: a mountain climber, a poet, an evening press reporter, a university lecturer but also a hippie' (p. 11).

Lacking a stable identity of her own, she assumed that of the man she was (most) enchanted with at any particular moment. In love with sensitive leftist Daniel, she took a position against the world's injustice. When Daniel quit his analyst job, she fixed her adoring gaze on the bank's Managing Director and became a careerist. As it turns out, she was persistently faithful to one man and one ideology. A modern Delilah, she was out for Samson's secrets in the service of Philistines.

Such lack of an enduring individual identity, muses the – neglected by Elin – Financial Deputy, could have been produced by a collision between her natural talents and her poor background, a contrast between nature and nurture, as it were:

What he sees as a weak self can have resulted from her youth and uncertainty. She is 27, her father is an unemployed bus driver who drinks . . . so she probably wanted to escape from it all, find another world, whatever the cost. She has an analytical talent. She immediately grasps the most complex situations and she remembers numbers – especially quotations – in a way that almost frightens him (p. 12).

The readers of Olivier Sacks will of course recognize the extraordinary capacity of the mechanical memory, usually accompanied by a complete inability to function in social life: Elin was not 'normal'.

She lied, she used 'feminine cunning' and blackmail. But she was not evil herself. If anything, she 'loved too much', as Robin Norwood's bestseller from 1989 put it. She had masochistic tendencies, begged to be mistreated, and yet abhorred the sexual exploitation of other women. She loved men but also loved ideologies: she cheated and exploited, but for a higher cause. A veiled Marxist, she condemned capitalism in general and her bank in particular, but saw no problem in manipulating the shareholders. As her US super-boss said: 'She was complex. She wanted to serve and to be appreciated – no doubt. But she was also vengeful and angry. . . . She was like a lion's paw: soft and pretty, but inside there was a claw that wanted to tear all of us to pieces.' (p. 225).

'The construction of Elin' can be seen as highly significant, as it reflects both the received image of today's finance world (inside and outside financial circles) and of people in financial services. In this image, extremely high intelligence (rather than formal education) is both assumed and claimed by traders and analysts. Elin is even more intelligent than most, thus reinforcing the conviction that, for the same job, women need to be twice as good as men. Her sexual intrigues also correspond to the image of a 'work hard, play hard', no-family oriented world; but while men are presented as ensnared in her sexual intrigues, Elin initiates them. Last but not least, lack of moral guidance is a trait supposedly prominent in financial dealings, but while young men seem to be *amoral*, Elin is *immoral*, but she performs all her evil deeds instructed by a man, the true master-mind behind the plot. Feminine after all: a will-less tool in the hands of a purposeful man.

While there is no doubt about the fictitiousness of Elin's character, the message (perhaps unintended) is clear: the world of finance is no place for women. Those who make it there are 'unnatural' – twice everything the men are, especially the vice, and not even aware of it. While the novel contains many thoughtful men, acutely aware of traps and dangers connected to this world, women, it seems, can only be the victims and the perpetrators in it.

The Reprieved

Linda McDowell (1998) has brought to our attention a British variation on the same theme. It is the spy story *Nest of Vipers* by Linda Davies (1995).

The female protagonist, Sarah Jensen, is a successful FX trader who is placed undercover in a merchant bank to investigate corruption. Sarah is a strong version of Elin; the blurb on the cover summarizes it well: 'One of the top foreign exchange traders in the City, she's addicted to risk as a way of blotting out the pain of childhood tragedy, while her glamour provides the perfect camouflage in the ruthless financial jungle.' (Davies, 1995).

Her morals are not those commonly accepted in society, but 'the child-hood tragedy' is her excuse. More intelligent than both Governor of the Bank of England and the Director of Counter-Narcotics Crime at MI6, she avoids direct evil deeds by unloading them on her *alter ego*, another brilliant professional woman, a hit killer. These deviant women are spared the fatal fate favored by Greek playwrights and David Lagercrantz. The hit-woman escapes to Brazil, and Sarah to Katmandu, in a re-run of the 1960s hippy dream. McDowell comments that an escape to a rural idyll was a con-sistent theme in the interviews she conducted with women in the City, and Linda Davies herself actually left a City career for 'the sylvan surroundings of a London suburb' (McDowell, 1998, p. 175). Similarly, Lagercrantz allowed the detective Daniel Mill to escape; differently, he left Elin no such option.

Why should highly stylized stories of exceptional women, presented in popular culture, be of interest for students of, for example, the management of finance? Let us reiterate the reasons we suggested earlier, in this particu-lar context. One reason is that popular culture – novels, films, mass media, and even how-to, and consultancy books – captures the dominant view of the financial sector at any given time. The other reason is to be found in the old dictum 'art imitates life and life imitates art'. While we believe, in a Tardean spirit, that people learn their jobs primarily by contact-imitation (Taussig, 1993), popular culture furbishes them with models and ideals. While the observation of everyday routines teaches everyday routines, popular culture, with its larger-than-life heroes, can provide material for dreams and rule-breaking behavior. As Linda McDowell put it, '[r]epresen-tations of fictional bankers influence the behaviour and attitudes of "real" bankers, and vice versa' (1997, pp. 39–40). Other professions are similar – as the female police detective in Martin Amis' (1997) *Night Train* suggests: 'TV, etcetera, has had a terrible effect on perpetrators. It has given them style. And TV has ruined American juries forever. And American lawyers. But TV has also fucked up us police. No profession has been so massively fictionalized. I had a great bunch of lines ready'(p. 18).

Why can't young people learn their jobs through reading work ethnogra-phies? Because contemporary ethnographies are modernist, as Manganaro (1990) rightly observed: complex plots, experimental structures, paradoxical resolutions. Popular culture, on the other hand, more frequently relies on strong narratives and traditional plots (even when the aim is to subvert those plots).

SUBVERTING STRONG PLOTS

In the previous sections we attempted to show how popular culture is related to organizational discourse and action through the mutual reproduction of strong plots. Now it is time to point out that this is not endemic to all popular culture; it can also offer alternative and critical readings that bring strong plots into question. This is particularly evident in the genres of popular comedy that parody organizations and managers. This mass culture tradition dates back at least as far as Charlie Chaplin's cog in the machine (literally) in *Modern Times*. In folk culture, this dates back even further to practices of the carnival and to the literature of Rabelais (Bakhtin, 1984a, b; Rhodes, 2001b). More recently, popular comedy has also been a site for the critique of dominant approaches to managing and organizing. To illustrate this we turn to two examples of US mass culture that have become global. The first is the comic strip character *Dilbert*, the second the animated television cartoon *The Simpsons*.[9]

Work is the sole setting for *Dilbert*, but both *Dilbert* and *The Simpsons* have organized work as a major theme. The former reports the everyday yet absurd working life of a white-collar employee in an unnamed organization. The Springfield Nuclear Power Plant (SNPP), owned and managed by C. Montgomery Burns, is the major industry and employer in the town of Springfield where *The Simpsons* is set. This company is characterized by an appalling environmental record, dramatically unsafe working conditions, an alienated workforce, and a despotic boss.

Both *Dilbert* and *The Simpsons* draw their comic appeal from a parody of working life, especially of managerial behavior. In *The Simpsons*, the main example is Burns, the arch-capitalist; in *Dilbert* The Boss, who has no name, but an ulimited propensity to adopt managerial fads.

The *Dilbert* Syndrome

The parody of leadership in business in the *Dilbert* books and strips can be summed up by what Dilbert's creator, Scott Adams, calls the 'Dilbert Principle': 'the most ineffective workers are systematically moved to the place where they can do least damage: Management' (Borowski, 1998, p. 1625). The principle builds on the premise that 'people are idiots', a drastic reformulation of the more orthodox *Peter Principle* (Peter and Hull, 1969). Whereas once managers rose to their level of incompetence, in

Dilbert the managers are incompetent to begin with. This theme is played out repeatedly in showing how the hapless worker Dilbert interacts with his un-named boss's tendencies to sadism, stupidity, and the thoughtless employment of management buzzwords.

> Dilbert: What did you mean when you said all employees are empowered? Does that mean I can control my own budget, make decisions without twelve levels of approval. And take calculated risks on my own?
> The Boss: No. It's just a way to blame employees for not doing the things we tell them not to do.
> Dilbert: No wonder you needed a new word. (Adams, 1996b: 4.4)

Adams has used his comic strip to poke fun at a range of fashionable management practices. Filipczak (1994, p. 29) suggests that 'Adams exposes many "cutting edge" workplace issues to the severe light of day, inviting us to laugh at re-engineering, cross-functional teams, business meetings, corporate buzzwords, management fads (. . .) The gap between executive rhetoric and employee reality is a favorite target of Adams' biting humor'. The following is a good example:

> The Boss: Great news! I've reengineered your job to make you more fulfilled! You'll no longer be limited to one little part of the value chain. You'll be involved in all stages of production!
> Dilbert: Oh Lord, you fired all the secretaries!!
> The Boss: Dust my credenza. (Adams, 1996b: 6.1)

For Adams, leadership is not depicted through the epic narratives about heroic leaders and entrepreneurs as it was for Maccoby. For him the leadership is a cover story for a dangerous combination of power and idiocy. Take the following discussion of leadership from *Dogbert's Top Secret Management Handbook*:

> Don't get me wrong. Leadership isn't only about selfish actions. It's also about empty, meaningless expressions. Here's a few you should memorize:
>
> ● Work smarter, not harder
> ● It's a new paradigm
> ● It's an opportunity not a problem (Adams, 1996b: 1.14).

For Adams, 'visionary leadership' is a rhetorical scam. His leaders create mission statements such as: 'We will produce the highest quality products, using empowered team dynamics in a new Total Quality paradigm until we become the industry leader' (Adams, 1996a). Overall, Adams is more than ready to play with the heroically emplotted narratives in which leaders are so often cast. For example, where management guru Stephen Covey (1990) has 'the 7 Habits of Highly Effective People', Adams has 'the 7 Habits of Highly Defective People' (Adams, 1996b: 2.19).

One reading of *Dilbert* is that it is a sign of a growing cynicism and increasing disengagement of workers from their employers; particularly in response to ongoing downsizing of corporations in the 1990s. *Time* magazine even referred to Adams as the 'Bard of downsizing' (Van Biema, 1996, p. 82). Daniel Feldman (2000, p. 1286) has said that *Dilbert* presents a view of business where 'many employees are highly cynical about the effectiveness of management and view large, bureaucratic organizations with disdain and contempt . . . [where] . . . cynicism is increasing as a new paradigm of employer–employee relations'. Thus Adams' workplace satire reflects an attitude amongst workers that managers are inept and have little connection with workers (Borowski, 1998). Dilbert's world is said to be one of 'vapid corporate-speak with no guts and no emotionally honest message' (Johnson and Indvik, 1999, p. 84). For some this is a sign that corporate transformation is only possible when management focuses on re-engaging employees (Miles, 2001). Others see Adams' vision as defeatist and in opposition to the possibility of moral progress in organizations (Borowski, 1998). It has even been argued that *Dilbert* cartoons are a cause rather than an effect of cynicism (Hutchins, 1999).

To our reading, however, such propositions miss one important implication of *Dilbert*: that it both identifies and critiques dominant stories and their heroic emplotment of leadership – such as the one we saw enacted in Analog. *Dilbert* problematizes these forms of emplotment by suggesting that they create role models which managers cannot live up to; again, the Analog story amply corroborates it. Such plots can alienate people as they try to come to terms with the messy realities of their work. Adams' plots reflect the ' "silent rage" of employees in the workplace . . . [where] managers pretend to know all of the answers' (Brown, 1996, p. 51). The issue is not that many people are disenchanted with jobs they perceive as futile, it is that the strong plots of management heroism fail to emplot the actual experience of people working in corporate organizations. It also suggests that when managers try to align their working lives in accordance with such emplotted narratives, the result is a paradoxical discord. Adams might be regarded as an 'anti-management guru' (*The Economist*, 1997: 64), but what he seems to be against is not business per se. He appears to be against particular emplotments of management and leadership narratives and how those narratives are abused in practice.

Adams seems to be following a democratic project. It has been suggested that 'whereas most business writers write for the one in ten people who are interested in management theory, he writes for the nine who hate it' (*The Economist*, 1997: 64). Adams says himself: 'all I really do is take what the employees are already thinking and just express it' (quoted in Filipczak,

1994, p. 33). And further: 'no matter how absurd I try to make my comic strip, I can't stay ahead of what people are experiencing in their own workplace' (quoted in *Fortune*, 1996: 99). His is said to be a 'protest voice . . . leading a revolt against traditional management' (Brown, 1996, p. 49). 'Because he has such an intense respect for the people on the shop floor or in the cubicle, he finds it galling to have to heed the words of bosses who refer to human beings as "resources" ' (ibid., 51). When asked in interview whether he thought he had become the 'voice of the American employee', Adams responded 'Yes, very much so' (Filipczak, 1994, p. 33).

What we see in *Dilbert* is the possibility for humor to be used as a way of bringing attention to the way that management work is idealistically emplotted in management narratives. This suggests that lived experience is not necessarily subordinated to strong plots. Adams offers a different and critical emplotment of more experiential veracity. He does so by claiming to give voice to the professional workers who are silenced by the loud din of management-speak. Adams' commentary is a rarely articulated practitioner-driven perspective that draws attention to the 'idols' of management theory (Kessler, 2001, p. 285). Adams is an iconoclast of the strong plots of mainstream management theory and the icon he targets is the heroism that they imbue in managers.

Samson/Simpson

The Simpsons is another telling example of the parody and overturning of strong plots in popular comedy (see Rhodes, 2001b). It provides an important reflection on contemporary society through the breaking of rules and experimentation with subjects traditionally seen as taboo for animation (Kafner, 1997; Cohen, 1998). As Korte (1997) has suggested: '*The Simpsons* works to encourage critiques, demanding that viewers be active in their consumption. Without hesitation or apology, it ridicules the advertisements, slated news stories, and inane talk shows that appear on their beloved TV set . . . very little is sacred on *The Simpsons*.'

It has been said that *The Simpsons* is the most 'morally exacting critique of American society that has yet appeared on television' (Marc, 1998, p. 193). In enacting this critique, *The Simpsons* starts by recreating a 'realistic' setting of American suburban life as its context. This, however, is a realism that is not intended to reproduce 'reality'. Instead, it reproduces dominant and identifiable social views of reality in order to question them (Hodge, 1996). In our terms, *The Simpsons* sets up strong plots so that it can question them, play with them, or even knock them down. This is particularly the case of the relationship between two of the main characters – Homer Simpson and C. Montgomery Burns. Homer is most often portrayed as a somewhat simple, bumbling, doughnut eating, beer drinking buffoon. Burns, on the other hand, is an old-style industrialist and a Yale graduate. At thirty-six, Homer holds the dubious honor of being the record holder for 'the most years worked at an entry-level position'.

There are many episodes of *The Simpsons* which demonstrate the over-turning and parody of 'normal' working life (see Rhodes, 2001b). Here we review one such episode – 'Simpson and Delilah'.[10] This episode takes the subject of corporate meritocracy and equality in career opportunities and turns it on its head with the help of another strong plot – the story of Samson and Delilah. In the original, Delilah takes away Samson's power by female cunning – by cutting off his hair, in which his strength lay, after a night of love-making. Also in the original story, meritocracy is a sanc-tioned plot of organizational promotion and recruitment stories. It relates to bureaucracy as the dominant mode of modern organizing, where the ability to hold a position is based on credentials (merits) rather than class, within the context of a modernity narrative that sees the bureaucratic organizations as having progressed from the class based systems of the past (Clegg, 1990). The desired bureaucratic plot is where the ability to succeed in working life is related to abilities and achievements rather than familial and class position.

'Simpson and Delilah' subverts both those strong plots. The normally bald Homer discovers a miracle hair growth formula. To his chagrin, he is unable to afford it at $1000. However, he defrauds the nuclear power plant's health insurance scheme and is able to get the formula. Overnight, Homer grows a full head of hair.

Meanwhile Burns is faced with the dilemma of having to promote one of his workers as a result of a clause in his contract with the union (the notion of meritocracy is thus re-cast in terms of adversarial employer–worker rela-tions.) Burns is of the opinion that 'none of these cretins deserves a pro-motion!' When he sees the newly hirsute Homer through his security monitor, however, he asks his assistant Smithers, 'Wait, who's that young go-getter?' Smithers replies: 'Well, it sort of looks like Homer Simpson . . . only more dynamic and resourceful'. Burns immediately decides to promote Homer. An announcement comes over the plant's PA system: 'Attention Homer Simpson. You have been promoted. You are now an executive. Take three minutes to say good-bye to your former friends and report to room 503 for reassignment to a better life.'

Homer hires an assistant, Karl, who further helps him refine his image (for example by getting rid of green polyester suits). Homer's first oppor-tunity to impress Mr Burns with his initiative comes when Burns announces the need to reduce industrial accidents. Homer's unqualified proposal is that accidents can be reduced by adding tartare sauce to the fish sticks served in the cafeteria. While Burns' hired consultants suggest 'a round of layoffs might wake up the idiots' and putting 'caffeine in the water cooler', Burns decides to 'let the fools have their tartare sauce!' When accidents do fall, Burns is so impressed that he even gives Homer the keys to the executive washroom. (This is a further symbolic parody of managerial hierarchy where even the most mundane bodily functions can take on a privileged form for those in power.) The real reason that accidents have fallen, as Smithers shows, is that Homer, no longer on the shop floor, is not causing them: 'Accidents decreased by exactly the number that Simpson himself is known or suspected to have caused last month. And our output level is just as high as during Simpson's last vacation.'

Eventually, Homer's 10-year-old son Bart accidentally breaks the bottle of hair potion while fantasizing about growing a beard. No diabolic women, no cunning, no sex tricks – just a domestic accident. Bart is not even a philistine. Homer returns to being bald. Without hair, no one takes him seriously any more. Burns demotes him back to his former position.

This episode makes one reflect over the old and new plots. What kind of strength did Samson possess that it could be taken away by simply cutting off his hair? Does male power always reside in superficial bodily ornaments? What counts as 'merit' and for whom? For Simpson, as it was for Samson, success is revealed as a matter of 'looks'. In direct opposition to a meritocratic discourse, the spectators discover that one's ability to 'progress' in this organization is about being the 'right personality'. The older spectators might even remember that they knew it, but simply forgot (just like they probably knew the Samson and Delilah story but did not see it as relevant). As Elisabeth G. Traube (1992, p. 73) pointed out, the success manuals and middle-class magazines in the US had already noticed at the turn of the previous century that '[i]n bureaucratic organizations such as large corporations, work is a necessary but not sufficient condition for promotion up the managerial hierarchy (. . .) Image or appearance became a central concern of the new success literature (. . .)' It was then, she says, that the new middle classes became obsessed with 'personality' as a replacement for 'character'.

When Homer's baldness returned, the normal hierarchical relations were restored. An interesting observation here is that Burns is also bald, but he retains his position of power in the power plant. The inference here is perhaps that 'true' power, that which is beyond appearance, is that of capital and tradition, whereas managerial power is fleeting. After all, Burns is more of a robber baron than a professional manager. This is again a direct opposition to the ethos of meritocracy.

The iconoclasm of *The Simpsons* consists in a refusal to take the commonplace emplotted order of work seriously. Its humor lies in a powerful counter-narrative that brings strong plots under critical scrutiny.

Popular Culture as Modern Carnival

Our reading of *The Simpsons* and *Dilbert* is that each derives its comic appeal from the overturning and transgression of particular strong plots. Both offer a carnivalesque parody of organizing, enacted by playing with the rules of what is expected in more conventional or official representations of organizations (Rhodes, 2001b, 2002). The use of such humor is important because in breaking the conventions of what is expected (that is strong plots), comedy can indeed draw attention to such conventions: 'Carnival, in order to be enjoyed, requires that rules and rituals be parodies, and that these rules and rituals already be recognized and respected. One must know to what degree certain behaviors are forbidden, and must feel the majesty of the forbidding norm, to appreciate their transgression' (Eco, 1984, p. 6).

Humor, however, is only one way that strong plots might be brought to the surface and questioned. More conventional intellectual and academic methods have also been used to achieve similar ends (albeit with significantly smaller audiences). It is to this point that we turn in the next and final section of our chapter.

RESEARCH AS AVANT-GARDE LITERATURE

We live in times when managers no longer seem to have character (Sennett's book is not about managers, but then he wrote it before Enron), but are Characters (McIntyre, 1981). In this setting, popular culture seems to be an all-purpose handmaiden. It perpetuates strong plots and it subverts them. It helps to build the dramatic tension and it works as a safety valve. It stages drama and carnival. It provides exemplars for both conformity and resistance. On the one hand, popular culture appears to be an undervalued and underutilized resource for the study of management. On the other hand, popular culture seems to outperform management researchers in the roles that many aspire to – as analysts, teachers and the providers of exemplars. What, if anything, is left for research literature?

One possibility is that which we are exploiting right now, in this text. Management studies can, and perhaps ought to, pay more attention to the two-directional relationship between popular culture and the practice of management. Another, and the one that has been exploited for some time, is that management research might function like the avant-garde art and literature in relation to popular culture. Research writing can be experimental and subversive; it might go beyond the received strong plots. Ours is not, however, an image of the research avant-garde as an elitist judge of culture that consigns the popular to 'the rubbish bin of aesthetic history in one easy totalizing and psychologizing gesture' (Docker, 1994, p. 111). Instead it might be an avant-garde that trades on, hybridizes and mixes the high and the low; the practice and the theory; the elite and the mass without necessarily belonging to any of them. Such an avant-garde experiments rather than repeats; it disrespects the canon rather than either following or opposing it; much of it vanishes but that which stays can revolutionize the institutional patterns.

Such research texts will not console themselves with the reproduction of strong plots in the sense that we have been discussing them. They will be marked by an iconoclastic desire to avoid such forms of emplotment and even to put forth what can be found in the spaces that lie outside of such plots. In this sense, they might be considered forms of avant-garde that trade in the cultural and the theoretical without being ensnared by either of them. Such management texts will neither emulate nor reproduce the hackneyed distinctions between popular culture and high culture – instead their exemplarity and originality will lie in their refusal to follow the plots that are handed down to them from either. To copy them would be futile, but it will be fully possible to be inspired by them – in both theory and practice of management. They will not be textbooks, but will inform future textbooks on management that will enter the circuit model of culture fully able to compete with other sources.

NOTES

1. An in-depth interview is a special kind of psychological interview intended to cover all the important events in life of a person. It usually begins with evoking the first memory.
2. He stepped down after the failure of Volvo's merger with Renault, and was replaced in the role of 'carrier of social character' by Percy Barnevik, the CEO of ABB. As Barnevik stepped down after a pension insurance scandal, Gyllenhammar has been reinstated in the gallery of national heroes.
3. One explanation might be that Ibsen was Norwegian.
4. The idea that literature precedes social sciences has been explored at length by Milan Kundera (1988).
5. The journal *Organization* has been especially open to this kind of endeavor, see for example the Thematic Issue on Organization as Science Fiction (vol. 6 no.4, 1999). See also Bloomfield (2003) and Metz (2003) on the relationship between science-fiction and management, and Rombach and Solli's (2003) search for leadership lessons in ten well-known movies.
6. In saying so, we defy many cultural theorists from both the left and the right. The Frankfurt School, and the Althusserian-Lacanian school takes mass culture to be an instrument for ideological manipulation. An opposing perspective sees popular culture as a new mythology, a shared belief system whose expressions might be produced by media elite but which belongs to the people (see Traube, 1992, for discussion of both). Beginning with Barthes (1957) and Hoggart (1957), a new approach claiming that mass culture is both the manipulative commercial product and authentic cultural creation found a powerful formulation in Hall (1979), and Jameson (1979) (for commentary, see Docker (1994).

7.   It is worth pointing out that both John Cleese and Lars von Trier have their own management consulting companies (Video Arts, Zentropa).
8.   This material was generated using the method of 'observant participation'. It involved an observation conducted by a practitioner under the guidance, and with feedback from a researcher.
9.   *The Simpsons* is America's longest running and most successful prime time television show. It is aired in more than 60 countries, and in 1999 *Time* magazine proclaimed it as the best television show of the 20th century. The *Dilbert* comic strip, first seen in 1989, appears in 2000 newspapers in 65 countries. There are a total of 22 *Dilbert* books with more that 10 million copies in print (Adams, 2003). The 1996 book *The Dilbert Principle* was number one on both *The New York Times*' and *Business Week*'s business bestsellers list.
10. Production code 7F02, original airdate 18 October 1990.

REFERENCES

Adams, Scott (1996a), *The Dilbert Principle*, New York: Harper Collins.
Adams, Scott (1996b), *Dogbert's Top Secret Management Handbook*, New York: Harper Collins.
Adams, Scott (2003), *Dilbert Web-site*, United Features Syndicate, www.dilbert.com, 17 July 2003.
Amis, Martin (1997), *Night Train*, London: Vintage.
Bakhtin, Mikhail (1984a), *Rabelais and His World*, Bloomington: Indiana University Press.
Bakhtin, Mikhail (1984b), *Problems of Dostoyevsky's Poetics*, Minneapolis: University of Minnesota Press.
Barthes, Roland (1957/1982), *Mythologies*, New York: Hill and Wang.
Bloomfield, Brian (2003), 'Narrating the future of intelligent machines: the role of science fiction in technological anticipation', in Barbara Czarniawska and Pasquale Gagliardi (eds), *Narratives We Live By*, Amsterdam: John Benjamins, pp. 193–212.
Booker, Christopher (2004), *The Seven Basic Plots*, London: Continuum.
Borowski, Paul J. (1998), 'Manager–employee relationships: guided by Kant's categorical imperative or by Dilbert's business principle', *Journal of Business Ethics*, **17**, 1623–32.
Brown, Tom (1996), 'The deeper side of "Dilbert"', *Management Review*, **85** (2), 48–52.
Clegg, Stewart R. (1990), *Modern Organizations: Organization Studies in the Postmodern World*, London: Sage.
Cohen, Karl F. (1998), *Forbidden Animation: Censored Cartoons and Blacklisted Animators in America*, Jefferson, NC: McFarland.
Cohen, Percy S. (1969), 'Theories of myth', *Man*, **4**, 337–53.
Covey, Steven (1990), *The Seven Habits of Highly Effective People*, New York: Simon and Schuster.
Czarniawska, Barbara (2004a), *Narratives in Social Science Research*, London: Sage.
Czarniawska, Barbara (2004b), 'Women in financial services: fiction and more fiction', in Karin Knorr Cetina and Alex Preda (eds), *The Sociology of Financial Markets*, Oxford: Oxford University Press, pp. 121–37.
Czarniawska-Joerges, Barbara (1989), *Economic Decline and Organizational Control*, New York: Praeger.

Davies, Linda (1995), *The Nest of Vipers*, New York: Doubleday.

DeMott, Benjamin (1989), 'Reading fiction to the bottom line', *Harvard Business Review*, May–June, 128–34.

Denning, Michael (1990), 'The end of mass culture', *International Labor and Working-Class History*, **37** (Spring), 4–18.

Docker, John (1994), *Postmodernism and Popular Culture*, Cambridge, UK: Cambridge University Press.

Eco, Umberto (1984), 'The frames of comic "freedom"', in Thomas A. Sebeok (ed.), *Carnival!*, Berlin: de Gruyter, pp. 1–10.

Economist, The (1997), 'The anti-management guru', 5 April, 64–5.

Feldman, Daniel C. (2000), 'The Dilbert syndromes: how employee cynicism about ineffective management is changing the nature of careers in organizations', *American Behavioral Scientist*, **43** (8), 1286–300.

Filipczak, Bob (1994), 'An interview with Scott Adams', *Training*, **31** (7), 29–33.

Fortune (1996), 'Dilbert's management handbook', **133** (9), 99–103.

Gabriel, Yiannis (ed.) (2004), *Premodern Stories for Late Modernity: Narrative Tradition and Organization*, Oxford, UK: Oxford University Press.

Gee, James P., Glynda Hull and Colin Langshear (1996), *The New Work Order*, St. Leonards: Allen and Unwin.

Guillet de Monthoux, Pierre and Barbara Czarniawska-Joerges (1994), 'Management beyond case and cliché', in Barbara Czarniawska-Joerges and Pierre Guillet de Monthoux (eds), *Good Novels, Better Management*, Reading: Harwood Academic Publishers, pp. 1–16.

Hall, Stuart (1979/1981), 'Notes on deconstructing "the Popular"', in Raphael Samuel (ed.), *People's History and Socialist Theory*, London: Routledge and Kegan Paul, pp. 227–40.

Hassard, John and Ruth Holliday (1998), 'Introduction', in John Hassard and Ruth Holliday (eds), *Organization-Representation. Work and Organization in Popular Culture*, London: Sage, pp. 1–15.

Hodge, Barry (1996), 'King-size Homer: ideology and representation', *The Simpsons Archive*, www.snpp.com, 18 July 2003.

Hogenson, George B. (1987), 'Elements of an ethological theory of political myth and ritual', *Journal for the Theory of Social Behaviour*, **17**, 301–20.

Hoggart, Richard (1957), *The Uses of Literacy*, Harmondsworth: Pelican.

Hutchins, Greg (1999), 'The Dilbertizing of the workplace', *Quality Progress*, May, 131.

Jameson, Fredric (1979), 'Reification and Utopia in mass culture', *Social Text*, **1**, 130–148.

Johnson, Pamela R. and Julie Indvik (1999), 'Organizational benefits of having emotionally intelligent managers and employees', *Journal of Workplace Learning*, **11** (3), 84–8.

Johnson, Richard (1986–87), 'What is cultural studies anyway?', *Social Text*, **16**, 38–80.

Kafner, Stefan (1997), *Serious Business*, New York: Scribner.

Kessler, Eric H. (2001), 'The idols of organizational theory: from Francis Bacon to the Dilbert principle', *Journal of Management Inquiry*, **10** (4), 285–97.

Korte, Dan (1997), 'The Simpsons as quality television', *The Simpsons Archive*, www.snpp.com, 18 July 2003.

Kundera, Milan (1988), *The Art of the Novel*, New York: Faber and Faber.

Lagercrantz, David (2001), *Stjärnfall*, Stockholm: Piratförlaget.

Maccoby, Michael (1976), *The Gamesman: The New Corporate Leaders*, New York: Simon and Schuster.

Maccoby, Michael (1981), *The Leader: A New Face for American Management*, New York: Simon and Schuster.

Manganaro, Marc (1990), 'Textual play, power, and cultural critique', in Marc Manganaro (ed.), *Modernist Anthropology. From Fieldwork to Text*, Princeton, NJ: Princeton University Press.

Marc, David (1998), *Comic Visions: Television Comedy and American Culture*, Malden, MA: Blackwell.

Margalit, Avishai (2003), *The Ethics of Memory*, Cambridge, MA: Harvard University Press.

McDowell, Linda (1997), *Capital Culture: Gender at Work in the City*, Oxford: Blackwell.

McDowell, Linda (1998), 'Fictional money (or, greed isn't so good in the 1990s)', in John Hassard and Ruth Holliday (eds), *Organization-Representation. Work and Organization in Popular Culture*, London: Sage, pp. 167–84.

McIntyre, Alisdair (1981), *After Virtue*, Notre Dame, IN: University of Notre Dame Press.

Metz, David (2003), 'From Lancelot to Count Zero', in Barbara Czarniawska and Pasquale Gagliardi (eds), *Narratives We Live By*, Amsterdam: John Benjamins, pp. 173–92.

Miles, Robert H. (2001), 'Beyond the age of Dilbert: accelerating corporate transformations by rapidly engaging all employees', *Organizational Dynamics*, **29** (4), 3131–321.

Norwood, Robin (1989), *Women Who Loved Too Much*, Flint, MI: Arrow.

Organization (1999), Thematic issue on organization as science fiction, 6/4.

Peter, Laurence J. and Raymond Hull (1969), *The Peter Principle*, New York: W. Morow.

Rhodes, Carl (2001a), *Writing Organization*, Amsterdam: John Benjamins.

Rhodes, Carl (2001b), 'D'Oh: The Simpsons, popular culture and organizational carnival', *Journal of Management Inquiry*, **10** (4), 374–83.

Rhodes, Carl (2002), 'Coffee and the business of pleasure', *Culture and Organization*, **8** (4), 293–306.

Ricoeur, Paul (1981), *Hermeneutics & the Human Sciences*, Cambridge, UK: Cambridge University Press.

Rombach, Björn, and Solli Rolf (2003), *Fiktiva förebilder: Reflektioner kring filmhjältar som ledare*, Lund: Studentlitteratur.

Sennett, Richard (1998), *The Corrosion of Character*, New York: W.W. Norton.

Street, John (1997), *Politics and Popular Culture*, Oxford: Blackwell.

Taussig, Michael (1993), *Mimesis and Alterity*, London: Routledge.

Traube, Elizabeth G. (1992), *Dreaming Identities: Class, Gender and Generation in 1980s Hollywood Movies*, Boulder, CO: Westview Press.

Van Biema, David (1996), 'Layoffs for laughs', *Time*, **147** (12), 82–3.

Varese, Federico (2004), 'Great mobility', *Times Literary Supplement*, July 2, 6–7.

White, Hayden (1998), *The Content of the Form*, Baltimore, MR: The Johns Hopkins University Press.

Whyte, William H. (1956), *The Organization Man*, New York: Simon and Schuster.

Wildavsky, Aaron B. (1984), *The Nursing Father: Moses as a Political Leader*, Tuscaloosa, AL: University of Alabama Press.

PART 4

Rethinking humanism

13. A philosopher in public management

Lars Vissing

I believe philosophers in public management to be a very small minority. But sometimes a false majority impression emerges. I found it perfectly adequate, when I was posted to Germany, to have a theologian as President of the Bundesbank. And when I hear Mr Greenspan brief the relevant committees of the US Congress on monetary issues, I often do recognize the language of the Church.

My reflection will be concentrated on a couple of questions related to humanities, to time and timing. The focus will be on today and tomorrow, with some excursions into history, and into our cultural basis.

The main idea will be this one: the link between management and humanities does exist today, but the main delivery from humanities is more likely to take place in a future situation of emergency.

WHAT IS THE SITUATION TODAY?

Humanities and management? Humanities inside management? Humanities providing something to management?

But is this 'something' lacking?

My first observation: this is not a situation where one would have doubts about the issue, about whether such connection exists or not. The question is rather to consider the contemporary characteristics of these links; to define them against those of tomorrow, and to consider whether they are an answer to a need, or not.

I am not sure if today's products – considered from the receiving end, and not from that of delivery, such as this volume – will generally come out in a positive light. But perhaps we are not here to exchange seasonal greetings, but rather to put the relevant questions.

What is today's delivery from humanities? Is it always possible to distinguish it – seriously – from other circulating fashion and lifestyle products?

Is it more than that? Or does it represent an immaterial value-added that puts it beyond the sphere of money- and power-making? Make it more than a spiritual service, more than the elements of a secular religion?

Let me give you an example. In June, I received from my Ministry the papers meant to prepare my colleagues and me for our annual ambassadors' meeting with government members. There was also a document calling for a common work to define our mission, our vision and values. Now, why would somebody – representing a state, a country, and not only a government – have to think about 'values'?

I happen to believe that the medieval division between spiritual and temporal powers remains a positive achievement, so close to the still valid basis of our culture, that I would have some apprehensions about seeing it further diluted, or even go. I was always jealous of my latin colleagues – Italian, Spanish, Portuguese – and also of the French, when I saw them being able to operate on the basis of the remnants of this distinction, that is, in a totally secular space, whereas I had to handle a universe where ethics and other religious ambiguities had a role.

Marsilius and Machiavelli provided solid lessons for contemporary management in this respect. These lessons are still valid, even if Erasmus, Luther, Calvin and the Church Reform generally, certainly did not solidify this fundamental distinction. When I see the influx of humanities into management, I ask myself whether this can compensate for a lack, without creating new civil religions, starting with the primitive acceptance of such non-sense concepts as 'values'.

The interests of a private company were previously defined narrowly as profit, market-domination or through similar concepts. Often now other inputs are desired, such as spiritual elements, in what remains otherwise a secular and business-oriented professional universe. This is of course instrumental in creating corporate culture and thereby loyalty and cohesion. How about the state, though? Do the extremely diversified interests and culture of a national state, its government and social and professional systems not provide enough cohesion and internal logic to inspire and shape an operational behavior? Does one have to add 'values' to this? Either we are the victims of a fashion, a trend, or we must admit that the Church is not doing its job any more.

I do believe that the present debate on management and humanities can help in getting beyond this primitive level. Another avenue is already wide open. I clearly sense that university programmes are being adjusted to meet a number of important needs. Universities as well as business schools are well aware of the need to offer a mix of disciplines. Such programmes very directly recycle humanities in university education and combine them with the traditional business, economy and political science disciplines. This is happening today. Ethnography, languages, sociology, history are back, and are now linked to management disciplines.

In some places, like England, this link was never totally lost. In my own field, foreign policy and diplomacy, I see the maintenance of this link as one of the major guarantees for a strong and incisive foreign service. Which is, by the way, what the UK has. Of course, the actual target is not to create responsibility for 'the beauty of the world' – but rather to increase cultural control on the business or negotiation partner. Political or cultural knowledge – ethnography or psychology – yes. But in the first place, to foresee the outcome of a deal, to avoid bumping into obstacles of an immaterial nature when you do what companies mostly do: earn money and increase corporate power.

WHAT IS THE PROBLEM TODAY?

The actual problem is – paradoxically – that in putting the question of management and humanities we are *not* acting to solve a fully deployed problem; we are spotting some needs, and shaping deliveries to meet them. But we are not handling a cultural emergency. I do fear that such a cultural necessity will have to appear, to ensure the seriousness of the product. There should be a compelling reason to make the enlargement of the management perception unavoidable. The essential characteristics of societies – not only of democracy – is *not to act* before a problem is clearly exposed and recognized: the bathtub has to flood the apartment before action is taken. Degeneration or policy change are the two opposite answers to such strong necessities. It cannot be just a wish to 'do something'. I thus do not foresee a major challenge for management, public as well as private, the major new factor in favor of a more general approach, before we are confronted with such an emergency. It could come – just one example among other possible scenarios – as the consequence of major man-made disasters, perhaps in 15–20 years from now, depending on the growth rate and a number of other factors. We will then reach a new situation with regard to the division of global responsibilites implied by our model of illimited growth – and limited attention to the environment, demography and so on. When we have filled up the bathtub, a more integrated approach to these problems and questions will emerge all by itself: an evident and major task for humanities, together with public and private management.

A FEW ELEMENTS OF ANALYSIS

This 'together' means going against the most fundamental tendencies of Western thinking. A couple of things should be remembered: already in Aristotle's *Metaphysics* 'being' is close to nothing, whereas acting, activating, measuring, establishing links is everything. *Machenschaft, Betrieb, Seinsvergessenheit* will be Heidegger's later conclusion on this cultural tendency. Other powerful factors – I am not going to list them – have consolidated this divide, especially the already mentioned medieval separation between Church and Empire. The burden of this divide, more than just a division of labor, is without doubt too heavy to yield to simple desires of influence, of a wish to 'make things better', or even thinking of getting back to the platonic idea of King-Philosophers, or to the sovereign function of the indo-european society, as analysed by Georges Dumézil: the amalgamation of spiritual, religious and sovereign functions inside a cast of Brahmans.

The difficulties in getting back to such an amalgamation are not based *only* on historical irresponsibility, conservatism, or in individual and corporate interests. They are based on solid cultural inertia, much older than the Anglo-American perception of management. Thus, today, we face a phenomenon that corresponds well to our times. We might have been close to new definitions of humanities' needs for management in the mid-1980s, when market economies were not in shape. At that time the acknowledgement of cultural factors and shared global responsibilities was increasing. But the fall of the Soviet Union and socialist economies gave our economic model a new perspective, a new lease of life, and new margins for expansion, at a crucial moment. This major event – positive as it was for market and cultural expansion – in fact delayed structural adjustment. I am talking not only about material structures, that is infrastructures, or production or economic structures, but also about mental structures. Our economy was given a new lease of life. And our civilization was authorized to remain confident and basically conservative in its approach.

Another dominant feature of our own perception, of some relevance with respect to the role of humanities and culture, is that culture was formerly a question of education and 'cultivation'. We have gradually developed a reality of cultural objects or products that can be imprisoned in museums as exhibits – in 'maisons de la culture', as they are called in France, where the prison formerly was also the 'maison d'arrêt'. Certainly this is not an educational perception. And who would speak today of a 'cultivated' person?

IS OUR CULTURE'S HERITAGE OF HUMANITIES FIT TO CONFRONT FUTURE CHALLENGES?

Some might believe that humanities will automatically deliver the supplements or complements that might help to adjust the traditional strategies and behaviors of business. But looking at their historic and cultural responsibility for the contemporary situation, some measure of doubt seems legitimate.

The delivery of a more balanced approach to management could well come from humanities, but not necessarily, and not everywhere. The opportunity *could* be missed. The outcome will depend largely on the adaptability of a number of disciplines, practices and perceptions. Here and there I can see clear signs of such adaptability, which I have already mentioned: the fast growing disciplines of higher education combining humanities with sciences, management, information technologies. This is a promising perspective. The effective way of establishing a larger basis for management will be through the university door.

It might not come fast enough for countries which – like France and Italy – traditionally shaped the mainstream school education on the model of the writer, author, poet: literature and poetry as the natural perspective, an educational basis for every child; literacy meaning literature.

I would hope, however, that the next move could be towards getting rid of the absurd divides at the secondary level, between 'humanities' and 'sciences'. There are places where I see some attention to these problems: one of the fast expanding consultancy sectors is that of sustainable growth. I think this is just one of the first important symptoms of the responsibilities that will be put on management. This is something beyond handling of anti-pollution filters: the first portion of shared responsibility for more than business strategies, the first sign of change of cultural software.

Responsibilities of all operators are bound to increase when societies move closer to the limits of what can be achieved with contemporary systems. These responsibilities will increase for the private sector, but certainly also for the state, and for the international organizations. I see no handling of our common future without new ways and contractual obligations among these players. In this future the major contribution of humanities will come in terms of an answer to a question, a reaction to an appeal, a response to a necessity. Relative speed will be essential. High speed, and a crisis scenario will appear. Moderate speed, and the transition can be handled.

This situation will be one where question marks should be put at every juncture of human thinking. Not in order to shape a new civil religion inside management: it would be absurd if humanities – responsible for confronting the Church, and for creating a new sound basis for civil management during the Renaissance – were now to be responsible for re-exporting religion, although in a new version, back to secular affairs. The target would rather be to help modify the ways of handling the world. Not through utopias but through adjustment of dominant cultural software.

A number of serious questions might then have to be considered: demography, health system and security ambitions; our model of growth and the future of market economies; the role of war and security policies, and many other fields. All considerations geared towards one aim: a critical look at our systems, principles and instruments. This is certainly a joint task for humanities together with private and public management. Only then will there be a 'heavy duty' delivery of humanities into management. And only then will such a delivery not mean a constant risk of slipping into a new 'vision & mission' religion.

This risk might not always be perceivable at academic meetings on management and humanities, where new critical questions are constantly brought forward and debated, but it is present at the receiving end – in the clienteles that collect and consume some of the strange products of the contemporary commerce between humanities and management.

14. The great narrative of the sciences and the history of humanities

Michel Serres

Last December, on my way through a city – I won't mention its name – famed for its natural history museum, while visiting its no less celebrated skeleton room I asked the attendant the age of one remarkably long and tall giant saurian. He answered: '120 million years, eleven months'. I then inquired: 'How did you calculate such a precise date?' 'Simple' – he said – 'the museum hired me to watch over this room in the middle of last winter. At that time a label still on the animal said it was a 120 million years old. Count yourself, why don't you.'

This good man had laid so much store by recent time that he completely lost any sense of proportion. We might laugh at his reckoning, but we think in the same way. We attach great importance to the 'news' we listen to so eagerly every morning, without ever really wondering what is truly new.

Now we find the word 'new' alongside the term 'humanities' in the title of our workshop. To reach a better definition of both terms, I will try to answer three questions:

- What was really new in the humanities when Renaissance Humanism invented them?
- What is so new today that we have to conceive of a 'New Humanism' and 'new humanities'?
- Can we speak of a 'new education'?

I

Invented at the beginning of the 19th century by the Erudite German School, the term 'Humanism' stands for the intellectual, philosophical, political and religious movement in the 15th and 16th centuries, represented by Renaissance men like Erasmus, Rabelais, Luther and Montaigne. They – and others – dreamed of a new education for young minds, an education that the same German school called the Humanities.

Preserved for a long time in our universities, this kind of teaching included the study of the ancient languages – Latin, Greek and at times also Hebrew and Sanskrit – their accompanying literature and fine arts, as well as an historical culture dating from the age when those languages were spoken.

Initially 'born again' and then classical, the humanities were further boosted by critical reflection in the Age of Enlightenment and formed the '*Bildung*' of a '*uomo di coltura*' (a cultivated person), until they shipwrecked – with all hands aboard, so to speak – sometime around the 1970s.

Now I find myself hunting round for traces of that culture, just as Diogenes in another age searched for a human being with a lantern in daylight. Educated mainly on economic and political 'news', the 'new elites' have never before been so far removed from that culture as today. The ruling classes are now sliding towards barbarism.

What happened during the Renaissance that created such a deeply felt need to invent a 'new' vision of the world and a 'new' education?

Between 1541 and 1544, three major novelties emerged: in Copernicus's new sky the earth started to revolve round the sun; on the cylindrical world map projected by Mercator, where the recent discoveries could be shown, the new Earth was represented in longitudes and latitudes; while the permission to dissect bodies granted at Louvain enabled Vésale to draw the exact anatomy of the new body. *Thus a new human body inhabited a new earth under new skies.*

At the same time, the new clocks measured the new time. Perspective in painting ordered a new space, and printing and musical scores organized voices and messages.

This set of dimensions supplied *a spatial–temporal information framework* making the Renaissance possible.

Consequently, accountancy was invented. Trade rose to new heights thanks to the complete transformation of culture. Thus to say that the economy made Renaissance and Humanities possible is putting the cart before the horse.

II

The Renaissance and humanist responses to these new developments had – in our eyes – some major flaws. The vision of the world's *space* at the time was only what Antiquity called the inhabited Earth, that is the Mediterranean, to which the New World had to be added, including the shock of its discovery. Since the humanities preserved the Greek–Latin tradition, they still considered other languages and cultures to be barbarian.

But most importantly, the *temporal* framework was remarkably narrow, since according to the biblical generations, calculated by Newton himself at the end of the 17th century, the world and history were still thought to have begun in the 4th millennium before Christ.

Today, those spatial–temporal frameworks are exploding.

Astrophysics and its cosmological models reckon the universe to be 15 billion years old. They are able to describe galaxies so far away from us that we receive their light from a time before the formation of the earth.

Geophysics has established when the earth was formed and reckons it to be 4 million years old.

Biochemistry has discovered a universal genetic code and dates the beginning of life to 3.9 billion years ago.

Paleo-anthropology has established the birth of human beings in Africa as dating from 3 to 8 million years ago and tells the story of a handful of families who left the African continent and then spread to the whole world.

As in the Renaissance, therefore, *new human beings, unitary – whatever their cultures and appearances – live on a new earth under new skies*.

Moreover, the formatting of information, whatever its meaning and contents, makes these new understandings possible.

To speak of the economy as the infrastructure, and to claim that culture depends on it and it alone, means making the same mistake of scale as did the attendant in the skeleton room.

Lastly, whereas during the Renaissance, Rabelais invented the word *encyclopédie*, based on the idea that the whole of knowledge formed a closed cyclical system, our whole of knowledge, projected into new time, forms what I call the 'Great Narrative'.

III

THE UNIVERSALITY OF THE GREAT NARRATIVE

Here are some contemporary new developments compared to those in the Renaissance. We are living at the time when people changed their knowledge base with the advent of new technologies; when, thanks to astrophysics and plate tectonics, they live in a new universe and on a new Earth; when the human body has changed more than during the whole history of mankind; at the time when Mercators, Copernicus, and Vésales are more numerous and more profound than their forerunners. At this time, we finally have a Great Narrative, aesthetically magnificent, which stretches into space and time further and is longer, more convincing and truer than ever before, as all the sciences ceaselessly work in parallel to rectify it . . .

and, as a supplementary miracle, no narrative has been more universal, more commonly shared by the whole humankind, as this one is since . . .

. . . since the Big Bang began to construct the first atoms, the matter of which inert things and our same flesh are composed,

. . . since the planets cooled down and the earth became a reservoir of even heavier matter of which our tissues and bones are made,

. . . since a strange acid molecule began to reproduce itself identically four million years ago and then became transformed through mutations,

. . . since the first living beings started to colonize the face of the earth at the same time constantly evolving, leaving behind more fossil species than the contemporary ones we could know,

. . . since a girl called Lucy began to stand up in the savanna of East Africa, unwittingly promising ground-breaking journeys for the future humanity, to all the emerged continents with their contingent and divergent cultures and languages,

. . . since some tribes in South America and the Middle East invented crops of maize and wheat (without forgetting the worthy patriarch who planted the first vineyard or the Indian hero who brewed beer, taming for the first time such a tiny living creature as yeast).

Then the common tree of the great narrative began to grow, a chronicle of unexpected density, real and shared, that could support a humanism and humanities finally worthy of the name, because it is a humanism in which all languages and cultures that originate from it can participate, which is unique and universal because written in *the encyclopedic language of all the sciences*, and which is translatable into *each vernacular language*, without any particularism or imperialism.

THE MOSAIC OF CULTURES

I can hear your objections: nothing in this great epic consoles us or protects us

. . . from not understanding each other, as we do not speak the same languages,

. . . from hating each other, because we do not practise the same religions,

. . . from exploiting each other because we have different economic standards,

. . . from persecuting each other because we do not have the same forms of government . . . Indeed nothing prevents us from killing each other for all of these reasons.

I hear your objections and you are right. Worse still, the ancient culture, itself founded on the horror of the war of Troy or the banning of human sacrifice under the fist of Abraham, the father of monotheism, has never spared us from that infernal violence which constitutes everyday history, from the massacre of the Gauls, Indians, Cathares and Aborigines, nor from Auschwitz or Hiroshima. The sciences do not provide meanings, only cultures can express them.

As for us, professors, at times fully-fledged humanists, we have neither political power, armed forces nor money . . . and just as well. We would not make any better use of them than anyone else. We have unfortunately demonstrated this thousands of times.

How few of so-called persons of culture realize that true culture can be recognized in not crushing anyone under the weight of that culture? All we have therefore is language, and at times, teaching.

We can thus only work in the long term. Precisely in the immensely long terms of the Great Narrative. How can we respond – with our specific means – to these painful questions, undoubtedly derived from the problem of evil, for which there is still no consoling answers? How can we work towards peace – the supreme collective good – not just thinking about it, talking about it, or meeting in inevitably pointless discussions, but really making a contribution?

I suggest pursuing our own action, as follows.

TOWARDS COMMON KNOWLEDGE AND COMMON EDUCATION

Concerned by the misunderstandings and wars between peoples, we believe that establishing a common stock of knowledge will gradually unite all people, beginning with the students, and will eventually encourage spreading of peace in the world. This universal humanism will contribute to creating a disinterested peaceful globalization.

We will ask the rectors of universities worldwide to dedicate the first year of teaching to a common programme enabling students in all disciplines and in all countries to have a similar horizon of knowledge and culture. They in turn will then spread this culture.

We will only suggest a general framework, to be adapted according to their specialization, culture and willingness. This framework is based on the following considerations:

THE GREAT UNITARY NARRATIVE OF THE SCIENCES

As the *hard sciences* have already achieved universality, we will take them on board as a whole and according to the general evolution of the world which the contemporary encyclopedia describes.

- Elements of physics and astrophysics: the formation of the universe, from the Big Bang to the cooling of the planets.
- Elements of geophysics, chemistry and biology: from the creation of the earth to the appearance of life and the evolution of the species.
- Elements of general anthropology: the emergence, spreading and prehistory of humankind.
- Elements of agronomy, medicine and the transition to culture: the relations between Human Beings, the Earth, Life and Humanity itself.

THE MOSAIC OF HUMAN CULTURES

As for *cultures*, they form a mosaic with a great diversity of forms and colours, reflecting the diversity of languages, religions and politics. The new humanist knowledge assimilates this set of differences.

- Elements of general linguistics; the geography and history of language families. The languages of communication and their evolution.
- Elements of the history of religions: polytheism, monotheisms, pantheisms, atheisms . . .
- Elements of political sciences: the various kinds of government.
- Elements of economics: the division of wealth in the world.
- Selected masterpieces of world wisdom and of the fine arts – literature, music, painting, sculpture, architecture . . . Sites: humanity's heritage according to UNESCO.

15. Post-humanist challenges to the human and social sciences

Karin Knorr Cetina

When we talk about humanism, we are pointed back to the past twice. First we are referred to the original 'umanisti', a 15th and 16th century reading movement that spread from the Italian city-states to the rest of Europe and identified with the Greek and Roman tradition in literature, history and public administration.[1] Second, we are referred to the pre-Christian antiquity, whose wisdom the humanists revered. We are now living in a time that is oriented to the future rather than to the past. Part of the recklessness and ontological insecurities we encounter on an institutional and individual level may have to do with the fact that the future does not provide the guidance the past offered to the original humanists, especially since we tend to define it in terms of innovations that break with the past. The future is not, of course, an empty space. When I say we are looking towards the future today it also means that there are many signals and indicators we draw on to assess where we are going – though they do not disclose where we will get to or what we will have become once we have gone further. It is some of these pointers and developments that I will address here. Many challenge humanism, if by that we mean the development of human virtue and the qualities associated with the modern word human – understanding, compassion and benevolence (communitarian values) as well as judgment, prudence and eloquence (rationality and reason).[2] What are some instances of post-humanist challenges? The first arises from the constitution of the subject in contemporary Western cultures. The second has to do with non-human objects and the role they have come to play in the social word. The third challenge arises from the information sciences which some think will require much change in that which we associate with 'human'. The fourth derives from the biological sciences. I will discuss it in the context of the notion of 'life' which I think is in the process of replacing humanist notions.

233

1. THE CHALLENGE DERIVING FROM THE CONSTITUTION OF THE SUBJECT

The challenge one can associate with the subject comprises two develop-ments, one challenging the powers of human reason and reasoning, the second challenging our notions of the human as moral selves. Several fields in psychology (cognitive psychology, evolutionary psychology and the psy-chology of emotions), but also some in economics (decision theory, behav-ioral economics and finance) have deconstructed the notion of rational man by demonstrating the number of biases, miscalculations and misinter-pretation humans are prone to, a series that is open ended. Sociology also has a hand in the deconstruction of reason, for example when neo-institutionalist studies expose the myths of rationality in organizations. As Elster (1998) put it, as *assumptions* of rationality give way to *research* into human cognition, homo sapiens loses IQ and gains visceral definition. One can also argue that homo sapiens has lost some of his or her moral sensi-bilities and the interest in virtue that renaissance and enlightenment thinkers hoped for. I want to illustrate that by a brief look at the notion of the moral and social self the social sciences have worked with in the past, a self that was guided by the norms and values of society. I will contrast this idea with the notion of an a-moral or post-moral self that is no longer pri-marily normatively guided.

The core model of the social and moral self of the period of high social-ity is the idea of the self as composed of an ego and an internalized 'other' that represents society and functions as an inner censor. In Mead, the inner censor is called the 'generalized other'; it is closely coupled to the intrasub-jective conformist past of the self and the self as an object, which Mead calls the 'me'. At the opposite end of this side of the self lies the 'I', the sponta-neous, unpredictable, disobeying self. The 'I' has the power to construct reality cognitively, and by redefining situations, can break away from the 'me' and the norms of society. The 'me' and the 'generalized other' can be likened to Peirce's 'you'; Peirce held the 'you' to be a critical self that repre-sented society and to which all thought was addressed. These notions are also roughly similar to Freud's 'super-ego', the rule-carrier which functions as a regulative principle in an internal dynamic of morality and deviance. In Mead's theory, the self first originates from such a dynamic. It arises from role taking, from taking the perspective of the other first interpersonally, when engaged with a close caretaker, and then also intrapersonally.

This 'I-you-me' system of the social self and its most sophisticated version (Wiley, 1994, p. 34ff., p. 44ff.) can be contrasted with a second model that understands the self, not as a relation between the individual and a moral society, but as a structure of wantings in relation to continually renewed lacks. This notion of the self can be derived from Lacan, but it can also be linked to Baldwin and Hegel (Wiley, 1994, p. 33). Like Freud, Lacan is concerned with what 'drives' the subject, but he derives this wanting not as Freud did from an instinctual impulse whose ultimate goal is a reduction in bodily tension, but rather from the mirror stage of a young child's development. In this phase the child becomes impressed with the wholeness of his or her image in the mirror and with the appearance of definite boundaries and control – while realizing that s/he is none of these things in actual experience. Wanting or desire is born in envy of the perfection of the image in the mirror (or of the mirroring response of the parents); the lack is permanent, since there will always be a distance between the subjective experience of a lack in our existence and the image in the mirror, or the apparent wholeness of others (Alford, 1991, p. 36ff.).

The two conceptions may seem similar in that both emphasize the discrepancy between the I and a model, but they are in fact quite different. From the idea of the self as composed of an inner censor results an ego subjected to feelings of guilt, experiencing rebellion, and attempting to 'live up to' society's moral expectations. In contrast, the self as a permanently reiterated lack gives rise to the desire, also permanent, to eliminate the lack. The former model would seem to result in actions that are perpetually curtailed as an ego attempts to adapt them to internalized norms; it will also result in deviant actions that transgress boundaries of which the actor is well aware. The second model yields actions spurred on by the unfulfillability of lacks, or by new wants opening up simultaneously with the (partial) fulfillment of old ones. In the first model, the actor's free fall from society is continually broken as he catches himself (or is caught by others) in compliance with social rules and traditions, and returns to their ontological security. In the second case, no moral society of this sort is in place any longer to provide ontological security. The 'you' is the idealized self in the mirror or the perfect other. The actor would seem to be freed from guilt complexes; but he or she is like a vagrant perpetually searching, stringing together objects of satisfaction and dismantling the structure again as he or she moves on to other goals. This search system is autoaffective and self-sustaining, indeed self-energizing; as a structure of wanting, the self is extended through continually renewed and discovered lacks that renew its motivation and affectivity. The Meadian I-you-me system neglects the autoaffective side of the self, which is not its self-love, but its willingness to become engaged in circuits that renew wanting. Note that autoaffection and self-energizing are forward-looking capacities; they appear consistent with financialized, credit-based economies oriented to the future and to growth rather than stability or sustainability or the wisdom of the past. In contemporary society, the Lacanian mirror is no longer either a physical mirror or the caretakers' activity of 'back-projecting', their activity of 'reflecting', like a mirror, the child's being in relation to parental idealizations and expectations. Instead, the mirror response has passed to the media and professional image industries that project images and stage 'wholeness', to knowledge disciplines that project the improvement and completion of nature and human life, and to a financial industry that projects the extension of wealth. In other words, the mirror is exteriorized in a media, image, finance and knowledge culture which all hold up models that are not moral in character but that are images of an improved and enhanced future. The challenge for humanism and the humanities is to come to grips with this shift from virtue-based, past-oriented moral models to promise-based, future-oriented, cognitive-emotional and aesthetic models.

2. THE CHALLENGE FROM NON-HUMAN OBJECTS AND POSTSOCIAL DEVELOPMENTS

Now the second challenge, the rise of the object world. My claim here is threefold. One, there has been an enormous increase of non-human objects in the social world; two, many of these objects need to be defined differently from our everyday concepts of objects as fixed things of a material nature, and third, these objects to some degree displace human beings as relationship partners and embedding environments – objects may also become the risk winners of the relationship problems that plague contemporary human relations.

The first claim is that there has been an enormous increase in the volume of non-human things in the social world – technological objects, consumer goods, financial instruments, scientific things, all exemplify this expansion. Consider for example scientific objects such as biologists' molecular structures, physicists' quarks or their Higgs mechanisms, astronomers' black holes and dark matter of the universe. Most of these objects (and they are internally differentiated further) have become available to us for discussion and inquiry only relatively recently, and they enrich and enlarge the natural world as a conglomerate of ever more detailed, more distant and invisible things. The social world has equally been enlarged by a tremendous increase of technological instruments, consumer goods, financial objects, and the like; one need only compare the number of radios, TV sets, telephones or cars in the average American household today with the late 1950s to get a sense of this expansion. The space shuttle of the late 20th century contained 10 million components, Rycroft and Kash (1999, ch. 4)[3] report, while the Eli Whitney musket of around 1800 had 51 components.

Expansion by itself matters, but the thing which matters more is how we define the non-human objects we encounter in today's world. The definition should take into account the increasing 'intelligence' of some objects and their complexity. But the definition I want to offer focuses less on present qualities than on another aspect, which has much to do with objects becoming binding sites for subjects' wantings. Let us start with scientific objects, as described by Rheinberger (1992, p. 310). Scientific objects are characteristically open, question-generating, and complex. They are processes and projections rather than definite things. Work with them reveals them by increasing rather than reducing the questions they raise. In this sense they are the polar opposite of tools like hammers and drills. These tools and instruments are like closed boxes. Objects of knowledge-based work, on the other hand, are more reminiscent of open drawers filled with folders extending indefinitely into the depth of a dark closet. Since objects of knowledge are always in the process of being materially defined, they continually acquire new properties and change the ones they have. But this also means that these objects cannot quite ever be fully attained, that they are, if you wish, never quite themselves. What we encounter in the work process are stand-ins for a more basic lack of object.

Why is this important? Contemporary Western societies are frequently seen as highly individualized and in the process of undergoing a further wave of individualization. I tend to think of this more as a process of desocialization; we experience, I think, a period of historical retraction of social principles and structures that follows upon a period of expansion of such principles and structures in the 19th and up to the middle of the 20th century. This retraction is manifest in the overhaul and dismantling of the welfare state, the disintegration of complex social organizational structures when these are replaced by information structures and conglomerates of networks of small units, and the emptying out of primordial social relations, what Lasch (1978) calls the 'collapse' of the private sphere and the devastations of married and family life . But the reverse side of these developments which is ignored by the commentators on individualization (for example Beck, 1992; Baumann, 1993; Coleman, 1993; Berger et al., 1974) is the expansion of object worlds in the social world, the changing nature of objects, and the rise of what I have called object-relations (Knorr Cetina, 1997; 2001). The strong thesis I want to put forward is that contemporary Western societies are to some degree a *postsocial* environment, which is one where objects displace human beings as relationship partners and embedding environments, or where they increasingly mediate human relationships, making the latter dependent on the former. This is made possible by the changing nature of objects (not all of them of course, not all the time). The argument here is that the open, unfolding character of such objects offers binding sites for desires. Post-industrial objects accommodate the post-industrial selves which I have described in terms of structures of wanting that are led on and extended by transmutational objects. The transmutational character of post-industrial objects illustrates the sense in which objects not only attract a person's desire, but allow wanting to continue, giving it its serial, chain-like structure. Object relations are also routinely enriched by a semiotic dimension (an object signaling what it still lacks and a subject interpreting these signals), role-taking (subjects putting themselves in the position of the object), cross-over (objects occupying a subject's mind), and flow-experience (the subject becoming a 'flow' of concentrated object experience). All these dimensions together account for the lure of object relations. Objects may also simply be the risk winners of the relationship risks that many find inherent in human relationships.

One area where one can find intimate object relationships exemplified is that of science, and more generally, that of knowledge-based work. It is difficult to imagine a successful scientist or a high tech specialist who is not intimately involved with his or her object of work. As the knowledge society expands and professional work encroaches upon home-life, object-relations are more likely to substitute for and mediate human relations. But object-relations are not limited to science and technology. They have long expanded into the domain of consumption. Many consumer objects make relational demands, offer binding sites for desires, and display similar qualities to those in knowledge-based work. Consumer objects frequently have a dual structure in that they are simultaneously ready-to-hand usable things and absent objects of inquiry developed further by technological research (cars, computers), artistic design (fashion, commercials), or analysis (finance). Thus, someone who develops an intrinsic relationship with a consumer object like a car, a computer, or a fashionable outfit will be lured into further pursuits by the continuous transmutation of this object into more attractive successor versions. These objects may also have an interior indefiniteness of being – a potential for further discovery and exploration (think of a computer) that involves a relational engagement of the subject with the object. Finally, there is the referential nexus of objects. Recall what Heidegger ([1927] 1962) and others have to say about objects' existence within referential wholes or systems of objects (see also Baudrillard, 1996): our instrumental being in the world implies not a single tool but the 'whole' of a workshop, where one tool refers to another and the whole constitutes an instrumental environment in which we are embedded. In a similar vein, we can argue that most objects we are surrounded with refer to further objects, as when an advertisement suggests a particular brand of a car and the surrounding images suggest that with that car go other objects indicative of a particular lifestyle and career.

To sum up the second challenge, objects are now part of the human world, not only in their instrumental and physical capacity but as relationship partners and elements of preoccupation and interference.[4]

3. THE CHALLENGE FROM THE INFORMATION SCIENCES AND POST-HUMAN DEVELOPMENTS

While the last challenge I discussed was about the increased relevance of the object world to which human beings are increasingly drawn, the next one is about the changing concept of the human itself and the transformation of humans into *cyborgs* (Haraway, 1991), *post-humans* (Fukuyama, 2002) or *trans-humans* (for example Baard, 2003). Such beings can be understood as human descendants that have been improved upon by the information sciences, in combination with nanotechnology, bioengineering and cognitive research (the 'NBIC' group of the sciences).[5] These sciences converge in investigating and developing devices that enhance, or as some advocates put it, 'augment' biological human nature. The challenge they pose is that they put into question sharp distinctions between humans and machines, and that they appeal to the plasticity of the organic and the technical. What the NBIC research creates are interfaces between these categories that blur the human-non-human distinction. While most technologies currently implanted in humans (for example neural implants for Parkinson's disease) or used as replacement parts for malfunctioning organs and the like have medical functions, it appears likely and is expected by some authorities (for example the United States National Science Foundation and Department of Commerce) that the convergence of the NBIC sciences will create opportunities to enhance normal human performance and will be used for these purposes. Such performance enhancements might occur through an expanded memory capacity, implanted links for direct access to telecommunication networks, much faster thinking speed or the capacity to see in the infrared and ultraviolet wavelengths. Such 'improvements' are not within immediate reach, but they may well be realized in some way in the not too distant future. Overcoming genetic diseases (such as asthma, cystic fibrosis, epilepsy, muscular dystrophy, Parkinson's disease, sickle cell anemia), congenital birth defects (resulting in Down syndrome, spina bifida, and cerebral palsy) and many other causes of human suffering, and overcoming the normal predicaments of old age and perhaps death, also provide motivation for the creation and testing of relevant devices.

Developments of this sort raise many questions about the rights extended to transhumans and the ethics expected from them.[6] Will those with a higher percentage of prosthetic parts or certain kinds of machine parts have fewer rights than biological cell structures? Will vacuum-cleaning robots be named and be taken on vacation (some are already now)? Why should biological cell structure serve as a criterion for drawing a distinction between human and non-human beings? These questions have steadily gained importance since the invention of the Turing machine, since the arrival of the personal computer and since the debates surrounding the discipline of artificial intelligence and its attempts to simulate brain output. We may consider such questions far off, the progress toward these new beings overestimated, and those who believe in the posthuman challenge out of touch with the realities of science and technology. But my claim is the fantasies themselves are important, and the humanities may eventually have to come to grips with the developments now in the making or lose ground to other disciplines.

4. THE CHALLENGE FROM 'LIFE'

One massive source of further fantasies and a challenge to humanism and the humanities that warrants separate attention is what one might call the challenge from 'life'. It points to the biological sciences, but it also pertains to a seemingly rising tide of ideas that are focused upon 'life'. The biological sciences produce a stream of research that inspires imaginative elaborations of the human individual as enriched by genetic, biological, and bio-technological supplements and upgrades. These ideas relate to the enhancement of life through pre-implantation genetic diagnosis and screening, germ-line engineering (genetic changes that can be passed down to an individual's offspring), psychotropic drugs that improve emotions and self-esteem, biotechnological means of enhancing the life span, and human cloning.[7] Serious research money goes into the halting and reversing of aging processes that give us the option of extending our physical and intellectual capacities beyond present levels. Much fantasizing and some research money goes into the improvement of cloning techniques, despite its condemnation by many segments of the population and some governments, and despite concerns about a 'dehumanized' future and the rights many think we have to a unique or unknown genome. The very debates surrounding the biological sciences bring into focus the perfectibility of individual life that the biological sciences promise.

The human, humanity and humanism have been integrative, centering concepts inspiring intellectual elites and whole disciplines for centuries. One of the questions we must ask is what are the equivalent concepts today, those that carry promise, inspire efforts and captivate the collective imagination?

In the last two centuries we experienced an expansion of *social* imagination that involved, since the enlightenment, hopes for the perfectibility of human society in terms of equality, peace, justice and social welfare, with the high point being Marxist visions of a socialist revolution. This social imagination focused upon human society. What it added to the earlier humanist ideas is a collective dimension. These ideas have not disappeared with the current retraction of the welfare state and the collapse of Marxism. But the promise and hope and the excess imagination that went into visions of social salvation have been extended to other areas where they find progressive inspiration. The biological sciences are one such area – and they turn around the notion of life rather than that of humanity or the human. The notion of life that is often applied to them when they are called life sciences can serve as a metaphor and anchoring concept that illustrates a cultural turn to nature and how it replaces the culture of the human and the social. What has become thinkable today in a break with enlightenment ideals is not the perfectibility of human society by societal means or the cognitive and ethical perfectibility of the human, but the perfectibility of life – through life enhancement on the individual level, but also through the biopolitics of populations, through the protection and reflexive manipulation of nature, through the idea of intergenerational (rather than distributional) justice. One can interpret a variety of developments in different disciplines as a manifestation of life-centered thinking; the notion of life stands for an open-ended series of phenomenological, biological, economic, and other significations and processes. This may be one of its advantages. The notion of life bridges divisions between several sciences. In the social sciences, 'life' thinking is illustrated by those areas that have turned the individual and its search for Ego and 'I'-related pleasures and affirmations into topics of investigation. But from a broader perspective, many areas focusing upon the subject can be seen to play into life-centered thinking – and in the social sciences today, the fantasized unit is more the subject than society. Theories of identity and identity politics and of the self and subjectivity provide examples of such trends, as do ideas embodied in the vast numbers of self-help books derived from psychology that counsel individuals about how to enhance their lives. Another development that plays into life-centered thinking in the social sciences is the renaissance of the notion of a generation – it serves as a counterconcept to the common concept of solidarity favored by social democratic and socialist parties in the last 100 years which is based on hopes for equality through the redistribution of resources. In contrast, generational concepts focus on sequentially related individuals. Hope and promise in reference to individual life also come from finance, where excess imagination – supported by the profession of financial analysts – is invested in financial scenarios as ways of enriching the self and the life course. What supports these ideas and life-course and generational thinking are institutional changes in pension schemes which move from solidarity-based principles, where income from the working population is redistributed to retirees, to personal investment schemes where one plans and pays for one's retirement benefits over the course of a lifetime. On a more conceptual and theoretical level, a return to human nature-based theories of rights and justice can be associated with life-centered ideas (Fukuyama, 2002), as can Heidegger's temporal notions of human existence as 'being towards death' and vitalist concepts (Lash, 2003) that can be linked to Bergson and Tarde.

On a popular level, the life-enhancement literature, bio-ethical controversies about the rights to enrich lives and genelines genetically and technologically, and the images of individuals searching for optimal experience through edgework (extreme sports and so on), suggest individuals and populations deeply involved in the appropriation of their lives and those of their offspring. For neo-Marxist thinkers, post-Fordist knowledge-based systems appropriate workers' lives rather than their labor, with work encroaching upon and difficult to distinguish from free time and coinciding with the individual's lifetime. Conflicts over the 'appropriation of life' (Lash, 2003) rather than over the appropriation of surplus value – between economic agents, individuals, *and* the state and non-human objects (such as viruses) – may well be what defines post-human and post-social environments.

CONCLUSION

The language of humanism, like the language of religion or anything that requires soul, was not predisposed to accepting post-human developments of the various kinds discussed. It is not predisposed to accept the expanding role of non-human objects, object relationships, post-moral persons, or identities that include, in central neural and other locations, non-human processors and parts. In particular, it is not predisposed to the orientation to the future informed by continually emerging and constructed *promises* (rather than important and stable values) that characterize the sciences and other developments implicated in what I said. In speech act theory terms, the felicity conditions, that is the conditions of success of a *request* – for example a request for virtue, or rationality, or ethical behavior – are quite different from the felicity conditions of a *promise*. Promises must concern future acts, they must concern things that the promise receiver really wants, and they imply that the promise giver articulates and intends to keep the promise. In other words, the desires of promise receivers, trust in the sincerity of the promises, and the future play a role in successful promising.

Fulfillment of the promise is the task of the promise giver and speaker, not of the promise receiver. With requests, fulfillment is the task of the receiver of the request, the wants or desires of the receiver play no role in the matter, and the future is only implicated in a trivial way – as when I ask someone to pass the salt and the passing has to be done after the demand is uttered. It would seem that promises are easier 'to sell' in the kind of times we live in. Or, to put this more strongly, I think that we have long switched from an environment strong on requests to one that is strong on (institutional) promises. And such an environment accords well with the lack-wanting self with which I started.

Perhaps one way out for the humanities is to consider a deep, transdisciplinary cooperation with the non-human sciences and the engineering and information fields that point the way to the future (see also Assman, 2002). One example that illustrates how one can achieve moral goals not by appeal to norms, but with the help of the information sciences, is the 'corporate fallout detector' just invented by a student at MIT's media lab. As reported by Wade in the *New York Times* (August 28, 2003, G5) the device combines a bar-code reader with an internal database of pollution complaints and ethics violations within a device that looks like an old Geiger counter. When the bar code of any product for which data are available is scanned, a clicking sound indicates whether the record of the corporation that produced the good is clean or blemished (strong noise indicates many ethical and pollution violations). Perhaps another way to confront the challenges the humanities encounter is the one some humanities disciplines appear to have embarked on, which is to redefine themselves as cultural sciences.

NOTES

1. The humanists saw reading as a social practice, a means to train memory, a step in the growth of personal knowledge, an act of reverence for the pre-Christian antiquity – and last but not least, an occasion for tasteful and showy investments (Resnick and Martinek, 2001, pp. 409–10). The term humanism, as cited in the Encyclopedia Britannica (Macropedia, 15th edn, vol. 20, Chicago: The University of Chicago Press, 1991, p. 665) was first employed by 19th-century German scholars to designate the Renaissance emphasis on classical studies.
2. See the definition of humanism in the Encyclopedia Britannica, Macropedia, 15th edn, vol. 20, Chicago: The University of Chicago Press, 1991, pp. 665–77.
3. Cited in Urry, 2003, p. 30.
4. One way in which this situation may have an impact on management education is when managers are not trained to understand the non-human world and the object-relations knowledge workers and others develop with that world. Consider NASA's problem with the Challenger accident 1986 and the recent Columbia disintegration, as described by Boffey (2003): The Challenger exploded shortly after liftoff, the victim of faulty O-ring seals that allowed hot gases to escape from a booster rocket and ignite the huge external fuel tank. The Columbia disintegrated on its way back to earth, the victim of a chunk of

foam insulation that broke off the external tank and hit the leading edge of a wing, allowing hot gases to penetrate and melt the innards. As the investigators of these disasters
declare, in both cases NASA managers ignored warnings by engineers concerned with
what they saw as potentially grave hazards and threats to shuttle safety in the concrete
cases, and they ignored signs of problems in other launches or classified them falsely as
maintenance problems. They kept launching the shuttles because they got away with it
last time (Feynman described the process as a form of Russian roulette). Managers were
more concerned with meeting launch and cost schedules than with the object side, with
listening to the engineers that were deeply involved with the objects and their fears.
5. For more information and summary descriptions of some of these and the following
   developments see the following website: http://incipientposthuman.com, z.B. http://incip-
   ientposthuman.com/physical.htm.
6. See again the website cited in note 5 for these and other questions pertaining to transhumanism and more generally websites on transhumanism movements.
7. The negative and collective dimension of biological research is indicated in the prospect
   of genetically engineered biowarfare agents and new weapons based on molecular nan-
   otechnologies.

REFERENCES

Alford, Charles F. (1991), *The Self in Social Theory: A Psychoanalytic Account of
   its Construction in Plato, Hobbes, Locke, Rawls, and Rousseau*, New Haven: Yale
   University Press.
Assman, Aleida (2002), *Menschenbilder. (Post) Humanität als Provokation für die
   Humanwissenschaften*, Mimeo.
Baard, Erik (2003), 'Cyborg Liberation Front. Inside the movement for posthuman
   rights', *The Village Voice*, 30 July.
Baudrillard, Jean (1996), *The System of Objects*, London: Verso.
Baumann, Zygmunt (1993), 'Wir sind wie Landstreicher – Die Moral im Zeitalter
   der Beliebigkeit', *Süddeutsche Zeitung*, 16/17 November.
Beck, Ulrich (1992), *Risk Society: Towards a New Modernity*, London: Sage.
Berger, Peter, Brigitte Berger and Hansfried Kellner (1974), *The Homeless Mind:
   Modernization and Consciousness*, New York: Vintage Books.
Boffey, Philip M. (2003), 'The gambles and gaffes behind two tragic space shuttle
   disasters', *New York Times*, Sunday 31 August, WK 8.
Coleman, James (1993), 'The rational reconstruction of society', *American
   Sociological Review*, **58**, 1–15.
Elster, Jon (1998), 'Emotions and economic theory', *Journal of Economic Literature*,
   36 (1), 47–74.
Fukuyama, Francis (2002), *Our Posthuman Future: Consequences of the
   Biotechnology Revolution*, New York: Farrar, Straus and Giroux.
Haraway, Donna (1991), *Simians, Cyborgs, and Women*, New York: Routledge.
Hayles, Katherine (2002), *Writing Machines*, Cambridge and London: The MIT
   Press.
Heidegger, Martin [1927] (1962), *Being and Time*, New York: Harper & Row.
Knorr Cetina, Karin (1997), 'Sociality with objects. Social relations in postsocial
   knowledge societies', *Theory, Culture & Society*, **14** (4), 1–30.
Knorr Cetina, Karin (2001), *Postsocial Relations: Theorizing Sociality in a
   Postsocial Environment*, in George Ritzer and Barry Smart (eds), *Handbook of
   Social Theory*, London: Sage.

Lasch, Christopher (1978), *The Culture of Narcissism: American Life in an Age of Diminishing Expectations*, New York: Norton.

Lash, Scott (2003), 'Empire and vitalism', *Proceedings of the Annual Meeting of the Eastern Sociological Society*, Philadelphia.

Resnick, Daniel P. and Jason Martinek (2001), 'Reading', entry in Peter N. Stearns (ed.), *The Encyclopedia of European Social History. From 1350 to 2000*, volume 5, New York: Charles Scribner's Sons.

Rheinberger, Hans-Jörg (1992), 'Experiment, difference, and writing: I. Tracing protein synthesis', *Studies in History and Philosophy of Science*, **23**, 305–31.

Rycroft, Robert and Don Kash (1999), *The Complexity Challenge*, London: Pinter.

Urry, John (2003), *Global Complexity*, Cambridge, England: Polity Press.

Wade, Will (2003), 'A good corporate citizen? This scanner can tell', *New York Times*, 28 August, G5.

Wiley, Norbert (1994), *The Semiotic Self*, Chicago: University of Chicago Press.

Afterword

Anthony G. Hopwood

The potential for a more humane understanding of the practices of managing infuses all of the contributions to this collection. Bringing together philosophers, historians, sociologists and management theorists, the volume challenges many prevailing notions of the knowledges and disciplines that are brought to bear on understanding and shaping the managerial world. By critically examining the nature of management knowledges, by questioning prevailing approaches to management education, by providing examples of new and different disciplinary linkages and by illustrating the insights that are capable of being provided by a humanistic view of the managerial art, the contributors together made manifest the very partial ways in which management is currently known.

The possibility of a different understanding is evident in the practice of management itself, as many of the essays in this volume make clear. Not only do the most technical of management systems invariably have an aesthetic quality that extends far beyond conventional notions of functionality, but also a system aesthetics is often a necessary aspect of mapping, ordering and arranging the complex linkages that are incorporated into today's management approaches. Almost all enterprises mobilize visual imagery in ways which both call on and, in turn, shape our wider aesthetic sensibilities. Patterns of organizational linkages derive from a profound sociability of the managerial practitioners. Indeed many of the most pivotal business institutions are reflective of deeper searches for sociability and human interaction; within London alone the Stock Exchange and the Lloyds' insurance market both have their origins in the coffee shop culture of the 18th century. Conceptions of organizational strategy are also invariably imbued with understandings of the cultural context in which the enterprise is embedded. We should always remember that some of the most successful businesses are those that can appreciate the shifting dynamics of the cultural world in which we live and the changing nature of the human condition.

My favourite example of just such a business is provided by the highly successful 18th-century British entrepreneur potter, Josiah Wedgwood (Reilly, 1992). Receptive to both artistic and scientific influences, he was a very active participant in a wider intellectual network known as the Lunar

Society (Uglow, 2002) that brought together philosophers, scientists, economists and men of letters. Such influences pervaded Wedgwood's conception of enterprise, his appeals to science and the establishment of a constantly experimenting enterprise, the insights which he had into the changing social condition and the emergence of more modern notions of fashion and taste, and, not least, the intrinsically human nature of organizing and the possibilities for creating what we would now see as a knowledge based workforce. The enterprise that Wedgwood created was attuned to the philosophical, social and scientific tendencies of its time. Indeed it could not have been created and still cannot be understood apart from them.

Such configurations of influences and interactions are only part of a much wider interdependency of economic, business and civil life (see also Bhimani, 1994). For we should remember that markets, as significant economics institutions, only emerged when a degree of stability had been achieved in civil society. When people no longer grabbed and plundered, but engaged in stable, repeatable transactions, the bases started to be created for economic and eventually business development.

But the humanities also provide a wider and quite different base for engaging with the managerial art: one of reflection and even critique. Management is not an unproblematic activity. As well as enabling, creating, ordering and co-ordinating, it can be constraining, fragmenting, and at times, undermining of the human potential. Managerial practices are ones that invariably need to be used with care, and their ambiguous nature can and should be illuminated by an historical appreciation of their emergence, by a philosophical analysis of their modes of construction and the concepts and languages through which they operate, and through the ways in which they are engaged with the wider human condition. Given the significance of the impacts and consequences of management, too much management discussion takes place within the internal logics of the managerial art and using the categories and distinctions of prevailing managerial language. Almost invariably such analyses are highly circumscribed ones, often failing to provide an adequate insight into the paradoxes that constrain management's own functioning, let alone providing a basis for appreciating, accounting for, debating and challenging the wider array of involvements of management into economic, social and political spheres. An involvement of managerial knowledges with the disciplines of the humanities offers just such a potential and for this reason that involvement is of enormous importance.

Many such aspects of this deep interpenetration of business life with the wider human condition are recognized and celebrated in the contributions to this volume. In most cases these contributions also reflect educational experiments underway. Throughout Europe, most likely more so than

elsewhere, scholars and management educators are striving to ground managerial understandings in the historical trajectories of their emergence,
drawing on insights from philosophical and literary modes of criticism
when addressing managerial problems and practices, and presenting the
possibilities for managing as part of a much wider process of human and
organizational choice. Management education is far from being a homogeneous craft and many fascinating enquiries are underway trying to create
new and different understandings of the managerial art.

Equally, however, one senses that a large part of the excitement likely to
be engendered by the pioneering contributions to this volume reflects not
only the marginality of such endeavours but also the pressures for them to
conform. There is a genuine sense of pleasure of the initiated being able to
write together. Despite the intellectual and practical potentials which a
more humane understanding of management offers, the prospects for a
wider interest in such a view are contested, if not constrained.

The potential is limited by the fact that much management education in
Europe takes place in stand-alone institutions which have little or no wider
intellectual hinterland. Of course, not all such institutions are characterized
by an anti-intellectualism. The Copenhagen Business School is an obvious
exception. But in many such schools, while individual scholars can be perceptive, experimental and entrepreneurial in their own domain, they often
have to function without a wider institutional legitimacy that being part of
a more all-embracing university is capable of conveying. They often have to
operate as lonely voices in what can sometimes be an anti-intellectual
wilderness. Such contexts are unlikely to change, however, so networks and
specialized means of communications between the committed are of vital
importance.

Business schools remain in many cases institutions that are still uncertain
of their own legitimacy. So many, rather than looking forward to their
own specific trajectories of development, look sideways to what compar-
able and often competing institutions are doing. Not having a strong
conviction in their own intellectual and knowledge positionings, business
schools invest heavily in homogenizing tendencies. Many of them seemingly want to look the same. They do not want to stand out too much, at
best aspiring to be the best of the homogeneous type. They usually feel duty
bound to reflect the latest management knowledge fashions, all rapidly
picking up modern finance theory whilst largely ignoring financial institutions and the sociology of financing, modern notions of corporate strategy
whilst putting less emphasis on the inculcation of strategic ways of thinking and behaving, modern notions of human resources, and so on, however
partial such knowledges may be. A configuration of forces has also resulted
in a new visibility of management education that has its own quite

significant consequences. As management education and business schools have become news for the media, such pressures for conformity have become ever greater. With newspapers such as the *Financial Times* and magazines such as *Business Week* seeking to promote themselves by selling rankings and ratings, institutions have found themselves investing ever more heavily in the processes of becoming similar. Increasingly these pressures, reinforced by state evaluative and regulatory agencies, have been brought to bear on research and knowledge creation directly. There is now an active politics of publication in 'A' rated journals and in those included in the most significant assessments and rankings. Other outstanding and important journals can be marginalized; scholarly monographs undervalued; wider pressures of dissemination ignored.

The implications of this can be highly specific, but often strong and powerful. Bocconi, the Italian business school, has instituted prizes for the best articles which its faculty publish in journals included in the *Financial Times* ranking of business schools. The London Business School gives hefty bonuses for publications in 'A' rated journals. Some aspiring business schools, of which the Tanaka School at Imperial College, London, is one, offer employment contracts embodying just such terms. And national research assessment exercises like that in the UK usually reinforce such tendencies. Such pressures for homogeneity are also evident in the rush to be accredited by an array of national and regional bodies, with European schools even aspiring for American certification. Through many of these regulatory initiatives, the forces of homogenization penetrate to the fine detail of the syllabus and the research agenda. More and more when I witness the rush to be the same I can't help but recall the biblical text used by Handel in the *Messiah*, 'All we like sheep . . .'.

In the midst of such forces it is easy to imagine more humanistic approaches to managerial knowledge being an endangered species. The simultaneous search for legitimacy and similarity is likely to reinforce the seemingly scientific, the outwardly rational, the economically oriented and the abstract and more readily generalizable. The latter tendency is of particular significance since many more modern forms of knowledge tend to be ahistorical, decontextualized and readily transferable, having few roots in particular institutional, cultural and national settings. Such developments offer particular threats to many European managerial knowledges grounded in the humanities which are often highly contextual in nature, providing strong bridges to history and particular institutional and cultural configurations. Not only can more abstract knowledges pose a direct threat to them in their own institutional arenas in some of the ways outlined above, but also the European knowledges are less transferable to other cultural settings, often requiring very detailed insights into historical origins, philosophical traditions and the many influences that give a specificity to the use of concepts and language. To the extent that this is true, many European knowledges enter with a disadvantage into the global politics of knowledge that is increasingly characteristic of the management field.

But all is not necessarily lost. The outstanding advantage of the contextual and highly specific nature of more humanistic managerial knowledges is their ability to engage more readily with pragmatic circumstances. They often can enter more easily into dialogues with communities of practice. They can illuminate the diversity of everyday practices. They can provide languages with which to mediate the relationships between the practitioner and scholarly communities. For the organizationally enabling potential of historically and culturally grounded knowledges is very real indeed and this might suggest that conversations with reflective practitioners could be useful and productive.

It is for all these reasons that the chapters in this volume are important as well as exciting. They provide a forum for development and reinforcement and for anticipating the potential of such approaches for research, education and application. Indeed their potential suggests the need for other means for stimulating and legitimating deliberations of this nature. My hope is that the availability of this collection will encourage other voices to enter the debate and to continue the development of the approach.

REFERENCES

Bhimani, Alnoor (1994), 'Accounting and the emergence of economic man', *Accounting, Organizations and Society*, **19** (8), 637–74.
Reilly, Robin (1992), *Josiah Wedgwood*, London: Macmillan.
Uglow, Jenny (2002), *The Lunar Men: The Friends Who Made the Future 1730–1810*, London: Faber & Faber.

Index